'There is scarcely a poor climb on the cliff and it will be pleasant to repeat the old favourites. Or lie in the sun by the llyn and watch the next generation take their girl friends up the climbs we thought hard. And although Arddu is, after all, only an unfeeling piece of rhyolite and the scratchings of the last few decades irrelevant to the larger scheme of things, there is an air of tradition about the place, of great deeds wrought in the past. On silent days when the cwm is deserted and the crags loom strangely through the mist it is easy to imagine the Abrahams peering in amazement down Shrike wall, or one of the great teams of the nineteen-thirties at work with the grass up on the West, or a young man from Manchester uncoiling his hemp rope below Vember.'

Jack Soper, 'Still More of Arfon', FRCCJ 1963.

Clogwyn du'r Arddu in Winter.

Photo: P.G. Martin.

WELSH ROCK

100 Years of Climbing in North Wales

Trevor Jones

&

Geoff Milburn

Pic Publications

Opposite above: Dinas Cromlech bathed in early morning light. Photo: Rowland Edwards.
Opposite below: Claude Davies and Joe Brown on their way up to a route on Clogwyn y Grochan. Photo: Trevor Jones.

First published in 1986
© 1986 Trevor Jones & Geoff Milburn

Pic Publications,
  25 Cliffe Road,
  GLOSSOP,
  Derbyshire.
  SK13 8NY

ISBN 0 951111 40 X

Produced by the Ernest Press
GLASGOW. G44 5QD

Distributed by Cordee
  3a De Montfort Street,
  LEICESTER.
  LE1 7HD

Front cover: Raped by Affection — John Redhead on the 1st ascent.   Photo: Dave Towse.

Rear cover: Ben Moon making his Statement of Youth, E7 6b, Craig Pen Trwyn.   Photo: Dave Summerfield.

Opposite: Gary Gibson hanging around on No Red Tape, E3 6a, Craig Pen Trwyn.   Photo: Gary Gibson Collection.

CONTENTS

ACKNOWLEDGMENTS

Many people have been of enormous assistance in this chronicle of personalities and events in Welsh climbing. They all had their vital roles, from octogenarians remembering events of over sixty years ago through the mental mists of time to teenagers flexing their iron-hard muscles on Pen Trwyn — fledglings poised in overhanging upward flight. Undoubtedly this book is a tribute to every climber who has ventured onto Welsh rock.

Our thanks particularly go to the photographers who so readily agreed to let their superb work go on show within these pages: Bob Allen, Steve Ashton, Mike Browell, Eric Byrom, John Cleare, Leo Dickinson, Mandy Dickinson, Rowland Edwards, Al Evans, Neil Foster, Gary Gibson, Pete Gomersall, Chris Gore, Chris Griffiths, Alan Hinkes, Chris Jackson, Dave Jones, Pete Livesey, Dave Lyon, Andy Newton, Elaine Owen, Peter Martin, Mike Owen, Gavin Peat, Andy Pollitt, John Sheard, Edgar Siddall, Ian Smith, Dave Summerfield, Dave Towse, Paul Williams and Ted Wrangham.

A bare list seems inadequate but the following are just a few of those who have backed us in so many ways: Dave Alcock, Bob Allen, Nat Allen, Jancis Allison, Hugh Banner, Geoff Birtles, Chris Briggs, Joe Brown, Jessie Byrom, Climber & Rambler, Climbers' Club, Claude Davies, Rowland Edwards, Fell and Rock C.C., Gary Gibson, Pete Gomersall, Peter Harding, High Magazine, Peter Hodgkiss, Guy Kirkus, Jill Lawrence, Sir Jack Longland, Chris Lyon, Bonny Masson, Colin Mathews, Mountain Magazine, Tony Moulam, Bernard Newman, Rucksack Club, Angela Soper, Jack Soper, Pete Whillance and Ken Wilson.

At a late stage of the script Johnny Dawes and John Redhead with extreme tolerance helped to put forward the latest philosophy, while Ken Milburn and Tom Waghorn made many helpful suggestions and proof-read the script. Dr Paul Clarke also helped a great deal with the later chapters. Our greatest thanks go to Geoff Birtles and Jim Perrin who did their utmost to steer us away from countless pitfalls, and to Paul Williams who enthusiastically worked until 4 a.m. one night to iron out some of the discrepancies and insert some of the more glaring omissions.

Opposite Above: Tim Freeman pulling up on Burning Sphincter, Pen Trwyn.
Opposite Below: Dave Lyon negotiating a tricky bulge on Wu-Shu Boys at Pen Trwyn.   Photos: Dave Summerfield.

INTRODUCTION

The world of rock-climbing is populated by larger than life characters whose thoughts and actions can be both colourful and eccentric. Mere historical dates and facts can never do justice to such remarkable climbers as Archer Thomson, Menlove Edwards, Al Harris or Don Whillans.

This book does not endeavour to give a balanced and analytical viewpoint of a hundred years of climbing in North Wales, rather it attempts to allow the climbers of each generation to bring to life the events which took place amidst the gaunt and sombre cliffs of Snowdonia. Later generations then spread further afield to the intimidating sea cliffs and the more hospitable limestone outcrops to the north-east of the mountains. In the last two years exploration has culminated in the conquest of the old slate quarries which contain some of the hardest and most serious rock-climbs ever recorded.

Trevor Jones with over thirty years experience amongst the Welsh hills has climbed with or known nearly all the most famous rock-climbers, while guide-book writer, Editor and bibliophile, Geoff Milburn has frequented North Wales for over a quarter of a century. Inspired by John Cleare's photographs in 'Rock-Climbers in Action in Snowdonia' the authors searched for a varied selection of interesting, humorous and historic photographs to complement the anecdotal material.

Some readers will find parts of the text controversial while others will notice either a bias towards particular characters, or even the absence of some familiar names. To be able to include such an extensive range of photographic material a compromise became essential. Instead of attempting a definitive history the writers have made a selection from their own experiences to give a personal viewpoint concerning some of the events which have shaped Welsh rock-climbing.

Opposite: John Redhead on the 1st ascent of The Clown, E7 6b, North Stack, Gogarth.   Photo: Dave Towse.

Part One — The Early Days

'He fills me with strength and protects me wherever I go. He gives me the surefootedness of a mountain goat upon the crags. He leads me safely along the top of the cliffs....'

Psalm 18.

Seen from the Gogarth cliffs the South Stack Lighthouse begins to cast its beam over a vast ocean.   Photo: Chris Jackson.

Let There Be Light

Wales is an old land and for centuries its mountains were unknown to all except a few hill-farmers, early miners and those who in times of war sought a refuge amongst the cliffs. In the north-west, Eryri, which has so aptly been described as the Mountains of Longing, encompasses the rugged ranges of the Carneddau, the Glyders and Snowdon. Rising to a height of 3,560 feet, Snowdon is by Alpine standards somewhat lowly. Nevertheless it was in time to become a focal point for the visitors who flocked in from afar.

One of the earliest recorded ascents of Snowdon was in 1819 by Captain Jenkin Jones, RN, who started from Llyn Quellyn at 2.15 a.m. one spring morning with a guide who charged five shillings for his services. On reaching the summit Jones wrote:

'I was so beautifully introduced by the rising sun that I felt a sort of ecstasy.'

He was very quickly brought to earth by his guide who implored him earnestly.

"For God's sake come down, the sweat in my hair is frozen and I do think I shall never recover my fingers and toes, and begging your pardon sir, I have finished the brandy."

The first proper rock climb had been unwittingly accomplished even earlier, in 1798, on the Eastern Terrace of the black cliff of Clogwyn du'r Arddu, which had been conquered by two humble clerics on a botanical excursion, the Reverend William Bingley and the Reverend Peter Williams. They were clearly more intent on discovering rare floral specimens than in climbing rock for its own sake:

'Every step now required the utmost caution....Mr Williams having a strong pair of shoes with nails in them, which would hold their footing better than mine, requested to make the first attempt, and after some difficulty he succeeded. When he had fixed himself securely to a part of the rock, he took off his belt, and holding firmly by one hand, gave the other to me. I laid hold, and with a little aid from the stone, fairly pulled myself up by it.'

There was a pause of several decades as Alpine climbing evolved, in which the British played a prominent part, but this was mainly during the summer months each year. In the early part of the nineteenth century, affluent English alpinists started to go to North Wales in the winter and discovered good snow and ice conditions — mainly in the icy gullies of Snowdonia. A perfect meeting point was the Pen y Gwryd, a hotel on the lower slopes of the Glyders at the junction of the roads to Beddgelert and Llanberis. It was ideally situated for the finest ridge on the mainland of Britain, the Snowdon Horseshoe, first traversed by a Pen y Gwryd resident, C.A.O. Baumgartner, in 1847.

The first proper access to Snowdon only occurred in 1830 when the road over the Llanberis Pass was built, and the Pen y Gwryd was superbly sited for the development of rock-climbing and mountaineering. In 1847 Harry Owen and his wife took over the hotel and ran it for nearly half a century, during which they saw the birth and lusty growth of Welsh rock-climbing. The developments by leading climbers at that time were to affect our attitudes nearly a century later.

During a local tour the wandering writer George Borrow went to Wales in the eighteen-fifties to gather material for his best seller, 'Wild Wales'. On one occasion he walked over thirty miles in one day and in the Ogwen valley he passed a 'wretched hovel', where the tenant's children were suffering from the 'Cryd' or ague. It was Helyg. Some seventy years later this humble cottage was to become a refuge and focal point for the best rock-climbers of the nineteen-twenties.

In December 1860 Professor Tyndall (who made the first ascent of the Weisshorn) and two friends went to North Wales where they obtained rudimentary ice-axes in Bethesda for four-pence from the local blacksmith. Tyndall, who saw Snowdon as a perfect minuscule Alpine peak, wrote in the Saturday review:

'Above and behind us the heavens were of the densest grey; towards the western horizon this was broken by belts of fiery red, which nearer the sun brightened to red and orange. The mountains of Flintshire were flooded with glory, and later on through the gaps in the ranges the sunlight poured in coloured beams. The scene would bear comparison with the splendour of the Alps themselves.'

Tyndall was one of the first of the intelligentsia to enjoy the Welsh mountains in winter and soon attracted other lovers of the hills from different professions. Already devotees of the P.y G. (Pen y Gwryd) had pronounced ideas of themselves as superior:

'We know ourselves to be a small sect and to be often laughed at; we reply by assuming that we are the salt of the earth, and that our amusement is the first and noblest of all amusements.'

In addition to scientists, doctors and the clergy, literary figures too were enamoured with the location. Tom Hughes, author of 'Tom Brown's Schooldays', showed a keen interest and in 1886 Charles Kingsley, cleric and novelist, went to stay at the P.y.G. Born in 1819 he had once walked the fifty-two miles from London to Cambridge in a day. He inserted Pen y Gwryd into his colourful account of Snowdonia in Victorian days in his novel 'Two Years Ago'. Lyrically he described P.y.G. as 'the divinest pigsty beneath the canopy'.

One of the first to visit Pen y Gwryd was C.E. Mathews in 1854. A future President of the Alpine Club, a rich Birmingham solicitor, a political friend of the Chamberlain family, and a tireless worker in public life, Mathews was to return again and again to P.y.G. for nearly fifty years. During this time he climbed Snowdon and Cader Idris in the region of a hundred times. He was the greatest influence in bringing the Alpine brotherhood to stay at P.y.G. for winter mountaineering from the 1860s onwards. This was a closed upper class society of climbers who were as sure of themselves as of their belief that the British Empire would last for ever.

In April, 1888 Mathews took his friend Melchior Anderegg, the greatest of Swiss guides, up an icy Snowdon:

'I led all the way and as the snow was deep and soft I hesitated. Melchior immediately forged to the front, but I emphatically declined, "No! I am the guide today, you are the Herr."

On reaching Crib Goch, there was the peak of Snowdon on our left, a great white cone in a blue sky. Melchior, whose knowledge of Swiss distances is faultless said, "We must go back, we cannot climb the final peak in less than five hours."

"Oh yes," I said, "we shall be there in an hour." "That sir, is quite impossible." Five minutes over the hour we were on the summit of Snowdon.'

In 1870 Mathews formed the 'Society of Welsh Rabbits' at Pen y Gwryd, the object being:

'To explore Snowdonia in winter and as near to Christmas as possible.'

And so they came from all directions: bishops and barristers, surveyors and solicitors, professors and parsons. Quite soon after they went in the summer as well and the sport of rock-climbing was born. One of their fascinations became the unclimbed and quartz-splashed thousand-foot precipice of Lliwedd.

On January 4th 1883 Stocker and Wall made the first ascent of the West Buttress. On the first assault they tried Central Gully, but not surprisingly they were repulsed by dampness and difficulty; it was to be another fifty-five years before it was eventually climbed. They then turned their attention to the West Buttress:

'We came to a ledge about six inches wide and four yards long, the rock above was nearly perpendicular with no handhold and nothing below. Somehow we got over, but neither of us wishes to be there again.'

Early exploration was often done with very rudimentary equipment. Ropes were only spasmodically used and tended to be any old rope which came to hand. Farm ropes were common and even clothes-lines were used. Often only forty feet long, they were made of hemp which stiffened quickly and kinked alarmingly when wet. The rope was held vaguely in the hands and passed round any convenient spikes to break a fall. This curious early attitude to a rope was amplified by W.P. Haskett Smith, who made the first ascent of Napes Needle on Great Gable in 1886:

'We classed ropes with spikes and ladders as a means by which bad climbers were enabled to go where none but the best mountaineers had any business to be.'

This objection to roping-up caused the first rock-climbing death in Wales on Lliwedd in 1888 when a party of three set off unroped. The third man got into difficulties, seized the second man's ankle, tried one more move, then fell to the scree two hundred feet below.

After a series of Alpine accidents Queen Victoria wrote to Mr Gladstone asking whether Parliament could outlaw mountaineering, but she was probably reluctant in case he addressed her yet again as if she were a public meeting...

At that time boots were casually nailed and many must have been lethal. The boots of Lord Francis Douglas, who was killed after the ascent of the Matterhorn, are in the Zermatt museum. Typically they have smooth leather soles with just a few flat-headed nails sprinkled round the edges. When the P.y G. regulars went to the Alps in the summer they usually climbed with guides, but guideless climbing by the better alpinists was soon on the increase. One president of the Alpine Club decided to try guideless climbing, but sadly could only tie a waist loop with a dangerous slip-knot. When challenged with this stupidity he replied, *"That's the guide's job."*

Amazingly, unstable human pyramids were used on frequent occasions and the topmost man was hoisted upwards in an endeavour to try to reach over the difficulty. It was this risky manoeuvre which was to cause the death of O.G. Jones.

Just four years after Stocker and Wall's conquest another climber was to make his mark on Lliwedd. Oscar Johannes Ludwig Eckenstein was born in London in 1859 and went on to study chemistry first at London University, then at Bonn his father's home town. In 1887 while staying at P.y.G. he made the first ascent of the Central Gully and West Peak of Lliwedd. During the next twenty years he continued to climb on the crag at regular intervals and by 1914 when there were forty routes on the crag Eckenstein had been on about a quarter of them.

Eckenstein's contributions were not due to his leading ability but to his highly-trained mind and he was the first man to carry out a deep analysis of climbing techniques and equipment. Geoffrey Winthrop Young wrote about him:

'...the first mountaineer in this or any country to begin discussing holds and the balance upon them, in a theory with illustrations.'

He invented and demonstrated the ten-point crampon and also designed a shorter ice-axe just over two feet long which could be used in one hand. In addition he examined rope techniques and the comparative efficiency of various knots. Amazingly his ideas were not generally accepted and English alpinists carried on the soul-destroying and laborious practice of step-cutting on steep ice for many decades.

As a character Eckenstein was blunt, tactless and contemptuous of the establishment, but nevertheless he commanded respect from others. He even went on an early expedition to the Himalaya with the infamous Aleister Crowley — The Great Beast — who wrote in his Confessions:

'Eckenstein was the noblest man I have ever known. His integrity was absolute.'

Eckenstein has a boulder named after him, a boulder as big as a removal van, below the wall between P.y G. and Pen-y-Pass, where he demonstrated his balance theories to anyone curious enough to take interest in his forward thinking.

Over some years one of Eckenstein's close companions was a schoolmaster. James Merriman Archer Thomson, the headmaster of Llandudno School, was a prolific innovator for nearly two decades from 1894 onwards until his eventual suicide in 1912. His first new climb, Central Gully on Glyder Fawr, was a bold expedition on a cliff shrouded in Victorian uncertainty. During the ascent his companions threaded the rope through a hole at the back of the capstone to protect him and he was then able to make the hard move in comparative safety.

Thomson had many outstanding achievements: eighteen new routes on Lliwedd and its first guide-book; sixteen climbs sprinkled around Tryfan, Glyder Fach and Glyder Fawr; and fourteen routes in Llanberis Pass, including The Black Cleft on Dinas Mot, then thought to be the hardest climb in Wales. The output of his new climbs was immense by Victorian standards and he and Harold Hughes, climbing only on Sundays, put up fifteen new routes in fifteen months on cliffs all over Snowdonia. A typical winter Sunday for them started off with a day's strenuous climbing on Lliwedd followed by dinner at the P.y G. A long walk back in deep snow then followed to arrive in Bangor at 4 a.m.

Their most sensational climb together was the first ascent of The Devil's Kitchen in March 1895 during the great freeze of that winter, when even the River Thames froze over. They borrowed the Ogwen Cottage coal hatchet to supplement their own axes (similar to modern two-axe technique), walked over the frozen Llyn Idwal and attacked the unclimbed Devil's Kitchen. They found the coal hatchet a much more effective weapon than their four-foot alpenstocks.

The final pitch took eight hours and it was pitch dark when they got to the top. It was too risky to descend the ice-bound lower cliffs of the Kitchen so they descended to Llanberis which they reached at 10 p.m. with their clothes in tatters. One of Thomson's hands was badly frost-bitten and he was unable to use it for several weeks.

Thomson was skilful and daring, but cautious and always chose his companions carefully. He also took great care in the nailing of his boots. In one respect however he was quite firm. It was common practice in the Lake District at that time for climbers to top-rope an unclimbed pitch prior to an ascent, as for example with Kern Knotts Crack. Thomson, however, would have none of this, and he climbed all his new routes from below.

Opposite Above: A celebrated gathering outside the P.y G. Hotel. T. Halliday, M. Black, F. Berrill, Roderick Williams (V.P. of C.C. 1930-34), Rev. J. Nelson Burrows (V.P. of C.C. 1905-08), M.K. Smith (V.P. of C.C. 1920-24), F.H. Bowring (V.P. of C.C. 1898-1905), C. Stewart King. Photo: C. Briggs, P.y G. collection.

Opposite Below: Ashley Abraham, C. Fox, W.J. Williamson, O.G. Jones and George Abraham on the lower slopes of Cader Idris at Easter 1897. Photos: Abraham collection.

Tales about Thomson's silence during days on the hill were legendary as he could go a whole day without ever speaking once. One man came back from a whole day with him and returned to Pen y Pass late at night. The man held out his hand and said "Goodbye". Thomson naturally shook hands...and merely smiled. Despite his taciturn nature he wrote prose which was often excellent, as in the description of an incident when he and Eckenstein investigated an unclimbed section around the Central Gully of Lliwedd:

'...a species of roofless cave with a steeply-sloping floor. From this cubicle there was no apparent exit. Eckenstein, who was separated by less than 30 feet, and had a long tail of rope trailing from his waist, joined me here to give me the benefit of his counsel and aid; pressing his back against one wall, and his feet against the other, he explained to me the exceptional security of his bridge-like position; it was one in which he could receive me in his embrace, if my attempt to climb out should prove abortive, and, as the next resting-place was obviously the heads of our companions below, I derived much courage and comfort from this assurance.'

Thomson's description of the crux of Great Gully, Craig yr Ysfa, will always remain a masterpiece of descriptive writing:

'By utilising a small foothold on the right wall the climber effects a lodgement on it, and then reaches its sharp upper edge by a struggle, in which he becomes near to defying all the laws of anatomy. A novel expedient is to lay the palm of the right hand on the block and, using the arm as a pivot, perform a pirouette to the south; the climber thus lands in a sitting position, with one leg thrust upwards to the roof to maintain equilibrium...any Galileo, however, will complacently demand a shoulder...'

Lliwedd was undoubtedly Thomson's favourite cliff and one of his best discoveries was Avalanche Route, so named because he was nearly struck by a flurry of boulders, which were dislodged by an inexperienced party. One of the culprits, George Leigh Mallory, was destined to be one of the greatest climbers of the future. Thomson described the crux of the climb:

'I stepped from my perch to the rocks on the right and rounding a corner encountered a vertical fluted wall. The position was extraordinarily exposed, for there stretched below three hundred feet of the open face which betrayed no ledge or furrow.'

Others came along during his long reign on the Welsh cliffs and he climbed with some of them to add weight to the party. Even in his fifties in 1911 he put up numerous new routes on Skye, but he suffered two nervous breakdowns and one evening, while alone at his brother's house in Surrey, he drank carbolic acid. Two hours later he was dead. He left no message and the coroner's verdict was 'Suicide while of an unsound mind'. One of his constant companions and friends during the first decade of the twentieth century had been Geoffrey Winthrop Young who wrote in the obituary for him:

'He led the era of exploration in North Wales from start to finish and he did not long survive its completion...the incomparable precipice of Lliwedd of which he knew every nook and cranny will be haunted...by the memory of a figure, solitary and smoking, crouched on some picturesque and inaccessible shelf, or moving with extraordinary lightness of foot...the grey curls drifting from the Rossetti-like head, or leaning easily outward in the middle of some gaunt and holdless slab...gazing upwards with a smiling intentness that seemed half critical examination and half remote and contemplative pleasure.'

Opposite: O.G. Jones with two companions on the Cyfrwy Arete, Easter, 1897.   Photo: Abraham collection.

Halfway through Thomson's long period of dominance a young, muscular physicist of Welsh extraction began to take an interest not only in the hills but more particularly in rock-climbing. O.G. Jones, or The Only Genuine Jones as he liked to be called, made his first ascent at the early age of twenty when he soloed the East Arete of Cyfrwy on Cader Idris. His early exploration in the Lake District constituted the basis for his book, 'Rock Climbing in the English Lake District', which was published late in 1897. Jones invented our present adjectival classification system, but at that time it had only four divisions: Easy, Moderate, Difficult and Exceptionally Severe.

On one occasion after he thought that he had developed frostbite, he dipped his fingers into boiling glue which caused them to be permanently misshapen. He trained hard and was very strong and even climbed round railway engines using rivets as handholds. His most extraordinary feat was when two climbers stood on chairs with an ice-axe across their shoulders as a horizontal bar. Jones then gripped the bar with three fingers of one hand, lifted his friend George Abraham under one arm, and then chinned the bar three times. It would be interesting to know how many (if any) present-day climbers could repeat this extraordinary performance.

During an attempt on a new route on the Aiguille du Plan above the Chamonix Valley the last man in the four-man team fell off, pulling off all above — except Jones who had a second or so to stop the tumbling Victorians. Standing in his steps and with only his hands he saved the party. After some time, one of them turned to another and said, *"Strong fellow, Jones!"*

Jones made useful contributions to Ogwen and just as important started the climbing career of two young brothers from Keswick. In a very few months George and Ashley Abraham became almost as skilful as Jones, because, like modern climbers, they spent fine-weather evenings practising on the crags and boulders near their Lakeland home. Jones took them down to the P.y G. and on one occasion they went to try the Great Gully of Craig y Cae. Nonchalantly Jones attempted to lead them through a waterfall but to their great relief he failed. On another occasion they had an expedition to try the Slanting Gully of Lliwedd. Unfortunately the weather turned bad and Jones left for Wasdale to honour a prior commitment. Before he departed, Jones most urgently advised the Abrahams, *"Whatever you do, leave Slanting Gully alone."*

History records that shortly after, on April 27th 1897, the brothers said they were going to potter about on Lliwedd and then succeeded in making an ascent of the notorious Slanting Gully.

'The last swing out onto the slab tested the arms terribly, for the feet flew back into space and there was a strange sensation as of a fly crawling on a ceiling.'

It was over-written perhaps, but the climb acquired instant respect as a hard and serious route.

Today it seems hard to believe that the Abraham brothers were not made to feel welcome at the P.y G., but one must remember that not only were they in trade as professional photographers but even worse — they kept a shop. The established upper middle class climbers did not like to see them produce a steady stream of excellent first ascents on a variety of cliffs. Some of their resentment was envy, the rest pure spite; and things got even worse when they decided to produce a book on Rock Climbing in North Wales. George commented:

Opposite: Starting the Devil's Kitchen.   Photo: Abraham collection.

'We have always found it most difficult to obtain accurate information regarding new climbs.'

The accommodation that was available to the ordinary man did little to make George feel at home:

'My experience of Welsh farmhouses has not been altogether a pleasant one. It has been associated to me with small windows, blinding rain and an inexhaustible diet of mutton.'

As the century closed a feeling developed that a more formal structure was needed for the Society of Welsh Rabbits at the P.y G. In 1898 forty frequenters of the Welsh farmhouse, the P.y G., met at the Cafe Monico in London and formed the Climbers' Club with C.E. Mathews as its first President. There were however objections from the Alpine Club's old guard who were firmly against rock-climbing:

'Why is it to the Alpine Club
Our C.E.M. no longer keeps?
Why should he found — himself the hub,
A Climbers' Club for chimney sweeps?'

The after dinner speech by Mathews followed the first annual general meeting of the Climbers' Club and he stressed:

"It is a sport that from some mysterious causes appeals mainly to the cultivated intellect. 'Arry or 'Arriet would never climb a hill."

Little did he realise that the great grandchildren of 'Arry and 'Arriet would lead the world in technical rock-climbing and that there would be 100,000 cousins flooding out of the northern cities every week-end to Derbyshire gritstone, Lakeland cliffs and Welsh granite — and not a few of them members of the Climbers' Club.

In the Lakes, not long before his death, Jones did the first ascent of Walker's Gully in icy conditions on January 7th 1899. Even today the route is still graded Hard Severe in good conditions. After many hours' struggle they arrived at the final crux pitch. It was so hard that Jones did the pitch in his socks although it was plastered in wet ice and running in icy water:

'I put my frozen feet into others' pockets, my dignity into my own.'

At Easter 1899, Jones went with a large party to Wales to work on a companion book on Welsh rock-climbing. He made first ascents of two gullies, Devil's Staircase and Hanging Garden Gully, and also made the second ascent of the Devil's Kitchen. On the first of these routes a boulder tumbled down the interior of the chimney, so close that it scratched some skin off his left ear...

Milestone Buttress on Tryfan was the next prize for Jones and the Abrahams. They tried Belle Vue Bastion and failed, then moved over to what is now Cheek Climb using the head and shoulders of the second. With the greatest of trouble they were up and around the first ledge in drizzling rain. They then climbed the second half by Terrace Wall Variant. It was tremendous, but it was beyond judgement; and feeling a responsibility, as was then the custom, they left no record.

At the top of the Devil's Staircase, Jones and George Abraham discussed a plan for a Himalayan expedition, but their climbing days had ended. Six months later Jones died in a terrible accident on the Dent Blanche when the leading guide asked him to help form a human pyramid to overcome a particularly difficult gendarme. The leading guide fell off, pulling his companions with him — including Jones. They slid soundlessly down an ice

Opposite Above: Nearing the summit of Snowdon. The railway and hut were built in 1895.
Opposite Below: Climbing on the Crib Goch Pinnacles: Photos: Abraham collection.

slope falling several thousand feet to their deaths. Incredibly the rope between the rest of the party and the last man broke over a sharp projection, leaving F.W. Hill as the sole survivor. Nearly two days later he staggered into Zermatt, still with the broken rope trailing behind him...

George Abraham wrote about Jones:

'His favourite theory was that all men should climb and would be the better for it, in contrast to the dog-in-the-manger attitude which then reigned in the climbing world, that the joys of the mountains were only for men of liberal education and from the higher walks of life.'

Jones too had realised the snobbish resentment of the Establishment towards the thrusting young Abrahams and their commercial interests.

The Abrahams returned to Wales to reconnoitre Clogwyn du'r Arddu which had been left to brood for more than a century. They first looked at the East Buttress and tried what was to become Chimney Route, but retreated before they had reached the first stance. George wrote:

'It has been said that this imposing mass possesses much interest for the rock-climber. It has been truly said that the easy places are too easy and the difficult places are impossible.'

One of the great contributions of the Abrahams was Monolith Crack on the Gribin Facet in Ogwen. They had such a struggle that they graded it Exceptionally Severe, under the system invented by their friend O.G. Jones, and thought it 'almost the stiffest problem in Wales'. George described his painful struggle:

'I got too much inside the narrow crack, and found further progress impossible. In fact it was a difficult matter to even extricate myself from the vice-like grip...As there was now little danger of falling out of such a quandary, we neglected the question of anchorage, and my brother mounted into the foot of the crack. It was an easy matter to climb over him and thus effect a splendid lodgement high up in the crack without undue fatigue...the upper portion demands every iota of surplus energy and strength.'

Tom Leppert's 1982 description was, 'A unique and legendary climb that requires both strength and a particular fighting spirit to succeed'. The main pitch he described as:

'This pitch will not be accomplished without a struggle. Face right and force youself into the dank claustrophobic depths of the cavity. Hopes do brighten, so make a bid for the daylight with a sort of vertical crawl and caterpillar-like movements. The originators were bolder; they climbed straight up! The second can be ignominiously stuffed into the tightest part of the cleft, then by clambering on top of him a wider part can be reached and completed on the outside, passing over the chockstone.'

George Abraham's classic guide-book, 'British Mountain Climbs', which was first published in 1909 and ran to six editions by 1948, included all the notable climbs in Wales. This book, which fulfilled the ambition of O.G. Jones, included the first meaningful graded list of climbs, the hardest of which were:

Exceptionally Severe Courses

Crib Goch Buttress, original route (120-foot rope).
Central Gully, Glyder Fawr (direct, without a threaded rope).
Devil's Staircase (direct) (120-foot rope).
Crib Goch Buttress (Mr. W.R. Reade's Route).
Great Gully, Craig yr Ysfa (direct except Door Jamb Pitch).
Three Pitch Gully, Clogwyn y Garnedd, East Face (120-foot rope).

Great Gully, Cyrn Las (direct throughout) (120-foot rope).
Eastern Gully and Hawk's Nest Ridge, Glyder Fach.
The Black Cleft, Dinas Mot (120-foot rope).
East Peak, Shallow Gully, Lliwedd (160-foot rope).
Slanting Gully, Lliwedd (120-foot rope).
East Peak, Central Route, Lliwedd (120-foot rope).
East Peak, Central Chimney Climb, Lliwedd (160-foot rope).
Central Gully, East Peak and Great Chimney, Lliwedd
Far East Buttress, Lliwedd (by the cracks) (160-foot rope).
Monolith Crack
Twll Du (160-foot rope).
Central Gully (Mr. W.R. Reade's Direct Route), Lliwedd.

Sadly about the time that the Climbers' Club was formed the owners of the Pen y Gwryd died and the cosy comfort and excellent meals became a thing of the past. After a while the P. y G. became associated with dirt and discomfort. Only a mile away however, at the summit of the Llanberis Pass, was the Pen y Pass hotel which had recently been extended and improved. Reluctantly the Climbers' Club transferred its base, but instead of a new beginning C.E. Mathews died and the social scene, which he had dominated for so long, fragmented.

Luckily a young successor, who could take on the role of social co-ordinator, was waiting in the wings, and Geoffrey Winthrop Young eventually took over the vacant mantle. As a boy he had been taken to Wales by his Alpinist father and before going to Cambridge he had made an early ascent of Napes Needle in the Lake District. In his formative years Victorian Alpine tradition became deeply engrained. Alpinism was sacrosanct and Young criticised those who merely rock-climbed. He had considerable literary ability and used his pen to spray the faithful with rigid dogma against pure rock-climbing.

'Long grey valleys of technique where the dry bones of dead sport await us, graphs, formulae and apparatus.'

Winthrop Young graduated from Trinity to teach at Eton and in 1903 stayed at Pen y Pass for the first time. Except during the First World War he went there for the next thirty-five years and was always surrounded by convivial gatherings from public schools and Oxbridge. They had the mountains to themselves which prompted him to write wistfully:

'Climbing then had the freshness of a dawn. Nobody was on the hills but a few farmers' herds and ourselves.'

Although he was rigidly against exclusive rock-climbing an extract from one of his poems still sums up the attraction of bare rock and difficulty:

'In this short span
between my finger tips on the smooth edge
and these tensed feet cramped to the
crystal edge
I hold the life of man.'

Although Winthrop Young always climbed with guides his Alpine record became formidable. In Wales he acted as a magnet and attracted new recruits from the Public

Schools, and others from professional and leisured backgrounds. Not only did he climb with the old guard which included Archer Thomson, but he also introduced many young people to the mountains. One such person was the son of the Rector of Mobberley in Cheshire. Even at the age of seven George Leigh Mallory was already climbing on the roof of his father's church!

One of George Mallory's first adventures was when, with two other young men, he ventured onto Terminal Arete on Lliwedd. It was the occasion when owing to their inexperience they dislodged several boulders and nearly wiped out Archer Thomson's party which was busy making the first ascent of Avalanche Route — hence the name.

Mallory was back in the Welsh mountains the next summer and stayed at Pen y Pass with his younger brother, Trafford, who later became Commander-in-Chief of the Allied Air Forces during the D-Day landings, shortly before he was killed. During that holiday Mallory, who was very absent-minded, left his pipe on a ledge. His solution was to solo back up to get it — by a new Very Difficult variation which is still called Mallory's Slab.

The extraordinary good looks of Mallory attracted the attention of Lytton Strachey who wrote ecstatically about them in a letter to Clive and Vanessa Bell, close friends of Virginia Woolf:

'He's six feet high with the body of an athlete by Praxiteles, and a face, oh incredible, the mystery of Botticelli, the refinement and delicacy of a Chinese print.'

Even Winthrop Young wrote enthusiastically about Mallory's climbing style:

'He swung up rock with a long thigh, a lifted knee and a ripple of irresistible movement. A perfect physique and a pursuing mind came together.'

Another route of Mallory's was a ridge named after him on Nantlle y Garn. It was Very Severe in standard and was not repeated until after the Second World War. Mallory eventually became a master at his old school, Charterhouse, and in 1914 introduced one of his pupils to the delights of Pen y Pass and rock-climbing. It was Robert Graves the poet who later wrote about Mallory and Winthrop Young in his autobiography 'Goodbye to all That':

'It appeared not merely in his preparations for an ascent — the careful examination strand by strand of the Alpine rope, the attention to his boot-nails, and the balanced loading of his rucksack — but also in his caution on the rock-face. Before making any move he thought it out foot by foot, as though it were a chess problem. If the next hand-hold happened to be just a little out of his reach, or the next foot-hold seemed at all precarious he would stop to think of a safe way round the difficulty. George used sometimes to grow impatient, but Geoffrey refused to be hurried. His shortness put him at a disadvantage in the matter of reach. Though not as double-jointed and prehensile as Porter, or as magnificent as George, he was the perfect climber; and still remains so.'

Clearly Mallory had a great future ahead of him in rock-climbing if he had so chosen, but his future lay in the greater mountain ranges of the Himalaya. After the war he went to Everest and became obsessed with the mountain which ultimately claimed his life. On his final attempt in 1924 he was last seen with Sandy Irvine going strongly for the summit. Eventually the mist rolled in and absorbed them into immortality.

Winthrop Young liked to give a literary touch to the naming of his new routes and on one famous occasion was the inventor of the term 'Thank God Hold'. He said that he had named it thus after a succession of Irishmen had used the same expression of relief

Opposite: Oscar Eckenstein as middle man during an ascent of the West Buttress of Lliwedd.   Photo: Abraham collection.

when each of them in turn had used the same hold on the rock below him. Another new term he coined was 'Purple Passage' because 'it was that kind of passage and better left out'.

Another climber from the Pen y Pass fraternity, who was perhaps Geoffrey Winthrop Young's greatest discovery was Siegfried Herford. His climbing ability quickly became awe-inspiring and he soon surpassed his fellow climbers.

In 1912 Herford spent over one hundred days in climbing but although his contribution to Welsh climbing was useful it was not spectacular. His new routes included: Alpha, a slab climb on Glyder Fach, a nice strenuous Very Severe crack on the Gribin Facet, and on the same cliff, Zig-Zag, a fine delicate route with a tricky crux getting into a groove. The latter has seen several nasty leader-falls onto the waiting boulders many feet below. John Laycock wrote in Herford's obituary:

'He climbed alone the Great Gully of Craig yr Ysfa, the first long climb he ever did. Such a thing would be madness except for one above laws. Herford could do such things and do them safely.'

Herford's fame was not to be earned in Wales and his great moment occurred as a result of another man's vision. Winthrop Young was keen to extend the Climbers' Club influence to Scafell in the Lake District and having seen the supple confident movement of Herford, he asked him to explore the Pinnacle Face of Scafell for a Climbers' Club guide-book. Herford's dramatic response on April 20th 1914 was the ascent of Central Buttress by the Flake Crack, best described by an extract from the 1984 Scafell guide-book: 'Probably the biggest single breakthrough in standard in the history of Lakeland climbing' — and even today it is still graded as Hard Very Severe.

Central Buttress, or C.B. as it is better known, was perhaps the biggest single step forward in the whole history of British climbing. Shortly after Herford's ascent, the war started and brought a cloud over the climbing scene. Herford subsequently joined the army and was soon in the midst of the bloody battle in France. In 1916 he raised his head from the trenches and was instantly killed.

After the First World War there was a mood of disillusionment throughout the country owing to the crippling loss of an emerging generation. The old order of climbing, forged in the leisurely Victorian times, was to be a thing of the past — destroyed forever in a bitter struggle when many of the young men lost their lives or limbs (as in the case of Winthrop Young) in the trenches. Although the old order had changed it merely meant that there was to be a lull before a new breed of climber was to emerge onto the scene.

In 1916, the same year that Herford was killed in France, a young eighteen-year-old Mancunian joined the Public School Battalion and became a sniper. Soon afterwards he was badly wounded in the hand but a long convalescence to recover from his injuries almost certainly ensured his survival. His hand eventually got better although it was always misshapen, but it did not inhibit the young ex-sniper from taking up climbing. Alfred Sefton Pigott had started on the climbing road which was to lead to a dazzling prize some ten years later on the unclimbed and forbidding precipice of Clogwyn du'r Arddu.

Not all climbing had come to a halt during the war as some people still managed to get away for breaks in the hills and surprisingly there was still hopeful creativity in the minds

Opposite: The Pinnacle Ridge on the Amphitheatre Buttress of Craig yr Ysfa   Photo: Abraham collection.

of a worried people. I.A. Richards, later to become a world famous literary critic, took part in the exploration of the unclimbed parts of the Idwal Slabs and its upper walls. His small group discovered Faith, Hope and Charity, three routes that were to achieve enormous popularity in later decades.

Just as the war was slipping to its agonising end in 1918 the first breach was made on the smooth uncompromising wall at the top of the Slabs, which they saw as a logical finish to Hope. Richards and Dorothy Pilley (who was later to become his wife) were reinforced by C.F. Holland, a first-rate climber who had been on the first ascent of Central Buttress with Herford and Sansom in 1914. There was a solitary holly tree growing out of a chimney crack, which was to give the wall its name. Below it a vague fault was to give great problems for those who aspired to climb it. Over the years the holly tree flourished on its tiny ledge and acquired much respect and affection from the thousands of climbers who passed by. Unfortunately in the early sixties a large falling leader stripped it from its precarious footing, which made the wall seem very bare and the route just that little bit less glamorous.

With the holly tree as the target a determined effort was made to get up the wall. For the take-off a risky ladder was improvised using an ice-axe held at arm's length by a second whose position was far from safe.

Richards became even more determined and climbed a corner crack to the right to a meagre stance. He knocked in a piton, then managed to traverse across to the holly tree. That simple statement of fact reveals the first use of a piton in Welsh rock.

'All went well. At the foot of the climb an uncanny thing happened. Tucked in a cranny an iron piton just showed. What mysterious person had left it there, and for what purpose? It seemed, on that haunting morning, a hint too clear to be ignored. Up above, where belays are lacking, and the climbing is delicate, I.A.R. sought out a crack for this iron Finger of Fate, and hammered it in securely with a stone carried up for the purpose. So placed, it was of no assistance to the leader of the pitch, but with my rope belayed about it, I could guarantee that, whatever happened, no serious harm could come.'

The piton was rediscovered by Ted Hicks in 1929 but later it worked loose and was reported missing. Colin Kirkus later commented:

'This venerable relic had too many historical associations to be regarded with any great distaste by even the most rabid purist: but alas! when getting frail and weak with advancing years it was uprooted by some ruthless vandal having no respect for the antiquities of a bygone age.'

A.R. 'Sandy' Edge replaced it in 1934 with a 'very graceful hand-forged one (price 1s 3d.)' but this was removed by Menlove Edwards who deemed it to be not necessary.

When the Richards party reached the holly tree they discovered that the leader could not get up the chimney to escape. In Dorothy Pilley's book 'Climbing Days' there is a charming account of the epic ascent but it was Holland who later wrote:

'First one tried to climb the fierce-looking crack, then the other. We stood on the tree in turn and sweated in vain attempts to ascend; in turn we fell exhausted into the safe but painful embrace of the tree. It was no use; the victory was with the enemy; we could do no more.'

The problem was finally solved by Holland who led the tricky wall on the left in nailed boots. He later confessed how he felt:

'...like a sparrow on the housetops, though without a sparrow's advantages as to the methods at his disposal of removing himself therefrom.'

Opposite: The Red Wall of Lliwedd.   Photo: Eric Byrom collection.

The Holland and Richards team had many lucky escapes in those days of minimal protection and there were some horrific falls and near tragedies which were all laughed off as part of the great adventure. Lliwedd seemed to be particularly suitable for bowling down the slabs at a great rate!

'...as at that instant he had no other holds, off he came. He landed luckily astride I.A.R.'s neck and the two of them managed to stay where they were...'

'Without a word Holland slipped down a little, then fell out backwards and came like a loose sack, head-over-heels, down the wall. At this instant I.A.R. noticed that the rope had again worked off the belay...I.A.R. avers that Holland was making a loud whizzing noise in his fall before he caught him, and that he swerved a great deal in his flight. There was no use now in worrying about the rope, the thing to do was to catch the climber.'

Dorothy Pilley also captured another superb incident on an early ascent of the Direct Route, Glyder Fach:

'He exclaimed, "Find me a rugosity! Find me a rugosity!" with some insistence. Slowly he concertina'd out until he was dangling at full arm's stretch by his finger tips. He made no attempt to return. Suddenly, with a grating screech (I have never heard a sound quite like it before or since) his hands slipped off and he dropped clear through the air onto the ledge below, where I.A.R. pounced on him with a rugby collar.'

The tenuous thread of new routes was to be maintained almost solely by Richards at the start of the nineteen-twenties. However, 1919 had seen the discovery of the delightful Tennis Shoe by Noel Odell before his long association with Everest began. It was good to see Noel still being sprightly in the Welsh mountains in 1985 at the tender age of 94.

Ogwen proved to be the most popular climbing area for nearly all the climbers for some time but one must remember that there were no climbing guide-books, and very little information was available except through two or three clubs which were at a very low ebb. There were not even any club huts or hostels in which to stay. However, even though it was tottering on the verge of extinction, the Climbers' Club had a nucleus of determined men.

In the post-war period George Mallory, who was President of the Climbers' Club, set up a small group which was soon irreverently dubbed 'The Demoribundisation Sub-Committee'. It consisted of Raymond Green, Maurice Guinness, S.A. Marples and of course Mallory. Its terms of reference were to get the club back on its feet again and to this end the group recommended: that there should be a regular issue of journals, a revival of club activities, new guide-books and lastly a club hut or cottage in North Wales. It required someone with dynamic powers to implement these considerable proposals.

Before long they found Herbert Carr, who was not at that time even a member of the Club. That was no problem. A survivor from the trenches and a keen member of the Oxford Mountaineering Club, Carr was the ideal man for the job. He had tremendous enthusiasm and boundless energy and was already engrossed in research for his classic work — 'The Mountains of Snowdonia'.

It was an historic moment when Carr first discovered Helyg, Borrow's miserable hovel in the Ogwen valley. An ideal meeting point, it consisted at that time of a single room, fifteen feet by twenty feet, to be provided with primus stoves for cooking and a spirit lamp for lighting. While Carr was in the middle of getting the hut ready for the grand opening he had a bad climbing accident in Cwm Glas. His companion Van Noorden, a brilliant young climber, was killed and Carr was seriously hurt with multiple injuries. He lay out in the open for two days and nights before his cries for help were finally heard. Later he was allowed out of hospital swathed in bandages to attend the formal opening of Helyg in October 1925. During the celebrations two Cambridge undergraduates happened to be passing, so Jack Longland and Ivan Waller were promptly invited in to join the festivities. Helyg was an instant success and before long it was not only a meeting place for members of the Climbers' Club, but far more than that, it was to be for some years the very hub of Welsh climbing.

The Climbers' Club did not, however, have the complete monopoly of climbing in Wales. Another powerful force appeared on the Welsh climbing scene. The Rucksack Club, based in Manchester, had a background of hard walking and its tough members had pioneered the development of many gritsone edges as well as being very active in the Lake District. In the nineteen-twenties they turned their attention to Wales. One of the leading lights, Fred Pigott, with his able deputy Morley Wood, was about to make a big step forward in Welsh climbing on the most challenging cliff — Clogwyn du'r Arddu. Herbert Carr had written of the crag:

'The East Buttress has never been climbed, the final wall (the Pinnacle) is quite impossible, but the lower two hundred feet below a broad open gallery may yet by conquered by a bold and expert party.'

As early as 1924 Morley Wood, who had a keen eye for a good line, had taken a close look at the East Buttress and picked out a possible route in the middle of the crag. It was grassy but climbable in its lower part before a pinnacle and an obviously fierce corner crack near the top. On Pigott's first attempt he climbed a hundred feet to a holdless ten-foot corner before retreating. On the second attempt in June 1926 a human pyramid was used to force the ten-foot corner beyond which they were able to assess the final crack:

'For the first few feet up it is the merest crack, with hardly finger room; but gradually it widens until at twenty feet a toe may be inserted.

At first, all efforts to get up this twenty feet were abortive. Even a human ladder, with the heavy-weights at the bottom, in boots, and the more lithesome ones daintly shod in rubbers at the top, met with no success.'

Again they retreated, but Lindley Henshaw had no doubts about the calibre of his friends:

'Pigott and Wood in combination are as unscrupulous as they are invincible. Nothing stops them and they stop at nothing, not excluding pitons and fixed ropes. If the threatened onslaught on the West Buttress takes place I shall not be surprised to see either of them turning up with the latest Sassolungo rock-drill and a whole belt full of pitons. Personally for their own sakes, I hope they do.'

Clearly Henshaw was looking beyond the East Buttress to the next big target which must have struck them as being a more serious undertaking. As to the no-holds-barred philosophy:

'The plain fact is that Morley Wood was alone responsible for the idea of putting chockstones into the crack, the evidence being perfectly clear on this point. It may be said that other members of the party were accessories after the fact: but Morley Wood was the one who conceived, organised, and eventually put into practice his diabolical plan; and if some of the

Opposite Top Left: Geoffrey Winthrop Young.
Opposite Top Right: Jack Longland.   Photos: Longland collection.
Opposite Bottom Left: Reputed to be Maurice Linnell.
Opposite Bottom Right: The Gwynant Crack.   Photos: Eric Byrom collection.

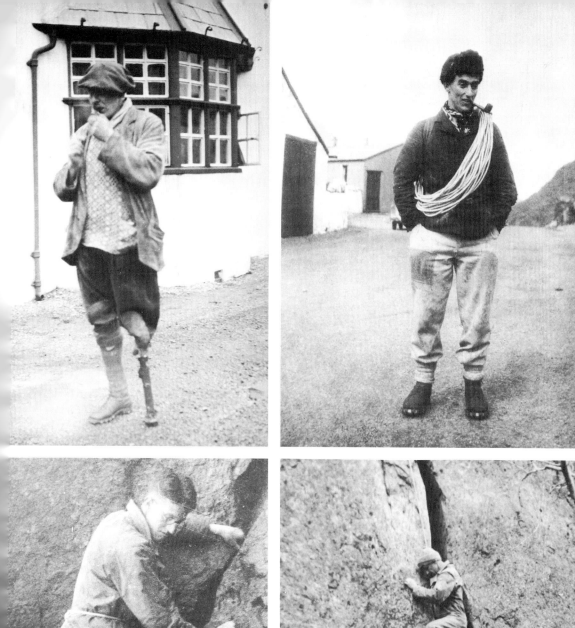

inserted pebbles did remain in, that can only be put down to Providence and not to any dexterity on his part.'

'On the next attempt conditions were foul and Pigott lay ill in bed. He encouraged the others to try again — almost to the point of offering his favourite piton from the dress-tie drawer.'

On the day when success was finally in sight Pigott was so confident that he insisted that Burton should go with them to take photographs. He also insisted that Henshaw should carry an ice-axe — just in case. Pigott skipped up into the weather-beaten noose as though it were a rigging, and reached a small ledge.

'Our leader having arrived exhausted at this point stood up on the ledge and called for a man with guts. Having none to spare below we sent up two chockstones slung in a handkerchief, one of which he inserted in the crack above, and secured himself by passing his rope through another six feet of Beale.'

On the last section Morley Wood threw the rope over a high notched rib so that his tired leader was protected for the final few feet. This breakthrough lifted the level of Welsh climbing which had lagged for so long behind the high standards already set in the Lake District. They had produced a climb which later became known as Pigott's and it could stand comparison with almost any other route in the British Isles. The final 5a pitch was the first to reach such a standard in Wales and although the route was not led free on the first ascent it stood as a tribute to Fred Pigott's muscular fitness despite his war-twisted fingers. One of the few routes that could supersede Pigott's was Herford's route on the Central Buttress of Scafell.

Where were the remnants of the traditional Welsh hard climbers of the pre-war era? Surprisingly they were emerging from the close-knit circle which was being reorganised by Geoffrey Winthrop Young. Young had been badly wounded on the Italian front and had lost a leg — a terrible blow for an active climber. This physical trauma caused him to hesitate in starting up the Pen y Pass parties again, but slowly he regained confidence in himself and restarted his joyful gatherings which included Jack Longland and Ivan Waller.

In 1927 all the praise was being heaped on the Rucksack Club elite for their success on the East Buttress of Cloggy. However that year Ivan Waller made his considerable contribution with three new routes which were all Very Severe. On two of them the ancients had failed miserably but of course Ivan was a rock-gymnast and a Whillans prototype of the twenties. He soloed one of the new routes on sight then on the more formidable Belle Vue Bastion he did the first ascent then promptly soloed it the next month. The same day he solved the first ascent of a new pitch on Long Chimney — also on the Terrace Wall of Tryfan. After soloing Belle Vue Bastion for its second ascent he took C.W. Marshall up it the same day. Marshall was clearly immensely impressed and wrote:

'...climbing for the next twenty feet is Extremely Severe, with an agonising step diagonally upwards to the left, which is very near the limit.'

Waller had made the first ascent with music to sooth him from a portable gramophone perched on the Belle Vue Terrace. In the concluding sentence of his article on the climb he wrote:

'We understand that in future any new climbs made to the gramophone will not be counted as such.'

Opposite: Determined jamming on Pigott's Climb, Clogwyn du'r Arddu.   Photo: Eric Byrom collection.

It ought to be pointed out that whereas Pigott's climb was mainly crack-climbing using inserted chockstones, Waller was quite out in the open and totally unprotected. On Belle Vue Bastion it required the utmost confidence, which Waller clearly possessed — as proved by his solo second ascent.

Waller's third great effort was up an impressive unclimbed crack on Clogwyn y Ddysgl, which had defeated Winthrop Young and George Mallory. This strenuous and classic cleft, Fallen Block Crack possibly his finest effort, was a masterly line taken in one pitch. Such wide cracks are not frequently found in Wales and years later V.S. leaders were to treat this pitch with considerable respect. Waller remained very casual about the whole affair:

'My second man was unable to follow me. I had never seen him before and I have never seen him since.'

When looking back at the considerable achievements that were shortly to follow it seems strange that modern climbers should not realise the extent of Waller's undoubted contribution to Welsh climbing.

The West Buttress of Clogwyn du'r Arddu was by then ripe for exploration and Herbert Carr who had visited the cliff on several occasions in 1919, when he climbed three routes on the Far West Buttress, had written:

'No breach seems either possible or desirable along the whole extent of the West Buttress, though there is the faintest of faint hopes for a human fly towards its left side.'

The Rucksack Club tigers, flushed with success on the East Buttress, were already planning an attack but others also had their eyes fixed on the same target. At Easter 1928 Jack Longland and Frank Smythe made the first reconnaissance with Winthrop Young as an observer of his young proteges. They noticed an entry on the extreme left-hand end but rain drove them away.

Two days later they were back, and Longland traversed across the repulsive, dripping foot of Black Cleft and sidled behind a bollard. They came to an unclimbed twenty-foot wide slab, tilted up at seventy-five degrees — there were overhangs to its right and a sheer drop into the Black Cleft on the left...Longland climbed slowly, digging out a turf overlay to reveal perfect small holds underneath. Smythe took over for more gardening then Longland returned to the lead once again, just as rain started to fall steadily and an abseil became necessary.

The following Whit-Saturday, Pigott and his Rucksack experts made the same entry to the West Buttress, climbed the gardened slab and were astonished to find the abseil loop. They gardened more unclimbed slabs for another three and a half hours and at one point Pigott remembered:

'To Henshaw and me far below, the clink of steel against rock heralded the advent of a crisis. Eversden advanced; paused; and descended. Wood, putting a rasp into his voice, called for the shock-troops, but Henshaw, as averse as ever to artificial aids, kicked out the pitons and demonstrated the fallacy of the security they seemed to offer. My suggestion of an artificial chockstone was received silently.'

After getting the rope firmly jammed they finally abseiled off to escape for the time being.

Longland spent Whit-Saturday taking the one-legged Winthrop Young up Route II on Lliwedd. It was a perfect day. Nowadays it would be incomprehensible for anyone to leave a half-completed route, when there was every possibility that someone else would step in and complete it. After the week-end and his successful ascent of Longland's, Jack wrote to his mother about the week-end, taking up nearly all the note-paper to explain his delight in taking Winthrop Young, his mentor, up a route on Lliwedd on such a perfect summer day. Then at the end in passing he mentioned that he had done a new route.

Whit-Sunday looked as if it might see the most intriguing race for a route in Welsh rock-climbing history — the Pen y Pass team of Oxbridge elegance versus the northern experts. The Pen y Pass team got off to a bad start when they had trouble with their cars:

'Of course, as he had two engineers in the party, all that could go wrong with the cars was duly suffered; the climax being reached when one car was derelict — its owner on some far-fetched petrol expedition — and the other which had presumed to go backwards in search of him, very coyly nestling in a ditch on the steep ascent to the Ranger track! However, there are always climbing ropes, and we had Geoffrey Winthrop Young to organise haulage parties...'

Consequently they arrived at the big cliff late in the morning. Pigott, Morley Wood and Eversden were already at the foot of the crag, minus Henshaw who had wandered off in a mood of contemplation. Soon Longland, Smythe and Bicknell reached the waiting Rucksack men and were able to answer the mystery of the in-situ sling which had been left after the abseil. In those more polite times, there was a charming scene of *"You first"*, *"No — you should be before us"*. Ivan Waller and Peter Bicknell insisted on standing down and the latter went off for a long swim with Winthrop Young, while the Oxbridge team politely suggested that the teams should combine for the assault. Pigott was adamant that as Longland had been on the route first he should lead the climb, so he flung a rope-end to him and told him to get on with it.

It was a fine warm day and Longland made short work of the lower parts of the climb that both teams had previously ascended but, as he wrote in the C.U.M.C. journal, the problems then began:

'My longest hesitation, on a little ledge below the rather unpleasant overhang which obviously had to be surmounted to secure a position on the next leaf of slab, was overcome by a triumph of organisation. To me, protesting, were first sent up on the rope a pair of rubbers; these were put on after a struggle (one hand being rather urgently needed elsewhere), and I cast round for a further excuse — *"But, there's no belay"*. There came a wicked smile upon the face of Morley Wood, at the sheet anchor end of the rope; this was the moment he had been hoping for, and he unslung his rucksack, which was hauled up, mysteriously heavy. I felt inside and found two chockstones: here all dead members of the Alpine Club turned uneasily in the grave.

It was none of your imported chockstones; no pudding stone from the Dauphine, or millstone grit from the steeps of Laddow, but sound Welsh rock picked from the foot of this very buttress. The first chockstone was a beauty, and fitted like a City man into his bowler hat. I sent down the other with my boots. My final complaint was at once answered by the appearance of a large clasp knife on a bight of the rope; and in pregnant silence I cut off a length, looped it round the chock, and passed my rope through it (the dead Alpine Club members meanwhile keeping up a high rate of coffin revolution.) Even so, the next pitch was sufficiently emotive, the crisis being a turn on small straddling footholds into an outward facing position, and then a very awkward pull over the little wall on the right to a minute ledge on the next slab.'

This was the one part of the climb where Longland felt pressed but he eventually dealt

Opposite Above: Before the climb at the foot of the West Buttress of Clogwyn du'r Arddu. T. Graham Brown, Ivan Waller, Frank Smythe and Jack Longland.   Photo: Longland collection.

Opposite Below: A party of Rucksack Club climbers beside Llyn du'r Arddu in the early 1930s. Could it be the Fettes blazer worn by Menlove Edwards?

Photo: Rucksack Club collection.

with the Faith and Friction slab. There he knocked in a piton above the crux, with a stone which he found on the ledge. Despite the abortive attempts by the Rucksack men, this was only the second piton to be knocked into Welsh rock. It was no premeditated affair, however, as Longland had picked it up in the Alps some time before and had carried it about in his pocket.

Down below, Pigott was anxious — as he had forgotten his matches and constantly needed to smoke. The battle was as good as won by then and in time they all united at the crevasse stance — Pigott happily smoking. It started to rain heavily, but they were well protected under the overhang and sheltered for a while. Only fifteen feet of overhanging rock separated them from safety.

'Our friend the overhang played his grim game to the last, pretending that the issue was still in doubt; but this was only bluff.'

Longland easily solved the problem and twenty minutes later they were all shaking his damp hand, just four and a half hours from the foot of the climb. The rain stopped and the sun came out to herald a new era in Welsh climbing. The East and West Buttresses had been conquered by the human flies.

Longland made further attempts on the big overhangs to the right of the Great Slab entry before it was first done. He even managed to get twenty-five feet up on one occasion, but three holds broke simultaneously — yet despite a nasty fall he was unhurt. Later, in 1933, Longland also made the first ascent of the direct start to Curving Crack which had defeated Kirkus. His companions were A.B. Hargreaves and Alf Bridge, and the route is wrongly recorded in the guide-book as having been done by Piercy and Woodroffe in 1940.

In those days when conditions were wet, which they often were, people climbed in socks but one disadvantage of these was they tended to roll about when a foot was placed on a hold. A.B. Hargreaves had the bright idea of placing several rubber bands on his foot to prevent the rolling effect.

Karabiners were still some years off and in fact Longland did not possess one until some years later when he clipped one to his climbing rope. It was soon spotted by an elderly Lakeland climber who spluttered:

"It's people like you who are the real vandals in the climbing world."

The Cambridge experts had the geographical disadvantage of being a long way from both Wales and gritstone and being at university had hardly any personal transport. Longland summed up the problem in a nutshell:

'We never came near to the habit of coming to Helyg week-end after week-end, from Liverpool or Cheshire and could not work steadily at a crag or a single problem. Nor do I think we had developed the mental attitude, as we certainly had not the technique that carried Colin Kirkus and Menlove Edwards on their triumphant wave of discovery. Our main planning and pipe-dream ambitions went towards each new Alpine season.'

This modest comment by Longland on his climbing ability does him less than justice for he was to pioneer the hardest pre-war climb in the British Isles. The last sentence of his extract neatly sums up the Winthrop Young influence which permeated the Pen y Pass group, of which Longland and Waller had become integral parts. Longland again:

'After the war break we had to learn our way about Lliwedd again as part of our admission fee to the privilege of joining Pen y Pass Easter parties.'

Opposite Above: Fred Pigott and a Rucksack Club team on Glyder Fach.
Opposite Below: Fred Pigott and a Rucksack Club team on Lliwedd.   Photos: Eric Byrom collection.

His own contribution, made at Easter 1928, was to pioneer the first pitch of Purgatory
— a '...*Very Severe pitch which A.B. Hargreaves described as the hardest single pitch
on the cliff, demanding a mastery of the special boot technique...possessed by very few.*'
   A.B. Hargreaves was one of the few people who spanned both the Welsh and Lake
District groups of leading climbers. He was also one of the very few men to have been
President of both the Climbers' Club and the Fell and Rock Climbing Club of the Lake
District. He was acutely aware of the respective standards at that time in the two areas:

'I have a clear recollection of the extraordinary low standard in North Wales before 1927. I
could see this because I climbed a good deal in the Lake District where the standard was much
higher.'

Pigott, Longland and Waller started to alter all that, but despite his modesty the plain
fact is that Longland put up the hardest rock-climb in the British Isles before the Second
World War. Climbing with two novices, Longland made the first ascent of Javelin Blade
in 1930. Perched picturesquely on the right-hand end of Holly Tree Wall, the Javelin is
set up and to the right of a shallow blind corner. Having just come back from studying in
Germany for six months Longland might have expected to be out of form — especially
as he was not with any experienced climbers of note — but things went very differently:

'Quite frankly, I'd lost the way. I'd come to the famous thread belay at the end of the first pitch of
the normal route, and I didn't know that the route ought to go to the right. I was, at that time, a
pole vaulter, which I think gives you pretty strong fingers, and I remember that the pull-out on to
the actual blade of the Javelin was very strenuous, though not dangerous — I had a belay about
forty feet below me.'

The route was the first Extreme in the British Isles although it was not appreciated as
such until many years later. There is a tiny notch just before the crux which grudgingly
accepts a modern nut, although twists and turns of the rope can easily flip it out.
Longland of course did not have even this dubious protection and the astonishing thing
about Longland's modest account is that a belay forty-feet below him actually gave him
confidence — a sharp contrast to modern pioneers.
   As Javelin Blade remained such an obscure route for so long and its difficulties not
appreciated it is interesting to compare the treatment given to the route by the different
guide-book writers.
   In the 1936 Cwm Idwal guide Menlove Edwards graded the Javelin Buttress as Severe
and merely noted for the Blade Finish that, 'The last part of the corner and the pull-out
are harder than the ordinary route'. Such an incredulous under-statement leads one to
believe that Edwards hadn't done, or couldn't do, the hardest pitch in Britain at that
time.
   As late as 1967 Tony Moulam's Idwal guide-book still only graded the Javelin Blade as
Very Severe and referred to the route as being much harder than the parent route.
   It took until 1974 for the truth to be revealed and Ken Wilson's guide-book set the
record straight for all time when he graded the route, Extremely Severe, 5b.

'An outstanding lead that stood as the most difficult piece of Welsh climbing for many years
though few were aware of it. It was only in recent times that its true difficulty became obvious
through the failure of a number of good climbers.'
'...moves are more gymnastic than fierce, and the pitch only claims its grade on account of the
distance from protection. It is best tackled on a warm dry day when moving well.'

Opposite Above: Alf Bridge, A.B. Hargreaves and Colin Kirkus.   Photo: A.W. Bridge.
Opposite Below: Members of the 1933 Gangotri Expedition, Richard Nicholson, Marco Pallis, F.E. Hicks, Dr Charles Warren
and Colin F. Kirkus.   Photo: Guy Kirkus collection.

Tom Leppert who graded the route E1 5b in his 1982 Ogwen guide has the final say in the matter:

'A remarkable route for its time. The crux comes at the end of a long run-out, yet one has to be relaxed enough to commit oneself with confidence.'

One can only ponder on what might have happened if Longland had been based in the North and had been able to apply his Javelin Blade abilities to other crags. Instead he spent much of his time in the Alps and greater ranges where he developed into a fine mountaineer. After several fine guideless ascents in the Alps he was selected for the 1933 Everest expedition and also visited Greenland with Wager and Courtauld. In later years Longland went on to a distinguished career in Education, becoming Director of Education for Derbyshire where during his years of office the Whitehall Outdoor Pursuits Centre became the first of its kind in the country. Not surprisingly Longland was to become in turn, President of the Cambridge University Mountaineering Club, the Alpine Club, the Climbers' Club and the British Mountaineering Council. In his ninth decade he still takes a keen interest in all mountaineering affairs but his fame undoubtedly hinges on a day long ago in 1928 when he pushed forward into the unknown on the West Buttress of Clogwyn du'r Arddu. As Fred Pigott wrote after the ascent:

'And so ended a great day for us. Great unclimbed cliffs are rare, so rare that one is indeed to be counted among the fortunate if allowed to practise one's craft upon them, to share with others the stimulation of defeat, the timeless tense hours of struggle, and the elation of victory — elation, — alas! always tinged with the inevitable regret that the rocks which have filled our thoughts for so long, can never quite mean the same to us again. Let us hope that the precipices of du'r Arddu were not the last of the great, untrodden, Welsh crags.'

Pathfinder

A few weeks after Longland's solution to the West Buttress a young teenager from Merseyside, Colin Kirkus, soloed a Severe — a hitherto unclimbed crack on Craig Lloer in a lonely cwm above the Ogwen valley. Kirkus's parents had a cottage near Ffestiniog and it is not surprising that he developed a keen love for the hills at an early age — by the age of nine he had already been up Snowdon and when eleven he traversed the Crib Goch ridge. There were two younger brothers, Nigel and Guy, but neither of them had the same infatuation for the mountains as their elder brother. During his early teens Kirkus went to explore the Berwyn mountains with his two brothers (Nigel was only eleven) having previously bought a length of clothes-line for fifteen pence. Colin pulled them both up a slaty buttress in the mist and hoped that they could not see the easier alternatives on either side.

At the age of seventeen he went on a family holiday to Bettws y Coed. There he broke free from the family for a day and cycled to Ogwen, where he left his machine, then walked over to Craig yr Ysfa. He tried to solo B Gully, a Very Difficult route:

'I scraped the mud out of a slight crevice on top of an overhanging boulder...I let go with my left hand, my right hand slipped numbly from the boulder...I was overcome by such a feeling of baffled rage at being thus ingloriously beaten that I rushed at the pitch again, only this time I fell and slid about thirty feet and stopped dangerously near the edge of the pitch below. I decided it was time to stop.'

This was the start of Kirkus's remarkably fruitful but fairly short career at the top of the climbing pyramid. He knew nothing of climbing or climbers but he was the first hard climber to produce dozens of new routes on large and small cliffs: Wales and the Lake District, gritstone and sandstone — even a 5b corner on Stanage Edge which would have been respectable if it had been done forty years later. Kirkus had the essential combination of not only superlative ability but also a keen eye for a new route — the latter at that time being the more important asset. He was able to pick out all the relevant features such as a crack, a rib perhaps, and then a slab — and then link them altogether into one superb line. Even on a climb he seemed to know instinctively which alterations to the line were needed in order to elevate the climb to greatness.

Whereas Pigott had been part of an elite Manchester group, Kirkus was quite alone to start off with and in his early days he had to learn everything by himself. It was a situation which suited his temperament, however, and he learned to cope with problems as they arose. Without partners he started soloing and not being in a club he was not exposed to disapproval. Luckily his natural talent on rock protected him and whenever he got into any kind of difficulty he had the coolness to get himself safely out of a potentially fatal situation.

'I got into a recess called the Javelin Gully (Idwal Slabs) though I did not know what it was at the time...The rocks became steeper and soon I reached a perpendicular section...I came down a little and saw a line of slightly nail-marked holds leading diagonally out to the left...Finally I seemed to have reached the end of all things..I found a piton...The rock above looked terrifying, then I saw a spike about twelve feet above me and after several attempts managed to lasso the spike, so down the rope I slid. Now for a do-or-die attempt. I climbed up the rope and managed to reach the spike and attacked the rocks above before I had time to change my mind...before I had time to realise it I was above the difficulty and safe at last.'

A.B. Hargreaves, 'The Little Man', who has been one of the greatest characters in the climbing world, was one of the first established climbers to take Kirkus in hand:

'I first met C.F.K. at Helyg in September 1928 when he would be about 18 and I, 24. I had been climbing a little over a year and had begun to lead a bit but he already had considerable experience of rock-climbing, mostly solo, and even had new routes to his credit...The Climbers' Club people seemed to think that he was a bit mad and our introduction was on that basis — possibly they thought I was too — anyway we were promptly dubbed "The Suicide Club"because our first climb together was the Holly Tree Wall in nails on a nice wet day.'

Kirkus still hankered after solo climbs however and went to investigate Craig Lloer which resulted in his closest shave:

'I had an urge for exploration and probably also wished to make a name for myself so I decided to have a look at Craig Lloer. It was about 200 feet high and had never been climbed. The main feature was a sinister-looking crack eighty feet up. The crack, forty feet high, overhung at the top...After an exhausting struggle I arrived at the overhang, there was a convenient chockstone and I tied myself to it, then I tried again. It was very strenuous and I struggled frantically, then just at a critical moment, my rucksack jammed in the crack. I worked it off my shoulder...

There was an innocent looking bulge above, I got half way up then realised it was much more difficult than it seemed. I could see a good hand-hold a little higher and made a grab for it. I was hanging by my hands. I felt I could not hang on much longer, I got into a panic and made a convulsive spring round the corner on the left, where mercifully my hands landed in a hold. I count that as one of my narrowest escapes.'

Kirkus was to excel at everything, whether it was the smooth open slab such as the Direct Route on Dinas Mot, or Pedestal Crack with its direct start which was still graded Extremely Severe some twenty years later. In March 1929 Kirkus was on Grooved Arete, Tryfan, where he soloed a super-direct pitch in a very exposed position. Later that year Hargreaves recalls a memorable meeting:

'In June 1929 Ted Hicks and Colin Kirkus met each other for the first time; this was on Tryfan's East Face, where Hicks was climbing some normal route with Warren, and they observed climbing alongside them, solo, this rather strange-looking young man. So, being responsible people fearing for his safety, they commanded him to join their rope. It then transpired that he had the night before cycled down to Helyg from Liverpool! Coming near to the Terrace Wall Kirkus suggested that the party should do Belle Vue Bastion, that excellent and difficult climb done a year or two previously by Ivan Waller; and he proceeded to lead them up it, thus tremendously impressing Hicks and Warren.'

The Cambridge party then moved over to Glyder Fach where Kirkus amazed them all by top-roping a steep right-angled groove which merged into an overhanging crack. He then led Lot's Groove with only Hicks being able to follow. Next day Kirkus led on sight the shorter and even more difficult Central Route on the Terrace Wall, which is still of a 5a technical standard. Kirkus was just nineteen and with these routes he became one of the top climbers in Wales. Hargreaves commented:

'Of course these were more or less stunt climbs and were not evidence of judgement, but on the 29th of June 1929, Colin led the second ascent of Longland's Climb on the West Buttress of Clogwyn du'r Arddu which most certainly required judgement. This took about four and a half hours and we had to shift tons of turf, soil and loose rock. Colin was maturing quickly. Later that year with Hicks and myself he did the eighth ascent of Scafell Central Buttress and the fifth ascent of the Gimmer Crack. Next year there was no stopping him...'

Alf Bridge, one of the leading climbers for many years, reflected on the early nineteen-thirties and wrote:

'I still think Colin was the best of them. He had all the right ideas. The reason I got to know him was that he ate three plates of porridge almost quicker than I could push them out...A lot of people think he was a contemporary of Menlove Edwards...it was five years after Colin did Lot's Groove that Menlove got going on his big series of climbs.'

As a climber Kirkus took things slowly and was occasionally awkward and ungainly in his movements, but he was not temperamental and never got rattled even under the most difficult circumstances. His eye for a new route was unmatched and he went from cliff to cliff picking out the best lines, but it was on Clogwyn du'r Arddu that he showed his true greatness. Kirkus started his exploration of Clogwyn du'r Arddu, on the West Buttress, with Dr Graham Macphee on June 22nd 1930.

'All the way along the foot of the cliffs the rocks overhung. Nobody had yet succeeded in overcoming this overhang. There seemed to be a faint chance in the middle, where a pile of blocks formed a kind of natural ladder. It looked a nasty place, but it seemed to me that, instead of climbing upwards, it might be possible to traverse out to the left, above the overhang. This would lead to a narrow slab, which ran up to the skyline and out of sight.

The traverse was Very Severe. There was one sloping hold where my rubbers would not grip at all, so at last I took them off and managed to get across in my stockinged feet.

I started up the narrow slab. It was far more difficult than it had looked, and wickedly rotten. I threw down every other hold. A thin ribbon of grass ran all the way up on the right, looking like a long and ragged caterpillar. I thought that even this might be safer than the rock and plunged into it.'

As Kirkus began to ascend, the 'caterpillar' began to peel off and slid down in a most alarming way so that Kirkus quickly vacated the vegetation and moved out left to the very edge of the slab. Unfortunately at that point he noticed the colossal drop below his feet, but undeterred he went on. After nearly all of the 120-foot line had uncoiled and crept up the slab, Kirkus had to stand about while Macphee tied on another 100-foot length. The situation was getting more and more hopeless and Kirkus was worried that he would not find a suitable belay point. Luckily just as he was despairing, he reached a suitable grassy niche where it was possible to bring Macphee up to join him.

The aim was to reach the huge slab which was still a long way up above them on the right, so Kirkus climbed a rib which appeared to go in the right direction. It quickly became clear that he would have to traverse right into a corner, but how was he to reach it?

'I got a long way across, and then stuck. The next move might be possible, by a kind of jump. It would be dangerous, but — well, a new climb was worth a risk. I looked at it a long time. It seemed to grow more terrifying and I was a long way from my second. I came back.'

Kirkus managed to find an easier way across, at a slightly lower level, but was faced with a twenty-foot corner of almost vertical grass:

'I made a mad rush at it. I had to climb up more quickly than the grass fell down. It was nasty and dangerous, but I dug in my finger-nails and toes (I was still climbing in stockings) and clutched and scrabbled until I reached the top.'

With the extensive slab in front the next pitch was not so steep and the turf split from the slab and began to roll up:

Opposite: Derek Walker on Lot's Groove, Glyder Fach.   Photo: Steve Ashton.

'It was rather like standing on a roll of carpet — with the carpet going on unrolling. It was very difficult and unpleasant but our reward was to come. We had two wonderful 100-foot pitches, right up and across the Great Slab, to its top left-hand corner. The rock was very warm and rough, and we felt profoundly happy and exhilarated. The climbing was just Severe, but it was easy after what had gone before and we seemed to glide up without effort. Macphee said I deserved a kick in the pants or a potato medal, he didn't know which.'

Great Slab was the culmination of all Kirkus's efforts so far and this route in particular inspired him to such an extent that he was thoroughly bitten by the new-route bug.

'Cooped up all week in an office, I would long for the next week-end. On a photograph of some cliff I would have all the known routes marked with dotted lines. The blank spaces in between fascinated me. Here was unexplored country; I longed to be the first to set foot upon it. I used to sit pretending to work, with the drawer slightly open, so that I could see the photo inside. Then I would plan a route.'

By 1930 Kirkus was the top climber at Helsby and with A.B. Hargreaves he published a guide to the crag in the Wayfarers' Journal. It was at Helsby that he gave much encouragement and advice to a prominent youngster who turned up there — Menlove Edwards. In later years when Edwards had taken on the mantle once worn by Kirkus they met at Edwards's camp-site in Cwm Tryfan where Edwards was working on the Tryfan guide. Kirkus offered Menlove a cigarette whereupon Edwards replied, *"You're the only person I take a cigarette from Colin."* When Kirkus had left Edwards remarked that Colin had been 'very decent' to him when others were stand-offish.

Bill Stallybrass, who climbed with Kirkus, summed him up well:

'Colin was a cheerful straightforward soul...and was as happy walking over comparatively low hills or leading a beginner up an easy climb as tackling a new route. Days spent with Colin were light-hearted, free of tension...'

Paul Work compared Kirkus and Edwards and came up with an interesting observation:

'Menlove felt his way up, Colin thought his way up. Both were fascinating to watch: Menlove because I could never see how he did it; Colin because I could, and so could he.'

Wilfrid Noyce, who did some of his first climbs with Kirkus when he was only fourteen, wrote:

'I watched each detail of the balanced slow movement of his body, and the shifting of his toes in slippery crevices. It was later that I learnt of his reputed astonishing use of the big toe at tricky points; on it he was said to stand for hours, spying holds. This time he bound elastic round his feet...moved forward over the slimy nobbles of Ash Tree Wall...On the smooth clean rock of the harder Dinas Mot nose I saw the same skill. Colin showed no nervousness...'

A.B. Hargreaves remembers another occasion when Kirkus and he were trying Javelin Buttress. It was a cold windy day and Kirkus got to the mantelshelf where he experienced some difficulty:

'He had the habit of flapping his hand behind him to restore circulation to them; unfortunately he flapped too hard and fell off.'

A.B. held him on the rope and fortunately Kirkus was unhurt. There were many adventures when A.B. and Kirkus were at large. A.B. used to take the train from Lime Street Station on a Saturday lunch-time in time to meet Kirkus at Helsby for an afternoon's climbing. They had an agreement to change in a public house — the Robin

Hood — but when they returned from the crag they habitually covered the floor with sand and were eventually asked to go elsewhere.

Kirkus frequently cycled to Helyg and back from Liverpool for a week-end. His brother Guy remembered that one week-end Colin walked to Helyg from Liverpool, getting so dehydrated in the process that he drank rainwater from puddles in the road.

After his success on the Great Slab of Clogwyn du'r Arddu he scarcely drew breath before attacking the smooth unclimbed Nose of Dinas Mot in Llanberis Pass. First attempted by Archer Thomson, Winthrop Young and the Abraham brothers, it had repulsed them all. They were all stopped by a hard move to reach a shallow groove running up the middle of the face, with the prospect of a very long run-out above. As long run-outs didn't worry Kirkus he soon dealt with the problem but the overall ascent took the party five hours:

'...should long remain a record. A ladder would make the final crack suitable for other than a few gymnasts.'

Kirkus did the top crack in socks which were often his normal footwear when things got tough, but this time he cut his feet badly wedging them into the crack. Above the route he tied his blood-stained socks to a little ash tree where they remained for several years.

In May 1931 Kirkus went up to the East Buttress of Scafell; it was convex in shape, dripping with water in many parts and still virgin. In a long and serious run-out he climbed the extra-delicate slabs of Mickledore Grooves, supported by Ivan Waller and Marco Pallis. Later that summer he was back in Wales prospecting on the remote crags of Cwm Silyn, which is out of the main Snowdon range behind the slate quarry village of Nantlle. On the beautiful curved sweep of slabs he left two classical imprints, the Upper Slab which is Severe and his fine V.S. on the right-hand section of the Great Slab.

Another outlying crag which Kirkus visited was the Amphitheatre Wall of Craig yr Ysfa where a tremendously steep wall cuts into the gully. At a higher level above a broad grassy terrace is an upper wall, with a steeply inclined quartz-splashed ledge running along at one-third height. It was an obvious entry and Colin tip-toed by himself along the ledge, made a long stride across a break, then arrived at a steep corner crack. The crux was a few feet up the corner, but underneath him was a drop of over two hundred feet to the rocky bed of the gully far below. Kirkus, who was fired in the furnace of soloing, did not hesitate long and easily disposed of the problem. He then continued more easily up a rough crack to the right to a spike-topped pinnacle which gave the route its name. The superb finish up an airy wall must have given a thrilling moment as he grasped the final jugs.

Kirkus and Edwards teamed up in August 1931 for Kirkus to attack a new line on the East Buttress of Cloggy — the chimney line which had repulsed the Abraham brothers. Referring to the assault Hargreaves wrote:

'Its ascent involved the removal of large quantities of turf, the insertion of at least one piton, and the giving of a shoulder by the second man, standing in loops fixed to belays not entirely above suspicion.'

Edwards injected a bit more humour into his report with such quips as:

'Crack becomes ornamental. Small piton (don't let it fall out) and sadly-depleted sod enable one to rise to a good stance and belay...Sweaty and rib-caving crack provides another old-fashioned

Opposite: Colin Kirkus and his fine Pinnacle Wall on Craig yr Ysfa.   Photos: Eric Byrom and Guy Kirkus.

interlude...Opportunities for lateral deviation are strictly limited throughout. Gardening operations were carried out incessantly by the leader, who therefore saw very little of number two below the sods. Cracks were greasy and the leader wore stockings...Rock all excellent except for the obvious rickety innards of the last overhang. There is no impurity except the piton and that will be found quite susceptible of removal by even the weakest purist.'

A few weeks after the ascent of Chimney Route he was back with Macphee to prospect Pedestal Crack — an even harder set of cracks and chimneys on the right-hand end of the East Buttress. He tried and failed on the direct start and had to work his way round to the right to get to the main pitch, but the failure on the start rankled and Kirkus returned soon after to force it. Twenty years later it was still graded Extremely Severe and is technically 5a by modern standards.

There were two other close friends of Kirkus and Hargreaves who showed great pioneering skill and technical ability, Maurice Linnell and Ted Hicks. In an even shorter period than Kirkus, Linnell showed great pioneering ability in his own right as well as climbing in support of Kirkus. It was a marvellous fortnight in June 1932 and on the 5th, Linnell followed Kirkus up the direct start to Pedestal Crack. Two weeks later, on his and Colin's birthday, they did Curving Crack and Birthday Crack during a week-end's bivouac at the foot of the cliff in company with Alf Bridge, A.B. Hargreaves, W.S. Dyson and lastly Marco Pallis who provided an all-olive diet for the week-end. Legend has it that on Birthday Crack a six-inch nail came in very useful as a belay at one point! Linnell made the third ascent of Great Slab with Pigott in 1933 and the following day removed the piton during an ascent of Chimney Route.

Linnell's expert eye for a new route focussed firmly on the unclimbed regions of the West Buttress, particularly the region of vast slabs and overlaps between Longland's and Great Slab. The easiest possibility seemed to be a series of grassy terraces which traversed this area at about one-third the height of the buttress. A start was made from the Eastern Terrace well below the entry to Longland's. This involved crossing the foot of White Slab, a difficult foot change, and a final spectacular jump onto steep grass. Only a climber at the top of his form would dare to do it and Linnell's Leap is a tribute to his boldness. The rest of Narrow Slab involved delicate slab-climbing and was undoubtedly Linnell's greatest contribution to Welsh climbing. It is a fine route, very exposed, and with the technical moves in airy situations. Nearly twenty years later Harding's guide-book described it in the terms of, 'As difficult a lead as any on the cliff,' and for many years Narrow Slab was regarded as the hardest of the Cloggy V.S.s. Some even insisted that it was Hard Very Severe.

In a few weeks either side of climbing Narrow Slab, Linnell followed Kirkus's example in unlocking more secrets from the East Buttress of Scafell, where he produced Overhanging Wall, Morning Wall, Yellow Slab and Great Eastern. Amazingly he capped these ascents by soloing the Bayonet-Shaped Crack at the top of Central Buttress, watched in astonishment by Ivan Waller and his party. This pitch is still technically 5b and well deserves its overall grade of Hard Very Severe.

The other climber who made a modest but useful contribution to Welsh climbing at the same time as Kirkus was Ted Hicks — yet another Cambridge man. A.B. Hargreaves well remembers his extraordinary physical characteristic; while Hicks was walking his hands could be seen swinging below his knees — a prehensile condition not thought to

Opposite: Sabre Cut, Dinas Cromlech. The final corner pitch.   Photo: Steve Ashton.

be in existence until the sloth-like movements of the Rock and Ice many years later. During his time at Cambridge he became an expert roof climber — as was the fashion.

'One night Ted was leading a fresher back across the roofs of Cambridge to St. Catherine's and crossing a skylight roof of a garage with ease. He warned his companion to take great care. With a great crash his companion promptly disappeared through the glass roof and Ted quickly descended to ground level by more orthodox means. Entering the garage full of fear for the safety of his friend, he discovered him sitting dazed but unhurt in the seat of an open Buick sports car — exactly where he had landed.'

Hicks became known to the rock-climbing fraternity on 5th May 1928 when he had a day's climbing on Gimmer with Warren, Bere and Spence. Late in the afternoon they descended to the 'gentleman's side' and found a Fell and Rock party on the first ascent of Gimmer Crack. After watching this they asked Reynolds and Macphee if it was interesting. The answer came "Yes, very!" despite the fact that it was perhaps the hardest route done in the valley at that time. A.B. Hargreaves takes up the story:

'So Ted and his party, "the fledglings and innocents abroad", said, "Right, we'll have a go". Now the sartorial fashion then was to wear Oxford bags — voluminous trousers with masses of material flopping around the feet. The Fell and Rock were able to observe, with something like horror, Ted proceeding up their new climb, rather nonchalantly, from time to time lifting the folds of his Oxford bags from under the tips of his rubbers — which was hardly the seemly sort of procedure then followed by the Fell and Rock! Anyway, Ted and Co. got up The Crack, casting down on their way a chockstone which the first party had used on their ascent, much to their annoyance as they watched events from across the gully. This hilarious story soon began to travel around.'

The Fell and Rock experts were completely taken aback by these antics and another version of the affair in the C.U.M.C. was as follows:

'They both seemed to be about seven feet tall, and they could reach all the wrong holds, and George Bower was dancing about in agonies of apprehension at the top, imploring them to use the belays...'

It wasn't long before Hicks was making his mark in Wales. After the historic meeting with Kirkus and doing Lot's Groove with him Hicks went on to do his own exploration. To quote A.B.:

'...an apparently weak spot was attacked light-heartedly in boots; after about an hour's hectic work, in which the Helyg poker played its part nobly, and during which the leader had changed into rubbers, a heaven-sent belay was reached, at a point where further progress seemed problematic. After several abortive attempts on a holdless corner above, an inspired lead across a rickety traverse and up an impossible-looking bulge, gave us Heather Wall.'

A.B. well remembered Hicks approaching the bulge along a thin crescent-shaped turf ledge, some thirty feet in length, which began to uncurl gently as Hicks walked gingerly up to its tip. Hargreaves had the gleeful satisfaction of later removing most of the turf with the infamous Helyg poker.

The effort that Hicks made to pioneer Rowan Tree Slabs with no protection was thought at the time to be at the limit of human adhesiveness.

On June 29th Hargreaves and E.A. Stewardson had done the second ascent of Longland's and A.B. was keen to do the true second ascent of Pigott's Climb (Fred had already led it twice). After meeting Hicks for the first time Hargreaves and Stewardson

went with him over the Glyders and Snowdon to reach Cloggy. The ascent went well but by the time they got to the foot of the final crack it was raining and windy. Not knowing of the existence of a good chockstone for belaying they threw the rope high over the arete to safeguard Hicks. Near the top he pulled on the rope and to his dismay it came away. It was only by a desperate grab for the top that he escaped falling off. If he had done so all three would have been at the foot of the crag in seconds. It was by far the narrowest shave that A.B. could remember in over forty years of climbing.

Alan Hargreaves also recalled:

'At about this time Ted had a really good go at Suicide Wall and very nearly got up it, but he would not risk the extremely difficult moves near the top with no protection except for me hitched to a little spike above that tiny ledge twenty feet below. I got down...and got a top rope down to him.'

It is clear that he had climbed the 5c first pitch which is the present crux of the climb but had not worked out the traverse to surmount the final wall.

On September 13th, 1931 Colin Kirkus again turned his attention to Dinas Mot and with Ivan Waller he produced another masterpiece. In concept West Rib was a very modern route being both sustained and delicate, and for many years it was to put off all but the best leaders. It is still graded as Hard Very Severe, 5a, and the modern guide-book describes it as:

'A committing and technical pitch which owing to poor protection needs a steady lead.'

The pitch is 105 feet long with continuous hard moves punctuated by mantelshelf-type manoeuvres which gnaw at a nervous leader. This tricky pitch was not equalled until Birtwistle's route Diagonal was put up years later.

The day that Kirkus and Linnell did Birthday Crack on Cloggy, the whole team clambered up the middle of the East Buttress just to the right of the tremendous sweep of Great Wall which is punctuated on its right-hand side by a series of cracks. Three of these were to be climbed by Kirkus. One line which was clearly quite enclosed in its upper section had a big pillar at the base of the crag. Kirkus, Bridge, Linnell, Hargreaves and Dyson all gathered together at the foot of the initial chimney on the left. As chimneys go this one was particularly uncompromising and at one point Alf Bridge wedged himself firmly in the chimney and even invited the others to use him as a human step ladder. They were still unsuccessful!

Without anyone noticing his disappearance Linnell slipped out of sight round the corner of the rib, and very soon amazed them all by peering down from the top of the pillar. He had calmly soloed a fine layback crack which made up the other side of the pillar. Very sportingly Linnell insisted that Kirkus should carry on leading the team up the rest of the route despite the fact that Linnell had done the crux pitch. Afterwards the voracious Kirkus was still not finished and wandered off along the foot of the crag. Alf Bridge was coiling the rope at the foot of Curving Crack when he heard a call for assistance from Kirkus who had climbed in nailed boots part of the way up the unclimbed Drainpipe Crack which is now the first pitch of Vember. By using Alf Bridge's shoulder Kirkus was finally able to make his way back down to safety.

During his halcyon period Kirkus did have falls, but fortunately in each case he survived. One of the more spectacular ones happened while he was in the Lake District with A.B. Hargreaves, on an ascent of Great Central Route on Dow Crag. The climb which is one of the great Lake District routes is in a deep amphitheatre with vertical walls which are often black and dripping with water. While attempting the South America Crack, a fierce 5b pitch, Kirkus missed a vital hold at the top of the crack and suffered a horrifying fall of some seventy feet. In an attempt to arrest his leader's fall Hargreaves had his hands badly torn and they were even burnt to the bone in places. As the shock came on the rope Hargreaves was twisted and pulled so that his nose was smashed into the rock face. Down in Coniston at the doctor's surgery the diagnosis was a broken toe for Kirkus, but A.B.'s injuries were far more severe, particularly his hands. The treatment was filling a bowl with carbolic acid and then scrubbing it into the wounds with a tooth-brush.

Another near disaster took place on Craig yr Ysfa when Kirkus lured A.B. Hargreaves up to the crag on the pretence of checking the grade of Amphitheatre Wall:

'I suppose I ought to have detected that there was something out of the ordinary in the lad's mind because he not only piled a lot more food than usual into the sack, but also a little bag which jingled, and the Helyg poker. This latter was quite a normal item of our equipment in winter because funds did not run to ice axes — but we did not usually borrow it in summer time — though the hearth-brush was sometimes requisitioned then. Well, it was a nice fine day, not too hot, and we talked a lot on the way over about Clogwyn du'r Arddu (and gardening, and about Menlove and his gardening activities on Idwal East Wall — blast him! — and about a certain young woman who had recently changed ownership)...'

After warming up on Amphitheatre Rib they went down to below the Amphitheatre Wall where Kirkus pointed out the crack that would straighten out his route:

'It looked a perfectly horrible place, and I insisted that we commence operations by my going to the top of the crack and fetching him up on a rope. This turned out to have been a wise move; it took about an hour, several pulls and lots of Colin's energy to get him up. He then reported that it would probably go if thoroughly gardened so I was sent down with the poker and spent another hour preparing the pitch for the lead...'

After a long tussle they dined on sardines wrapped in sliced tongue, and then jam sandwiches laced with Nestle's milk and were just about to start on the next course when:

'The aforesaid little bag was produced and I was surprised and rather shocked to see that it contained a little hammer and a couple of flat pitons. I say shocked because we two were generally agreed that steeplejacks' ironmongery was out of place on crags, British crags at any rate, unless there was something that could not possibly be led safely without such aids, and which, if it could be done, would result in the completion of a climb...Anyway this was the first time to my knowledge that C.F.K. had thought of using the things.'

Kirkus tackled a steep groove and eventually hammered in a ring peg while he hung on with his other hand.

'He tried once — and came back into the niche — he tried again (harder) with me holding the rope taut — and then — (a loud "ping" and a "whirr") — the piton was out and Colin was in mid-air...I was able to get some rope in during his gracefully parabolic descent...He landed on his stomach at the very edge of the Terrace and just as the rope came tight on him he bounced over the top of the Direct Start crack...The brakes held, but only after I had been dragged several feet with the belay rope stretched like elastic. I can still see his legs waving in the air...But although the leader was saved — at the usual cost in second man's hand-skin — a disaster had occurred; the bully-tin had got kicked overboard during the proceedings so we had to eat the Carlsbad plums neat...'

Kirkus had trained assiduously for the forthcoming Everest expedition of 1933 but the expected invitation never came, even though Longland campaigned strongly for his inclusion. 'Too inexperienced' was the trite judgement. Alf Bridge wrote a furious letter to the Alpine Club suggesting that they expected Everest to be climbed from the playing fields of Eton. Later in a letter to the Wayfarers' Journal, Menlove Edwards most charitably and cuttingly commented:

'Liverpool nearly sent her greatest climber to join the Everest expedition.'

Kirkus had Alpine experience, but the mountaineering establishment had rigid rules. Kirkus was below the salt as he had neither been to public school nor university — merely to Liverpool College, a reasonable school, but it was not good enough. Looking back, one wonders what might have happened if the team of 1933 had been stronger and if Colin Kirkus had been included...

Kirkus's sustained period of new route activity came to an abrupt end with a tragic accident during the winter of 1934 while he was climbing the cornice of The Castle on Ben Nevis. Kirkus fell from the cornice pulling off his partner, Maurice Linnell. Kirkus had serious eye injuries and was unconscious for quite some time...On coming round, he was utterly dismayed to discover that his great friend had been strangled by the rope and was already dead. Finally in shock and hardly believing the reality of the situation he made his own way down to Fort William.

Kirkus was so badly affected by the death of his friend that he did no more routes for some eighteen months, and sadly for all he did not pioneer again to the same high standard as before. Eventually he settled down to training young people to climb, although he did finish writing the fine 1937 Glyder Fach guidebook, and carried on doing new routes in Ogwen, but at a more modest standard. As late as 1938 he did several new routes in Cornwall and one was a typically determined effort in the old style. He made a solo attempt on a V.S. now called Nameless and only retreated when very close to the top of the climb.

During the war Kirkus joined the Royal Air Force as a navigator and bomb aimer, despite the fact that his eyesight had been badly affected by the accident on the Ben. Typically he memorised the lines of the eye test which he could not see and came through the rigorous medical examination with flying colours. He was soon attached to the elite Pathfinder group and was proud that he had never failed to find the target or to coax his machine back to base. Having lost his elder brother in an attack on Kiel in 1939 he was determined to avenge the loss. By 1942 Kirkus had survived nearly twenty-five 'Ops' including the first 1,000-machine raid on Cologne. In September 1942 he was finally reported as missing after a raid on Bremen.

Perhaps it is fitting to close with Colin's words, written after an ascent of Snowdon in winter, and picking up his path along Crib Goch:

'The hard snow was piled up to a knife-edge on the crest, while on the right it dropped in an almost vertical wall of white. The slope on the left was easier, but still quite steep. The snowless valleys were almost invisible, so that there was nothing to be seen in front but this narrow gleaming moonlit edge, dropping down into nothingness. I felt as though I was poised in the air, on the very top of the world.

All around were snowy summits, dropping weirdly into the inky blackness beneath; they looked almost like clouds...It was 5.30 now and beginning to get light. The moon seemed to have lost its brilliance, and the snow was a dead unearthly white, cold and spectral. A chilly wind had sprung up and I shivered as I forced my way into the old wooden hut on the summit...

The east window was almost covered by a framework of feathery icicles, and I kept watch through a ragged hole that was left in the middle. All the valleys were filled with mist, with the peaks standing up clear above, like islands. It got slowly lighter, but no warmer. Then presently a scarlet glow appeared above a level purple bank of cloud lying on the horizon, and soon the red sun came into view...'

A Great Effort

One person in the history of rock-climbing stands very much apart. To many he has become a cult figure, the very epitome of feats of great strength and endurance where man challenges the elements. Loose rock and vegetation were a delight to him and he revelled in the rotten and vegetated rock of the Devil's Kitchen as well as opening up the Three Cliffs of Llanberis Pass which had to wait many years before they were stripped of their insecure surface layer to become safe for lesser mortals. This dark and brooding figure was to dominate the climbing world for some years while an inner mental battle raged.

John Menlove Edwards was a vicar's son from the village of Crossens near Southport, Lancashire, and as he developed he began to show intellectual promise. Eventually he won a scholarship to Fettes, a Scottish public school where he won a swimming prize and finally obtained an exhibition scholarship to study medicine. Curiously, although he was unhappy there, he continued to wear his multi-coloured Fettes college blazer almost to the end of his life over thirty years later.

During his mid-teens he started climbing in the Lake District so that by the time he went to Liverpool University he already had some experience of climbing and he became a founder member of the university climbing club which was inaugurated in November 1930.

At the age of twenty-one he was four years older than Kirkus had been when he broke through into the top echelon of hard climbers. Fourteen new routes in 1931 was a respectable number by anyone's standard and Western Slabs on Dinas Mot was a particularly important effort as Colin Kirkus failed to make the second ascent. Paradoxically, Kirkus traversed off left to escape and completed the West Rib which was technically harder and potentially more dangerous.

The same day as the Edwards team did Western Slabs they also traversed the Nose to produce a Girdle which Edwards described as being, 'Pleasant…at about Difficult standard'. The route is now graded as Very Severe!

One of the new routes in 1931 was a superb and relatively easy climb on the right-hand side of Dinas Cromlech the 'columnar cliff'. Climbed during December, Flying Buttress was to turn into perhaps the most popular route of its grade for decade after decade of young climbers. Edwards wanted to call it Sodom, but the Climbers' Club guide-book Editor of the day set a precedent and rejected the name, so the bland name of Flying Buttress had to be substituted. The names 'Menlove' and 'Sodom'…when we think of his homosexuality it is almost too painful not to point out the connection.

During that year Edwards explored Mynydd Mawr and climbed Adam Rib on Craig Cwm Du. His description of the route was unusual to say the least.

'Quite a pleasant climb; though easy it is steep and admirably loose.'

No other climber except Edwards would have dared to say 'admirably loose'.

By 1931 Edwards had become a member of the Pen y Pass elite parties of Winthrop Young, and it seems proper that, seventeen years after Herford's superb innovation, another Pen y Pass young tiger should dispense with the rope loops and encumbrances and layback cleanly up the satisfying flake at the top of overhanging enormities. Kirkus wrote magnanimously:

'Dear Edwards, Congratulations on C.B. It was a most marvellous achievement to lead the Flake Crack direct. Herford did it on a rope without (the sling), but even he failed to lead it throughout. I have sometimes thought of it, but I expect I would have funked the beastly thing when I got under it. To do it straight off without exploration was a most marvellous feat. Three cheers for the Climbers' Club!'

Another hard pitch which Edwards managed that year was the Right-Hand Crack finish to the Direct Route on Glyder Fach. It still gets a 5b grading and involves some brutal jamming and laybacking. Edwards thought that the route:

'...can be horribly strenuous, indeed quite unbelievable for balance climbers.'

Kirkus commented that he felt Menlove was a much better climber than himself and was very safe. Although Kirkus's routes were at least as hard as those of Edwards and were done in a relatively short span of time it could be said that Edwards was safer than Kirkus as Colin had some quite horrific falls. There is no doubt that luck played a great part in Kirkus's not being killed while climbing, particularly on the Ben Nevis fall when Linnell was killed. There is in fact only one record of a serious fall by Edwards. A.B. Hargreaves neatly sums up Edwards:

'My recollection of Menlove is that it never occurred to him that he might fall off. He was just accustomed to sticking on, despite holds breaking, points of attachment slipping...it never seemed to matter to him what he had on his feet. He must have done many very hard climbs in battered old boots with a sprinkling of wobbly nails.'

Surprisingly Edwards kept away from Wales for the first six months of 1932 but he returned to Helyg when his exams were over. Kirkus was also there in July and pioneered both Birthday and Curving cracks on Cloggy, then The Crack on the Pinnacle Crag of Cwm Cywion — three V.S.s in just two days. Although Edwards was also at Helyg and stayed for the rest of the week he strangely did not climb and spent the time swimming. As Edwards never had a wrong word to say about Kirkus, who had led him up the first ascent of Chimney Route on Cloggy the previous August it is strange that they did not climb together. Whatever the cause of Menlove's reticence that July week in 1932 it is a case of sadness for what might have been...

Happily in August there were to be two fine additions to the Ogwen climbs, Procrastination Cracks on Glyder Fawr and the excellent Grey Slab. The latter, a 150-foot slab which is often wet, Edwards did with a fourteen-year-old boy:

'...it was on this route that a small boy showed very notable courage in trusting himself entirely to the pull of the rope for a hundred feet.'

Three days later there was a subtle seduction when Edwards fell in love with a loose, repulsive thing — The Devil's Kitchen — and his whole attitude was profoundly affected by the experience:

'It has every natural advantage, being steep, composed of pretty rocky sort of rock and covered with vegetation. It is the sort of place where one can feel the full glory of stepping in perfect safety on someone else's opinion.'

The Devil's Buttress was his first new route on the cliff and, after doing it on a rope while wearing boots, he then soloed it. In time Edwards clocked up twenty new routes

Opposite Top and Bottom Left: Menlove Edwards climbing at Helsby.   Photos: Jim Perrin collection.
Opposite Top Right: Menlove in a more relaxed pose.
Opposite Bottom Right: Menlove on the Procrastination Cracks of Grey Wall.   Photo: G.L. Bartrum.

on this cliff and to his credit he was not afraid to ask for a rope from above when he got into difficulties. Guy Kirkus who later pioneered the Right Wall of the Kitchen remembers an Edwards effort on an unclimbed section of the cliff. He had to drop a rope to Edwards who had got into difficulties. Edwards tied on to the end which snaked down to him and then continued...He came off, penduled on the thin rope which started to fray at one point, and then forced his way stoically upwards through unclimbed rock. Edwards had good cause to remember the event:

> 'There was a nasty accident, when the leader got a little too high up in surroundings with which he was not adequately in touch. There came a rope from above, and the doughty explorer continued jerkily upward for the next hundred feet to the sound of heavy breathing in triplicate.'

Edwards described many of the loose and revolting parts of the cliff with a great relish:

> 'The Devil's Dump is nice: the steep bit is an interesting study in mosaics, but they did not finish it off very well. Alternatively it may be regarded as an excavation in the Dump, and you get holds on the bits sticking out: it is decidedly decomposing. Herein lies its charm...
>
> ...On Dump Crack it is not easy to force a way through the forest of plants...A tall spike rises above the fernery on the left...Straight up into a good cave which has not been wiped for years. Up its messy depths...'

For those stalwarts who shrink away from dry sun-drenched rock Waterfall Climb on Craig y Rhaeadr has a quite unique attraction. It did not escape Menlove's eagle eye:

> '...in fine weather it is wet, and in wet weather it is pouring: and when we went it was coming down in bucketfuls all over the place, and even so the stream stood out strongly by comparison, falling sheer onto a ledge half-way up...
>
> ...the ominous cessation of the noise of running water often occurs in the good old gullies, and it means that the aforesaid water is being soaked up by the body of the leader in mid-stream: like a sponge. And the irony of the situation is that the lad cannot do otherwise, he may be absolutely unwilling to vacate his absurd position; as like as not he has been nailed to the rivulet by the hand of fear...
>
> ...The grass on the second pitch is long and rank, and serves admirably to hold the rock together: but really it is a fine cliff, and gives one an excellent swim in bad weather.'

On that cold, wet and windy day in November, the hapless second, one A.B. Hargreaves, was marooned high on the cliff, unable to communicate with his leader above the roar of the wind. He almost fell off his perch with astonishment when Edwards suddenly appeared at the foot of the cliff and started making reassuring noises.

The good thing was that he had first tied off the rope at the top of the cliff, having finally completed the final 180-foot run-out. Edwards had the last word on the matter when he commented that 'the rain had been very rowdy that day and they simply couldn't think what to call the climb!'

Edwards made the second ascent of Great Slab on Clogwyn du'r Arddu, again with Hargreaves who narrated what happened:

> 'I got from Kirkus a full account of the climb...I was the manager of the party. Menlove made no bones at all about that slippery little slab and the long green caterpillar, but it was when I joined him at the top of it that I first saw an exhibition of his enormous strength. Our third man (Rennie Bere) weighing fully fifteen stone, just made a dash at the slippery slab and shot off into space on the end of 150 feet of line. This antic not only fused my hands, but locked me to the belay and I was helpless except to hold on. Menlove came down to me and without even shouldering the rope, lifted that chap with his hands until he was able to get hold of something.'

Opposite: Don and Barbara Roscoe on Grey Slab, Glyder Fawr.   Photo: Steve Ashton.

About this time Edwards was climbing with a rather nervous second on a steep cliff. When Menlove finally stopped at the top of the pitch the tremulous one asked if he had a belay. There was a long pause:

"Well, yes. A psychological one."

When the second arrived at the stance he discovered to his horror that the belay consisted of an unstable pile of stones with the rope coiled round it.

In the early part of 1933 Menlove became well and truly obsessed with water...cliffs running with water...and the force and fury of an icy river in full spate. At Easter he went up to Scotland and amazed his friends by swimming through the Linn of Dee — a foaming cataract of melt-water from the thawing snowfields of the high Cairngorm plateau. For a hundred yards of its length the river roars through a rock gash, only fifteen feet wide at one point. Edwards wrote casually after the event:

'Jump into the Linn straight from your car, let the stream take you down in its arms, then jump out again.'

He tied one end of a climbing rope to a tree and the other end to his waist — then jumped into the torrent...the rope slithered snake-like across the wet slabs as Edwards disappeared from view. He did a full circuit of one whirlpool then was swept down again, but he finally managed to get out without help. He mentioned casually that the main problem had been a struggle to get the writhing coils of rope away from his neck. He must have 'enjoyed' his experience as he later did a similar performance with a roped swimming-tumble down the Swallow Falls at Bettws y Coed.

Prior to qualifying he had worked for up to fifteen hours a day and still found time for new routes on the awe-inspiring faces of the Devil's Kitchen. Edwards qualified as M.B., Ch.B. in July 1933 and the Dean of the medical faculty wrote that he was confident that Menlove would make a very reliable physician and surgeon. Tragedy struck the family while his brother Stephen was on his way to watch the degree ceremony. He was in a collision with a tram and two hours later when he died, Menlove was at his side. Life continued, however, and for the first six months of 1934 Edwards was Clinical Assistant at the Isle of Wight Mental Hospital and so was infrequently in Wales.

During this time Menlove did manage a few routes, such as Slow Ledge Climb, which was so named because if a person sat on it he would slowly slide off...This six-month gap ended earlier associations before future, deeper, and more emotional events took over. Edwards summed up most of the good and bad times in his article 'Young Climber'.

'It is perhaps not generally realised that there are in the climbing world one or two seconds who display more courage and sagacity in the face of emergencies...than ever has been shown by the most reckless of leaders...They are responsible for many of the best climbs. Their leader dare not do anything else. If, in evil pass, he says, *"I think I had better come down"* this second says, *"Oh,"* and the leader has to try again. And if a little later he says, *"What do you think? Had we better go on?"* the second simply replies, *"Yes, let's,"* or, *"Oh, we might as well,"* and again what can the leader do but go on if he can and fall off if he cannot?'

Edwards also high-lighted what is often a memorable time for a climber — the drive for the hills on a Friday night or the race home after a week-end away:

'Not that these are the only dangers attaching to the sport: there is that terrible over-confidence that may attack one after a good route. I remember the car got that once. It drove us faster and faster through the wilds of Denbigh until, screwing its accelerator to the sticking point, the

Opposite: The 1st ascent of Suicide Wall by Chris Preston. 'In 1945, without runners, climbed in gym-shoes, utterly serious and far, harder than anything else in the country, it was an astonishing lead.'   Photo: D.M. McKellar.

graceless vehicle turned against the hand that led it, and after a short decisive battle, pitched us head first out onto the road. But that is quite another story. Incidentally, it was rather a famous car on account of its small size and curious appearance. I hear that only a week or so ago, in a like mood, the little car charged into the back of a sheep, and, unhappily, with fatal results. The car never regained consciousness.'

Edwards in fact, like many climbers, had never had any idea whatsoever of safe driving and the second he gently poked fun at was A.B. Hargreaves.

Later in 1934 Edwards returned to Liverpool and became a clinical assistant in the psychiatric department of Liverpool Royal Infirmary. In addition he set up in private practice as a psychiatrist. It was at this stage that one of his closest climbing friends (still alive) went to consult him professionally. He came away utterly convinced that it was Edwards who needed the psychiatric treatment, not himself. Perhaps this was the first time that the mental stability of Edwards was beginning to falter.

Although 1934 was a lean year for Edwards as far as new routes were concerned the following year resulted in entirely different circumstances for him, starting on an April week-end when he met Wilfrid Noyce.

Noyce was a cousin of the Kirkus brothers and his first pair of boots had been specially bought to a specification laid down by Colin Kirkus who took him up his Direct Route on Dinas Mot. At the time Noyce was only seventeen — one of the youngest climbers to start off at such a high level. During Easter 1935 Noyce went to stay at Helyg and at breakfast asked:

"Can I be taken up something good?"

He had been disappointed at being taken up a lowly Difficult — Ivy Chimney on Tryfan — and as Edwards was there Noyce plied him with one question after another..."*How about Clogwyn du'r Arddu?"* Menlove thoughtfully replied:

"The upper part of the Pinnacle Face would go some day."

Edwards was intrigued enough to ask Noyce to climb with him on the Llanberis Pass cliffs the following day. Edwards commented:

"I always go to a cliff where there's a downhill path if possible."

After meeting Winthrop Young at Pen y pass and promising to return for tea the two climbers went down the Pass to Clogwyn y Grochan where Edwards had his eye on a possible new route. He soon launched out on steep wall watched keenly by Noyce:

'It was an unspectacular technique and one of wrestling, with every appearance that the battle was a losing one. Then suddenly he was on top. That day, as often, he was climbing in clinker-nailed boots which made the struggle more audible. Moreover, with what seemed a pointless and exasperating patience he would hang on, scrabbling, and peer round for any rock projection that would take a hitched rope. Sometimes the result did not look secure, but it had a habit of working...

...I thought Menlove awkward as I looked up at him. I had seen the holds, I could do it. But when used, they seemed all wrong...

...He worked upwards very slowly, clumsily almost, and I can see now that it was strength of arm alone that kept him to the rock. At the time he seemed to be making a mess of it...Boys of seventeen, however, are not naturally modest and I did not appreciate the difference between his method of climbing and mine.'

The route was Long Tree Gate and it must have been a hard lead in clinker-nailed boots. Inevitably Edwards graded it as Severe, but it was later graded as Very Severe, although it must have been a grade harder than that in his nails.

Opposite: Soapgut, Milestone Buttress.   Photo: R.F. Allen.

Next day they went to the Milestone Buttress to a grass-filled crack on the left of the buttress. It was green and very greasy. Fortunately Noyce was well belayed as on the last section Edwards had to make a jump for a turf ledge. He slithered off and the pull nearly tugged Noyce off his belay. On the second attempt he managed to finish Soap Corner which was eventually named Soap Gut when they returned to climb the direct start the following year.

Under the older man's guidance Noyce led Belle Vue Bastion, later describing how the crux felt:

'The route after the shower was slightly greasy, even to socks. Down a little I thought, and steady. Try another hold. A little grab and draw up, quickly. Got it.

...Meanwhile the second watches and wonders as his thigh numbs against the grass, until he forgets almost what he would do if the leader did fall...Mallory, O.G. Jones and his guides, Mummery, Merkl. Thank God the leader is safe and we can warm our blood racing over the dark fells.'

Unfortunately Noyce suffered very serious accidents in 1937, 1939 and 1946 and just before his death he had a most bizarre accident on Clogwyn y Wenallt. He had gone up to take a photograph of Don Whillans while he was climbing the bottom pitch of Bovine. From the wide ledge Noyce somehow stepped back and overbalanced into space. He sailed down for ninety feet and crashed into the scree, breaking several bones in the process.

Certainly Noyce gave the impression at times that his mind was far away and appeared somewhat vague and absent-minded. Shortly before he went on his last expedition he attended a C.C. meeting and went up to the Cromlech with Trevor Jones. Wilf mused rather distantly that the last time he had gone there was with Menlove some twenty-five years earlier. Jones was under the distinct impression that they were going to do Sabre Cut but all of a sudden Wilf asked, *"Which is Glyder Fach?"* Jones for once was speechless. *"Aren't we going over the tops?"* Wilf queried, in a rather touchy tone. *"No! Certainly not!"* Jones retorted in amazement. The two faced each other with looks of disbelief.

When the C.C. meeting came to an end and they were all strolling out, Noyce caught up Jones and said, *"Trevor, can I have a word with you?"* Within a few seconds Noyce had jumped into his car, then suddenly stuck his head out and said, *"Goodbye"* — and promptly drove off without another word.

On Carreg Wastad both Shadow Wall and Crackstone Rib were pioneered by Edwards on the same day. He thought that the latter with its five holly trees was the harder climb. Both climbs were to become trade routes as many generations of climbers traced their way up the awkward sheaves of rock which are so typical of the cliff. After a fine run of climbs on the three low-lying cliffs of Llanberis Pass Menlove turned his attention to the Ogwen valley and did not return for some five years.

Although in 1936 Edwards rowed himself in a boat from the Scottish mainland to the Island of Harris (It took him 28 hours for the forty miles and three days later he rowed back again.), the forthcoming Cwm Idwal guide-book must have been uppermost in his mind. When it came out that year at least eleven of the routes were under-graded when compared with a recent guide-book. Kirkus on the other hand got the grades in his

Opposite: Looking down on the final exposed slab pitch of Main Wall, Cyrn Las.   Photo: Steve Ashton.

Glyder Fach guide-book more or less right and he dealt with the hard routes in a very responsible manner. For example, Lot's Groove:

'A climb of great severity including one of the most difficult pitches in Wales. A preliminary inspection on a rope is probably advisable. Standard: Very Severe (exceptionally so).'

Although the modern climber may frown at some of the grades of the routes, one must remember that the Cwm Idwal guide was the first of its type and Edwards was breaking new ground. Without a pause he then went on to write a further guide-book to Tryfan in collaboration with Wilfrid Noyce.

An event which was to cause heated debate was the visit of a party of Bavarian climbers in the summer of 1936. On the first wave of their assault on Tryfan the two leaders, Teufel and Sedlmayr, placed two pitons which they used for aid to complete Munich Climb. This event became a matter of national pride and it seemed as if the Kaiser had won after all. The question became, how long would these pitons defile defenceless Tryfan rock? Edwards came to the rescue in September and on the crux pitch managed to lasso a loose block on a ledge before climbing round a nose which had required the Teutonic iron crosses on the first ascent. Immediately after Edwards had triumphed, the second man knocked out the offending iron with the faithful Helyg poker and also retrieved an added bonus in the shape of a bronze karabiner. With the lasso in mind Edwards reflected:

'...has the advantage that the leader can climb with a rope above him all the way. I do not know why leaders do not make their rope precede them more frequently in this way. Saves a lot of trouble.'

Jim Perrin's comments in his historical section of the 1982 Ogwen guide-book are extremely interesting when it comes to weighing up Edwards:

'The fissile, the dank, the rotten and the vegetatious drew him when his life seemed thus, when touched by love and affection his life too became lighter, more delicate, more airy.'

Oddly the Tryfan guide was the only one that Edwards wrote the grades of which would be reasonably acceptable to the modern climber. Perhaps it was on account of the fact that it contained mainly other people's routes and Menlove did not have the personal mental problems regarding the routes as he did with his own creations.

In a few short weeks in the high summer of 1936 Noyce, with Edwards on occasions as an unlikely second, made great contributions to Ogwen — almost in keeping with his cousin Colin Kirkus. Six routes were done in three weeks, the brightest jewel being Scars — a route with precarious crab-like moves on a crux that a well-known climber was to fall from nearly twenty years later.

During 1936 Edwards basked in the halo surrounding his protege, the young Noyce, and while Wilfrid flowered on the ancient buttresses of Tryfan his friend's talent lay dormant.

It would be wrong to assess Menlove Edwards without quoting at some length from 'Great Effort', probably the finest article that he wrote, on the stresses and strains of putting up new routes. As an analysis of a leader's thought processes it is unique.

'...Some people prefer to go up hills at a steady ten miles an hour, as if they were an army tank cruising or Scott hauling sledges in the Antarctic. I do not. During each rest I gazed at the cliff, exploring from a distance how the route might go. Then when quite near the cliff I stopped again and looked up at it more slowly, heavy with the fresh air, and it looked at me, and it slid about in my eyes as a cliff sometimes does, and was difficult to focus. I shall go there and there, I thought, and then perhaps coming to the steeper portion, I shall go there, or perhaps it will be too hard for me to go there then I shall not go there but will go there instead...

...So in the middle of the mountains upon a pile of rocks I sat down. A certain tendency to inertia in the mind can have great force...Then later I got up and walked to the foot of the cliff meditating carefully where to start. Then tied the rope on, flung the loose end down the slope, and arranged it so that its coils should open without snags...

...After twenty minutes I had advanced about fifteen feet and was trembling slightly, not sure of my position. The rock now before my face was ordinary rock, surfaced at an angle of sixty to seventy degrees, fairly smooth. Heaven was above, the earth a few yards beneath, and I remember nothing of either. As for myself the forepart of my right foot was planted well on a square ledge, the heel overhung into the air and demanded a constant muscular effort at the calf; my left foot was three feet higher and one and a half feet to the side put against a small sloped piece of grooving. In appearance therefore, had anybody been passing, I was about to step up. In practice I had been trying to do this for ten minutes but had not yet succeeded. It seemed simple, the need was clear, holds were there, but they were small and I am not a man in any way to make a move until satisfied that it is safe, so that to remain in this statuesque and still position was my only choice for the time being. Every minute or two, when my right leg began to tremble, I pulled the left leg down from its unserviceable height, bent myself this way and that a little to relieve the strain, then put the leg back again, using the action also as a gesture of purpose...

...so I began to struggle. Oh, good heavens, good heavens, I thought, what on earth am I to do; this is not very good, you are being a coward, an arrant coward and cannot, must not continue...Then I began to struggle again. I thought, what is wrong, there is something missing, there is no spirit, I am heavy and unable to move; perhaps if I launch out and become sufficiently frightened...So I made several attempts to launch out but nothing happened. Then I thought perhaps if I eat my sandwiches that will improve me...So standing still on my footholds and feeling firmer than I had done for some time, I got the tin of sardines out of my pocket, twisted the lid off in the usual way but carefully because of the position and ate the fish one by one with my mouth...

...Now how will it go I thought, every excuse is exhausted...Now if there were an onlooker, that would make an effort worth while, perhaps — is there anyone in sight? no, not a soul, not one in the whole valley: there is no representative of the human race, none to praise, nobody to look surprised at cowardice or to laugh at folly, to provide me with a gibe or comparison or stage: there is a sheep, but the sheep do not know about these things, a little bird but she is away out of sight already. So I stood on waiting, unable to move...I stood on that hold for a long time. Then quickly, with the sweat standing out on my skin and my heart beating, I moved up on to the next holds and then the next and then I did not see what to do and the movements stopped again...

...I made a final effort. Look at yourself I said, and do you know what this is, this is schizophrenia, the split mind: I know but I do not care what I said: it is stupid: what could you do if you did get ten feet higher up, the rocks have not started yet to become difficult, take yourself off from this cliff: oh, this climbing, that involves an effort, on every move the holds to be spotted and often there are none, then every limb placed, the body set into the one suitable position found but with trouble, then with the whole organism great force must be exerted, before anything happens, and this is to be done while the brain is occupied sick and stiff with its fears: and now you have been doing this for well over an hour and a half and the strain must be telling: get down therefore.

My mind made up, it only remained to go, not always an easy thing to do. But as it has often been remarked God may be merciful and is so sometimes when you least expect it; and on this occasion it happened that feeling in behind the heather I almost immediately found a good enough spike of rock for my rope and was able to get back down again in no danger. Then I walked a little way up the hillside slowly, rested and walked home.

But the resilience of man is great, and his ingenuity. So I was not done yet and on the way back setting to work I soon picked up my pride in this way, by thinking, today the victory has been to the devil, but tomorrow is not to him yet, also by thinking: it has been said that the secret of life is in detachment from it, good.'

1937 was to be the tragic year of great injury not only to the relationship between Edwards and Noyce, but also to Noyce himself when he had one of his most serious accidents. Edwards had gone for a while to Norway on a climbing holiday and on his return went up to the Lake District to join Noyce. On September 21st they set out for Scafell and on the way paused to examine the first-aid equipment on Sty Head Pass — they idly wondered if they would ever need it.

First they decided to try Mickledore Grooves, Colin Kirkus's great climb. As one often finds, there was moisture on the cliff and Noyce needed a shoulder to climb one corner; it was still wet and Noyce's socks crinkled on the holds. The run-out on that big pitch is a most serious one hundred and forty feet...He came off!

Edwards did his best to gather in the rope as quickly as he could, but two strands of the three-strand rope parted and Noyce's head and face were smashed against the rock. After three days unconsciousness he finally awoke and began the long road to recovery.

After his exertions in the Ogwen valley and two guide-books to Cwm Idwal, Edwards turned his affections to Lliwedd, a pillar of Victoriana. Most of his routes were done in August 1938 and included six Severes, four Very Severes, and two Hard Very Severes — nearly all done with F.J.R. Dodd. The piece de resistance of this batch was the much tried Central Gully Direct. Dodd climbed the final overhang on a rope. Then Edwards led the lower half of the climb and Dodd the final overhang which he had previously inspected. It might be thought that there would have been an ever-increasing number of people wanting to climb the route. In the twenty-five years after its first ascent, there were only two repetitions. By contrast Cenotaph Corner, climbed in 1952 by Joe Brown, up till 1968 had several ascents on nearly every week-end.

It is useful to quote from Harold Drasdo's historical introduction to Lliwedd which gives insight into both the routes done by Edwards and also into the man himself:

'His climbs do not always have the classic lines of those of Kirkus...

...he undergraded a number of his routes outrageously, minimising the degree to which the difficult climbing had been extended...

...a number of criticisms of the Edwards' guide might reasonably be made, starting from the disturbing truth that climbers continued to get lost on the cliff.'

To explain this, a quote from an Edwards description of the East Ridge of Bracket Gully:

'This is an indefinite article. The rocks...rise in discontinuous and brief series with innumerable incidental factors and no common factors.'

In 1946 the guide-book editor, Nully Kretschmer, tried to correct the imbalance of gradings of Lliwedd compared with Kirkus's Glyder Fach guide-book. Severe on Glyder

Fach meant anything from Hard Very Difficult to Mild Severe on Lliwedd, while V.S. on Glyder Fach could be anything from Mild Severe upwards on Lliwedd.

If one ignores the Lliwedd and Devil's Kitchen routes, then Kirkus and Edwards each put up twenty-five new routes in the Severe/Very Severe category — an appropriate dead-heat situation.

While the new routes put up by Edwards gradually got better in quality his mental state sadly declined correspondingly and there was little but gloom, despondency and soul-searching for him in the remaining years of his life.

As one generation declines so another appears and a nailed boot hard man from Manchester University was emerging on the climbing scene. Arthur Birtwistle really did first ascents in nailed-boots, but what would one expect from a Mancunian expert who had been trained to perfection on Derbyshire gritstone? His contribution to Welsh climbing was minimal but immense — a slab and just one crack pitch — and the awesome quality of both instantly lifted Birtwistle to immortality.

In 1937 Birtwistle paid a visit to Cloggy and made for the Drainpipe Crack on the East Buttress, a problem that had defeated Kirkus on the occasion when he was rescued by Alf Bridge. Using all his gritstone skill he succeeded on the crack which is now taken by Vember. It defeated him eventually but he showed great determination and was not put off by the overwhelmingly steep wall on which he was at work. In those days the Drainpipe Crack had no protection and was a 110-foot lead-out. It was still 5a with hard moves at the start and a smelly seriousness emanating from its dank interior.

Birtwistle also made a good attempt on White Slab getting about thirty feet above Linnell's Leap and one can only wonder what he could have done with just the odd peg for protection. His greatest effort, however, was to superimpose Diagonal onto Dinas Mot. It well deserves its modern guide-book tag of 'magnificent' and like the Drainpipe Crack it was not repeated for ten years...The climbing is all too obviously very open and the mantelshelf on the third pitch still has a nasty habit of stumping modern leaders. Birtwistle eventually wrote the first analytical account of hard and technical rock-climbing for the 1950 Rucksack Club Journal. It was simply entitled 'Thoughts on Leading up Difficult Rock':

'It is only by leading that a climber can get to know himself and until he does know himself, it is the instinct of fear which will dictate when a return should be made...with increasing experience and practice and especially continuous and regular leading, some men get to know accurately their own physical and nervous strength.

Eventually daylight dawns and the leader becomes a thinking-climbing machine. Given plenty of practice, physical strength is easy to judge. Nervous energy is infinitely harder to judge, but it is of at least equal importance. When a leader's nervous energy gives out, fear takes over and there is little chance of avoiding a fall, even though some physical strength is left.

To climb really up to the safety limit, demands a good deal of determination. What is not generally appreciated is that after the leader has climbed to the safety limit and then decided to retreat, all the determination used in getting up has now to go into reverse to get down.'

Much of Birtwistle's philosophy is just as relevant in the nineteen-eighties as it was when it was written thirty years ago.

One of the leading Oxford undergraduate climbers who was active at the same time as Birtwistle was David Cox. While up on Clogwyn du'r Arddu, Cox noticed an unclimbed crack on the extreme left-hand end of the East Buttress. In mid-June 1938 Cox and

Robin Hodgkin, in the company of Clare and Beridge, the daughters of George Mallory, started up the unclimbed line at 8.00 p.m. They finished the route that night and with Sunset Crack they thus ended a four-year period of stagnation on the cliff. The next month Cox soloed Spiral Route on Craig yr Ysfa — a fine delicate V.S. on the left-hand side of the Pinnacle Wall. As a sequel to this fine effort Cox wrote an amusing article entitled 'Raw Deal for a Precipice' which suggested:

'All good crags face north. Craig yr Ysfa has to pay the price which this rigid ill-considered convention among precipices demands. One would like to see the whole cliff transplanted turned carefully through 180 degrees so as to face south and then towed a mile or two to the obvious site now unfortunately occupied by Pen Yr Oleu Wen. If the contractor could tilt it up twenty degrees Craig yr Ysfa would become another Clogwyn du'r Arddu.'

At the height of the Battle of Britain in August 1940, Edwards gave us two remarkable routes on Clogwyn y Grochan. The main part of the cliff is unbelievably steep, but Menlove's expert eye picked out the lines of Brant and Slape — Cumbrian dialect for 'steep' and 'slippery'. The notorious little wall of Slape's second pitch is still 5a and tricky. Grudgingly Edwards gave it 'Severe, possibly V.S.'. The bad weather in August did not prevent Edwards from unlocking the secret of the grey wall which bulged out from the central part of the Grochan. Brant was climbed in a fine drizzle and was a virtuoso piece of route finding. Despite his mental decline, Edwards produced Brant, Slape and his sole Cloggy route, the Bow-Shaped Slab — three of his greatest contributions.

The visit to Cloggy was a rare one and with John Barford and Nea Morin he went to prospect for new routes, particularly up the unclimbed sheaves of rock of the West Buttress. He made a typical Edwards entry by lassoing some blocks to swing across a mauvais pas, but then had to retreat. On the third attempt — with Jack Cooper, a young Manchester climber who was on his honeymoon — he was successful and gave us Bow-Shaped Slab which has a nasty 5a pitch in an intimidating position. Many leaders in future years left it until they had done all the other V.S. routes on the cliff, and even then did not always get up Bow.

Edwards collaborated with John Barford on an interim guide to Clogwyn du'r Arddu in which they tried a numerical system of grading which did not catch on. It was supposed to replace the old adjectival system but looking back it was clearly far ahead of its time and too sophisticated for a wartime generation to digest. Priorities lay elsewhere. The basic idea can be seen from the table below:

Adjectival Grade	Numerical Grade	Examples
Medium Severe	VA	Sunset Crack
Hard Severe	VB	Curving Crack, Longland's, Bow-Shaped Slab
Very Severe	VI	Pigott's, Chimney, Pedestal, Narrow Slab

All four climbs in the fifth grade are quite clearly at least V.S. by anyone's standards, and the system suggested, although an excellent one, was spoilt by undergrading.

In the foreword to this interim guide to Cloggy Edwards made a nice point about competition:

'The wave of intensification has intensified competitiveness, and the bad as well as the good side results of that: jealousies, and so on one side, an unbalanced concentration on the most obviously and crudely competitive points in development...But these things, big and little, stand half-submerged perhaps already, like the boulders of the moraine, as the fresh washings creep over them of earth and goodwill.'

Edwards went to Cornwall for a brief holiday and wrote, 'marvellous bathing in bits of waves mostly; best fun I've had for years and years'. He allowed himself to be washed onto the rocks by the waves and at their highest point would seize hold and climb out of reach of the next surge. Only a super-swimmer such as Edwards could have enjoyed such danger. Three Royal Marine commandos who tried to emulate him were drowned.

In 1941 Menlove was registered as a conscientious objector and the child guidance clinic where he worked in Liverpool closed down. Edwards was out of a job. He decided to rent Hafod Owen, a lonely little cottage in the Nant Gwynant, from Colin Kirkus. Just after this one of his friends, Tony Leggate, was killed on active service at sea. Edwards wrote one of the most touching obituaries that one could wish for:

'Archie was a bad climber. He had no knack for finding holds on rocks or for using them when found. This may have been accountable by his loose build perhaps: he was long and thin; or by his lack of strength, or by other such things, but the immediate and outward result was that under the suggested physical danger that climbing entails, he fell into a state of paralysing fear and profound mental demoralisation.

Jackets ripped, trousers were torn, his knees knocked, blood like water, desperation was arrived at, was passed, to where effort ceases to last, success, perhaps, a tense interval on a stance, then another pitch. Then the day far spent, at the top, flinging time away, we would eat and, as mortals should who have stormed Olympus, we laughed and laughed until we could not laugh. A magnificent fellow to climb with, he would see a joke, could make me see one.'

Edwards went to Skye in 1944 and made a solo traverse of the Main Ridge, but couldn't resist the siren call of the sea which surrounded the island, so he set off in a rowing boat to Rhum in a solitary eighteen hour epic. Before long he left Hafod Owen and went to work at the Great Ormond Street Hospital for sick children in London. He was not happy there and so in October he resigned and went to stay with his brother in County Durham. There he tried to commit suicide and his regular climbing pattern was finished.

During the war David Cox became Commanding Officer of a mountain Commando Training Wing in Llanberis, and was in charge of two ace climbers — Jock Campbell and Chris Preston. Preston became superlatively fit during his duties as a mountain instructor. He was determined to solve the long-standing problem of Suicide Wall which had defeated the efforts of Kirkus and Edwards as well as an almost successful attempt by Ted Hicks. The latter had got onto the grassy ledge at the top of the first pitch, the same point that Edwards reached during a war-time effort.

Preston inspected the line by abseil, then climbed to the ledge, but his seconds were unable to follow and he had to accept a top-rope from David Cox, who as his superior officer had ordered the abseil. The following week-end on October 7th Preston, who was as determined as ever, resolved to make his final attempt.

Of the Suicide Wall team a strong party consisting of Dick Morsley and Jack Haines had done great deeds. Haines broke the Welsh 3,000s walking record on a very hot day and finished it wearing nothing but his boots. When he approached the final summit of Snowdon the ladies in the welcoming party suddenly discovered the fascination of the view in the opposite direction!

Opposite: Chris Preston slips, high on Suicide Wall.   Photo: D.M. McKellar.

Preston eventually got onto the tiny grass ledge which splits the big pitch and brought up Morsley and Haines, safeguarded by pitons banged into the grass. The superb picture of Preston leading the final few feet shows his fine figure pressed sideways hard against uncompromising Idwal rock — a posture only possible by someone at the peak of his form. It was E2 5c — not only extraordinary boldness but a leap forward in wall-climbing — the hardest climb in Britain for over a decade.

Ironically Preston crashed his motor-cycle on the way back to camp in Llanberis. Cox was able to breathe again and only ten days later on October 17th 1945 went back with Campbell to attempt the unclimbed White Slab on Clogwyn du'r Arddu.

When Campbell and Cox reached Cloggy they swung across the old-fashioned Bow-Shaped entry using the rope, but found the first moves up the corner of the White Slab too hard. Instead they followed grooves up to the right to a chimney, then determinedly traversed back left to a thin crack in the White Slab itself. Campbell carried on until it got much thinner so came down and tried the V-groove on the right. He had to lean horizontally to use the only hold on an overlap to the right...an irreversible swing and a wild pull up led to a ledge and belay. A layback then led to another overhang similar to that before. On one attempt on the groove above Campbell jumped off while retreating and twisted his ankle badly. Cox later related his predicament:

'...the awful possibility began to dawn on me that I might be called on to try and climb it. I was roused to make my one contribution to the day's success.'

He had noticed a good foothold way out to the right and by an enormous straddle got his foot on to it but could not complete the move. Even with his injured ankle Campbell did the big stride, pulled round and was above the difficulties on the easier upper ramblings of Narrow Slab. They called it Sheaf after Jack Longland's description of the West Buttress as:

'...a series of sheaves of rock overlapping from left to right.'

After the war Edwards returned to his old haunts in Wales from time to time and in 1949 climbed the Central Gully of Clogwyn y Grochan with Roy Beard and a few days later also did Rift Wall on Craig Ddu. The latter which was known for a long time as Anthropology is now a highly popular V.S. with a two-star rating. Not long after these routes he went to stay at Cwm Glas Cottage, a Climbers' Club hut on the hillside facing the Grochan. There he tried to commit suicide with a drug overdose.

The years were becoming increasingly depressing although Edwards did still return to Wales infrequently. On one such occasion in 1952 he went up to the high cwms to visit Clogwyn y Ddysgl. There he produced the amazing Route of Knobs to the right of Fallen Block Crack. Typically it was graded as Hard Severe by Edwards and for twenty years the route lay shrouded in mystery. No-one admitted to having either done it or even failed on it. While the 1978 Pass guide was being compiled Joe Brown honestly revealed the fact that on what was presumed to be the second ascent he had found a few problems. Later it transpired that the route was well worth a Hard V.S. grade for its open start and a tricky traverse higher up. Clearly Edwards had not lost his strength by the time he did the route. For some time he stayed with Paul Work in Beddgelert and even moved a half-ton boulder up a hillside with just a crowbar. He also took Roy Beard, the Custodian of the new C.C. hut, Ynys Ettws, up to do Fallen Block Crack. Afterwards he described the ascent in the hut log-book:

Opposite: Tony Ashton traversing out from below Pillar Chimney on Manx Wall, Clogwyn Du.   Photo: Steve Ashton.

'On the F.B. Crack the hon. warden, nobly seconded No. 1, wedged massive in crack on slight hold: then following, accosted the steep bit, mounted inch by inch, struggled heroic, horrible to look upon, long time, then movement upward ceased, movement downward inexorably began to supervene, and eventually brought him to the stance again. He took off several layers of clothes and sent them up on the rope: No. 1 got to the final ledge and tied by double rope, with legs secure in a place where the greatest possible leverage could be exerted. Hon. Custodian then accosted the steep bit again. He mounted inch by inch, then came struggles longer, more heroic if possible, more horrible to look upon than the first. I heaved with all my force at his command. Then movement upward ceased, movement downward inexorably began to supervene, and some time afterwards brought him to where he stood, dejected, massive, symbolic, with the Fallen Block.'

Later a Liverpool climber Ken Pearson climbed with Edwards on the Grochan, where they tied on to Menlove's khaki-coloured rope which had a great bulge in it. Edwards explained that it was the one that had been almost cut through during Wilf Noyce's horrific fall from Mickledore Grooves. Edwards had re-spliced the severed ends and wrapped the whole untidy joint with a thick swathe of insulating tape.

That his climbing powers were still in superb shape is borne out by one of his climbing companions of the thirties, Evelyn Leech. In 1955 she was soloing Grooved Arete on Tryfan when she saw Edwards soloing Belle Vue Bastion — a fine effort for a forty-five year old. Unbelievably about the same time Colin Mortlock saw Edwards nonchalantly soloing DOWN the Bastion in a decrepit pair of old boots.

Perhaps it is fitting that just before his suicide in 1958 Edwards did his last new route on the Devil's Kitchen with Arvon Jones. The route combined both rock and water — the two things that meant so much to him. An extract from one of his own poems of the thirties, seems fitting for his demise:

'A great heavy snow flake, down she came carefully swinging like a dancer, majestically down like a pearly shell in the sea. Settled on a grey damp boulder, and there like a liner in the ocean, she lay down, she tipped up and sank.'

Part Two — The Human Flies

Black Rocks to Black Cliff

After the Second World War there was a dramatic change within the climbing world brought about by new clothing, equipment and safety methods. The pre-war climber had hemp rope and nailed boots and for more difficult climbs rubber-soled plimsolls and careful judgement were the main means of staying alive and remaining in one piece if a leader ventured onto hard rock.

Cliff assault methods were developed for the commandos in the war years and karabiners were an essential part of their equipment as well as camouflaged anoraks and windproof trousers. Later all these desirable items became available to the post-war climbing generation. Almost at the same time, nylon climbing ropes were developed which gave a greater safety factor as they were more resilient than hemp and nylon's greater extension under load made them much safer for absorbing the energy of a falling leader.

Footwear too changed just after the war; nailed boots were superseded by the moulded rubber soles invented by a Milanese climber — Vitale Bramani — shortened to Vibram, although the British version was the 'Itshide' sole which was designed for Army boots. There was initial opposition to Vibram-soled boots as it was thought that they would be useless on slippery Welsh rock. However, they came just in time to save a lot of Welsh climbs as hundreds of vital holds on innumerable routes had already been drastically worn away by the abrasive action of metal clinkers and tricounis. The worst examples of this heavy abrasion are still to be seen on the Idwal Slabs.

Tweed jackets and floppy trousers were soon discarded in favour of camouflaged anoraks and trousers. Another innovation which became available was an important camping item, the so-called Yankee Bivvy, a robust American bivouac tent made of thick olive-green cloth which was so heavy that the tent did not need a fly-sheet. When the buttoned entrance was closed it provided a cosy, almost pitch-black interior against the worst weather that Wales could unleash.

With the added advantages of nylon for climbing ropes, so it was with nylon slings for running belays as they could be more easily threaded round chockstones or pulled over spikes, pinnacles or flakes to give a leader more confidence. Peter Harding, the leading rock-climber of the forties, summed it up neatly in an article entitled 'The New Generation' in the 1948 Rucksack Club Journal:

'I may add here in conclusion a few points on a sling technique which I have found to be very useful. This is the use of a number of small slings of cord or thin nylon line. On the ascent of a formidable new route these are attached, wherever possible, to the smallest of spikes and pimples, and in extreme cases to pitons. In the event of a fall they are completely useless...but as retreat slings they are invaluable.

We all know that a good leader should always be able to retreat and should always keep a reserve of strength for this purpose. This is however often difficult on a hard climb; here the little slings give an extra margin of safety and so allow one to press matters a little further, knowing that if retreat be necessary the slings can be used as emergency handholds on the way down. In a real emergency the leader can always be lowered from one of the slings to rest until he has regained his strength sufficiently to have another go.'

83

Peter Harding is thought to have made another important contribution to climbing — the invention of the modern method of hand-jamming which has been wrongly attributed to Joe Brown. Harding explained this technique also in the Rucksack Club Journal of 1948. It was a technique which he had developed in the mid-forties before Joe Brown had even started climbing. In Harding's words:

'So few climbers, unfortunately, have mastered the useful art of making their hands jam in cracks...The secret lies in the use of the thumb. By pressing the thumb towards the centre of the palm and using the fleshy part of the thumb in conjunction with the back of the hand a perfect jam is obtained in the right-sized crack. It is possible to hang comfortably at arm's length, with a cigarette between the fingers, from a hand-jam made in this way. This type of hold is of course limited to cracks of a certain width; in practice, however, it is found that with careful selection of points of hold quite a large range of cracks can be dealt with by this method. The larger sizes of fissure can be overcome by the clenched fist, but this is not as satisfying, especially on overhanging sections.'

It might be thought that as soon as the war was over the few members of the post-war generation would be poised to make a big impact in North Wales, but food and petrol rationing were to carry on for several years and the travel restrictions that lack of petrol caused were to slow development in North Wales to a snail's pace compared the lightning speed of movement on motorway links by the top climbers of the nineteen-eighties. In addition very few people were lucky enough to have their own cars. A far greater factor however was the Saturday morning shift for many working men.

Some quite revolutionary ideas concerning rope technique and belaying were outlined by Ken Tarbuck in his article 'My Technique With Nylon Rope' which appeared in the 1947 Rucksack Club Journal. His ideas were fundamental and some of the principles he outlined have influenced rope techniques and rope management to the present day.

Instead of tying on to the main rope by passing it round the waist and then tying on with a bowline knot, Tarbuck suggested that a better method was to have a long length of hemp cordage which was wrapped six or seven times round the body and then tied with a reef knot with the free ends tucked into the lay of the cord. Attachment to the main rope was then made with a screw gate karabiner to which was tied the main rope. This meant that the karabiner could be easily moved round the body and was better for belaying with the attached mechanism at the back of the body on stances. This was in fact therefore a rudimentary harness and was an improvement on previous techniques.

For attaching the climbing rope to the karabiner, Tarbuck developed an adjustable knot which gave greater shock absorption. Under test with properly-tied Tarbuck knots dead-weight strain was between 80-90% of the strength of the rope compared with 60% for a bowline knot.

The important thing about a Tarbuck knot was that it could be slid up and down the main part of the rope to tighten up a belay. Tarbuck also recommended that a waist belay should be used instead of the time-honoured 'over the shoulder' technique. Another point was that the use of hemp cordage got over the problem of nylon-to-nylon heat generation during a leader fall. Tarbuck's sliding knot which tightened as strain came upon it was also extended to the use of running belays, to help reduce the load on the main rope during a leader fall. The Tarbuck knot is now part of rock-climbing history, but his other sensible suggestions have only been overtaken by mechanical devices such as the Sticht Plate for belaying, and we must admire Tarbuck for his vision nearly forty years ago.

During the war an apprentice joined the Rolls-Royce works at Derby in 1942. This young man, Peter Harding, was soon to become the leading climber on both Derbyshire gritstone and the North Wales cliffs. He had to work nights and a five-and-a-half day week was compulsory. During his early teens he was also a keen cyclist and he met Veronica (Ronnie) Lee with whom he started to walk and climb regularly.

In 1944 he started climbing in earnest at Black Rocks, Cromford, and despite the arduous wartime work at Rolls-Royce he went to Black Rocks twenty-eight times that year, usually catching the 7.10 a.m. milk train from Derby to ensure that he got a really long day. Soon he started to do the harder routes on the crag, but concentrating on climbing did not detract from his work at Rolls-Royce where one year he won the best apprentice award. At Black Rocks he met Ernie Phillips and the Dyke brothers who used to cycle there from Mansfield. A new face began to appear regularly at Black Rocks; his name was Tony Moulam. Although at that time he was still at school he was soon to become Harding's regular second. Later, just like Harding, he changed his emphasis from the Peak District to North Wales.

On August 16th 1945 Moulam was called up into the Army the day after the Japanese surrender. Just before this Moulam had gardened an unclimbed crack at Cromford, but as King and Country had called him away before he could complete it, he generously left a message for Harding to lead it — which he did, and so by proxy they produced V.J. Crack.

Their greatest effort was the relentless siege of the Promontory Traverse which they eventually completed on 12th July 1945 and even today it is still graded Hard Very Severe, 5b.

They had ten days in Wales at the end of July but there was a problem as at that time copies of the guides by Edwards were hard to obtain. This was because during the war it had been thought that the guides could be of use to the enemy. They still managed to lead Munich Climb and Soap Gut which was then described as 'the hardest climb on Tryfan'. They also spread themselves onto other climbs on the Idwal Slabs and then onto the tricky Original Route on Holly Tree Wall. Their long apprenticeship had started.

In the autumn Harding went to Wales again for a week and during one of his trips in 1945 saw Chris Preston top-roping Suicide Wall before his successful first ascent. Just after this Dick Morsley, who was with Preston on the first ascent of Suicide Wall, put a top-rope down Cenotaph Corner and although Preston did it several times he still pronounced it to be quite impossible.

In early 1946 he went to Cratcliffe where he was attracted to the perpendicular unclimbed wall to the right of the Bower which had also been named Suicide Wall. He did it on a top-rope and cleared out vegetation to reveal a good vertical crack. On May 5th he was ready but as other climbing friends on the crag seemed unenthusiastic Harding set off with his girlfriend Ronnie Lee. On the top wall his rope jammed and Ronnie had to climb out of the Bower to tug it free. From the flake a jammed knee, then the final overhang, with its magnificent finishing jugs, brought success to produce a superb Hard Very Severe, 5b, by modern standards. It was to be a tremendous fortnight for Peter. A week later he put up the Cave Superdirect at Stanage and on May 19th

Opposite: Steve Ashton leading Sucide Wall, Route 1.   Photo: Steve Ashton.

made a rare trip to Helsby where he made the second ascent of Jim Birkett's Morgue Slab — a tricky slab set high up on the cliff with no protection. Harding showed that he could excel at all types of problem and all standards of difficulty, not just solving unclimbed cracks with his new hand-jamming technique.

In July he went for a ten-day holiday and stayed at Helyg, the only Climbers' Club hut in North Wales at that time. The Climbers' Club members realised that Harding was the leader of the new climbing generation as no-one before had done so many of the top routes of the day in such a concentrated period of time. He started off with Longland's then the day after polished off West Rib, Western Slabs and Nose Direct on Dinas Mot, all with Tony Moulam who was on leave from the Army. The following day with Tony they went back to Clogwyn du'r Arddu and did Narrow Slab. The weather turned bad and the cliffs streamed with water, so Harding did the first ascent of Lot's Groove in nailed boots in rain, hail and high wind. It was fitting that on his last day he went back to Clogwyn du'r Arddu.

'Ivan Waller and Macraith Fisher appeared and whisked Charles Warren and me round to Llanberis. Mac Fisher apparently thought that the only object of the trip was to test back axles for two gentlemen called Rolls and Royce. Ivan drove the huge car almost up to Cloggy (I thought *"He'll never get this past the 10-foot corner!"*). On reaching the cliff Ivan directed me to lead Pigott's Climb...From the top we took the usual way to the summit by the Direct Finish to East Pinnacle. After the first pitch I worked out to the left round the corner and onto the Pinnacle Face. Moving up, I eventually reached a huge flake. Ivan, however, recalled me to follow the traditional route, remarking that Colin Kirkus had got him into trouble like that. I made a mental note to return to East Pinnacle Flake, but I never did. So it was with many things. Pinnacle Flake has now been climbed by the new generation: one can always rely on them to fill the gaps. All too often they are criticised for doing just that; some of us forget that we ourselves were once the new generation.'

Peter would have carried on except for the fact that Mac Fisher was a novice on his first climb. During this ten days Harding had a look at Preston's Suicide Wall on a top-rope then tried to lead it.

'With A.J.J.M. secured at the top I had a look at it with the comfort of a top-rope. The climbing seemed of a high technical standard with fingering which required some learning. However, with the impatience of youth, and Moulam as second, I decided to have a go at leading it. Some fair way up I made a silly mistake: I mantelshelfed, intending to slip my toe into a small hold, straighten up, and attain the halfway ledge. But the toe-hold wasn't there! I had made my move too early...The ground below slopes down steeply. I glanced at Tony, squatting on the scree to my left. It didn't look very far away. With a hand push I leaped backwards, turning half-about in mid-air, to make a splendid three-point landing. Tony tightened the rope at touchdown and there was no bounce. But I ate my lunch standing up: 30 feet is farther than it looks. Afterwards we decided to leave the second ascent of Suicide Wall for another day. In any case it wasn't listed in the guidebook so we couldn't have ticked it off if we had done it.'

It had been a wonderful ten days; perhaps Harding had done just too much to absorb Suicide Wall as well.

Although Harding had been accepted by the Climbers' Club which, at that time, was still a bastion of Oxbridge tradition he still found time to poke a little fun at the code of that era.

'Tradition had it that one started on the easy climbs and gradually worked up the scale. It was common to make reasonable progress from Moderates to Difficults, but it was when one came up against the Edwardian Very Difficults that the trouble began. Tradition seemed to dictate that one battered away trying to do those incredibly difficult routes until one became either too old or too tired to climb at all. One then joined a climbing club. Nowadays tradition has gone.

The young climber can go straight onto V.S.s and even X.S.s without having to bother with those terrible V. Diffs. One can fall off Severes without having had the benefit of a public school education, romp off to the Himalaya without being a rugger blue, and even lead new E.S.s without even being a member of a senior club.'

In 1946 Harding went back to Wales in the middle of September. There he finished off his season on Clogwyn du'r Arddu with Chimney Route and Sunset Crack, both with Arnold Carsten who had just done the Central Rib finish to Great Slab. It had been a bumper harvest for Harding on the Black Cliff: Longland's, Narrow Slab, Pigott's, Chimney Route and Sunset Crack; together with Lot's Groove in nailed boots, West Rib, Western Slabs and Nose Direct. One can only regret the Pinnacle Flake that might have been if he had had Tony Moulam with him. Harding even tried the then unclimbed White Slab by its left arete above Linnell's Leap, but had to use a piton to retreat.

Also during September in Ogwen he did 3,500 feet of climbing mostly solo. As well as the three summits of Tryfan, Glyder Fach and Glyder Fawr, the climbs included: Lot's Wife, Terrace Wall Variant, Tennis Shoe, Holly Tree Wall Original Route and a slide down the recesses of Monolith Crack.

As the autumn shadows lengthened over Maen du'r Arddu he felt one more urge to return to the East and West Buttresses. Arthur Dolphin came to Wales to join him and although the crag was streaming with water they did Longland's and Curving Crack in nailed boots on which they shared the lead.

The early months of 1947 were gripped in the severest winter of the century and week after week the temperature dropped below freezing point so that everywhere was carpeted in deep snow. The Stonnis Club went to Wales for Easter and stayed at George Dwyer's cottage, Tal y Waen, in the Ogwen valley. George was a professional climbing guide who had climbed with Kirkus a lot in the thirties. The weather was still not good so Harding climbed in nailed boots which helped his technique after the long winter lay-off.

Months later the weather improved and on a fine, sunny week-end he arrived at Helyg with his old Stonnis Club friend, Ernie Phillips.

'The break came with a week-end in May when Ernie and I made a second ascent of Brant on Clogwyn y Grochan (the first ascent in boots).'

Before doing Brant he had climbed the groove above the start of Slape which now forms the first 5a pitch of Hangover. Harding reached the small holly-tree belay and then retreated.

'The amusing thing about that week-end was that Ernie and I eyed out the route of Spectre, which we estimated as being a nice pleasant V. Diff. requiring rubbers and a dry day for its full enjoyment. Since it was raining at the time we kept our boots on and did Brant. Returning to the Grochan next day we changed into rubbers, for the weather was fine and the rock was reasonably dry...

The first pitch went easily. With Ernie tucked in by the side of a huge sharp-edged flake I traversed right and shinned up a slim crack to an overhung niche with a sloping floor. Realising that I had now done the easy part I hammered in a peg high up in the crack. At first I decided to attack the overhang direct and then to swing out to a ledge on the right. However, I could not

make it go, so gingerly I traversed round a bulge on the left and delicately across to a heather groove. Near the top of this I espied a great jug.

"Once my fingers are on that" I thought "this Spectre is as good as exorcised."

Ernie encouraged me from below so I climbed up to slide my fingers thankfully round the top of the jug. It moved. I retreated rapidly on tiny finger-holds, to pause a few inches below. Almost before I had calculated the next moves the block of rock which was my 'jug' toppled from its perch. It narrowly missed my rope. Glancing down I saw it smack the flake a fraction from Ernie's head, fortunately just on the opposite side of the knife edge.

"Thanks" said Ernie.

I merely grunted and moved upwards rapidly. I reached the good holds at the top of the groove and pulled up onto the slabs. I lit a cigarette and then belayed.

"You're on next" I shouted.

The next pitch was easy slab-work to the foot of a crack — the crack which is such a prominent feature of the route as seen from the road. The upper part of the crack was full of earth and plants and was rather difficult to reach. I fixed a running belay and pulled up to do some gardening, slipping a small peg into a thin crack on the right with my fingers to use as a balancing point for my right foot. My left foot was toe-jammed into the main crack. I dug out handfuls of earth and assorted greenery. There was a nice bunch of lupin-like plants in the back of the crack but they did not seem safe enough to pull up on. In search of possible holds in the very bowels of the crack I stood up gently on the peg. It promptly slipped out, leaving me dangling on two handfuls of mud.

A good thrutch and I was well and truly jammed in the wide part of the crack head first. Another thrutch, and I was almost falling out of the crack, but at least from a few feet higher up. Not many cracks can withstand the onslaught of a well-executed series of thrutches. At last I pulled up on those good finishing jugs. The rest of the climb was a matter of course.

Spectre remained as top climb in North Wales for three or four years, defying all attempts to repeat it for nearly two years. I seconded the second ascent by Mervyn Hughes in 1949. Since then I have done the climb four times, once with Richard Meyer when a new lower pitch was added, once with Ken Herbert when he added a different start and a different finish, once behind Vin Ridgeway (before breakfast) when I went directly over the overhang on pitch 3, and once solo when I did the same again. I have never found it to contain the difficulty it gave Ernie Phillips and myself in 1947. By careful analysis of the difficulty I would rate it not more than just a little harder than Diagonal Route on Dinas Mot, which Arthur Birtwistle had led nearly ten years previously. However, it was acclaimed by popular vote the hardest climb in the valley until Joe Brown's generation came along with their own inventions.'

Peter Harding's guide stated:

'Exceptionally Severe. Exposed, strenuous and delicate also. Probably the most difficult climb in the valley.'

At that time it certainly was. Its reputation was enhanced when John Lawton tried to do the second ascent. He fell from the crux pitch traversing left from the niche. The rope cut through and he crashed to the ground a hundred feet below sustaining severe injuries from which he slowly recovered.

Harding only had five week-ends in Wales in 1947, together with a week's holiday in August. As he was at Loughborough College and the petrol-rationing restrictions were at their greatest his new-route activity was severely restricted. During the week's holiday he did twenty climbs in four successive days which put him in fine form.

On Friday 29th August he did four routes on Dinas Cromlech and had a good look at the unclimbed corner to the right of Cenotaph Corner. He solved this with his old friend Ernie Phillips. Ivy Sepulchre was graded as Exceptionally Severe, the same as Spectre, and in his guidebook Harding described it thus:

'A very serious and difficult climb. The crux involves some loose rock, vegetation, overhangs, a fight with a holly tree and delicate wall climbing.'

Pitch 3 in particular has a unique description:

'110 feet. The crack is wide and hard to start. Progress is made by a bridging type of layback movement, an occasional hold of doubtful nature appearing now and then. At forty feet the angle relents to a small niche below the overhang; no belay. Start the overhang by bridging using holds in the crack: there is a piton above on the right which gives both protection and direct aid. The climbing at this point and above is exceptionally severe, strenuous and in a very exposed position. Above the overhang the crack narrows and after one good hand-jam the pull out is made on small fingerholds on the right wall; the leader may rest on good footholds. A short groove leads to the foot of an old rickety holly tree and after a struggle with this and the crack behind it good holds can be reached on the left wall.'

Later, on Christmas Day, Peter and a strong Climbers' Club team went all the way up to Craig yr Ysfa specially for an ascent of The Grimmett. The team consisted of those with whom he was to climb on many occasions during the next three years: Tony Moulam who was still in the Army, Arnold Carsten who had just produced a new guide to Helsby, Dick Meyer and Norman Horsfield. Various combinations of people did The Grimmett on Christmas Day for the next three years. In 1948 there was a jolly party of nine people in perfect weather conditions. They carried balloons, wore paper hats and tied an effigy of Tony Moulam (who unfortunately couldn't be there) onto the rope. Sadly the effigy fell out of the rope and they had a solemn memorial ceremony. During their Christmas dinner Alf Bridge, who used to do a climb with Colin Kirkus over the Christmas period, sent them a telegram wishing them 'Happy landings'.

Alf Bridge was one of the most enthusiastic Secretaries the Climbers' Club had had for many years and despite the age gap he forged strong links with Peter Harding and his young contemporaries. Unfortunately Alf came under pressure from a certain pressure group in the Climbers' Club not to dilute the Oxbridge mainstream with the surging proletariat. Eventually the pressure on Alf became even more intense and he resigned both as Secretary and from the Climbers' Club itself which was much the poorer. Alf had bridged the gap between climbers of the twenties and thirties and subsequently with the hard men of the forties. Alf had finally turned his back on the 'Mandarins' as he called the old Establishment.

Another great name still appeared occasionally at his old love, Helyg — Menlove Edwards. Peter Harding still remembers his ungainly climbing style, so individual, so forceful, so awkward, but never looking as if he would ever come off. It seemed as if each individual point of his contact had a natural unbreakable adhesiveness with whatever the rock or however unfriendly or slippery the surface might have been. At Helyg Harding recalled one of Menlove's extraordinary feats. There is a perched loft above the Helyg kitchen which reduces the height of the ceiling to about seven feet for half the kitchen length. In the loft wall facing the fireplace was a stable door which when closed had a projecting lip of floor boards of perhaps four inches. It was a challenge in those days to leap up, grasp the lip and try to mantelshelf into the loft with legs flailing in free air. Once a bent-arm position was attained it was possible to use the inside of the door posts. However, when the door was closed no hold was possible except the straight mantelshelf. Edwards was one of the very few people who could do it.

1948 was another great year and by April Harding was back on new-route form and started the season with the first ascent of Trilon on Carreg Wastad. Three other good climbers appeared on the Welsh new route scene that year. Geoff Pigott had inherited his father's abilities and became interested in the unclimbed parts of the Llanberis cliffs. In contrast to his father's route on Clogwyn du'r Arddu Geoff's Phantom Rib on Clogwyn y Grochan is a succession of delicate moves up a very exposed rib. The modern guidebook description sums it all up:

'An excellent exposed climb on small holds. The crux is very committing and is in a superb position.'

The older traditions of the Climbers' Club produced Mervyn Hughes from Oxford. He was undoubtedly the finest climber that Oxbridge produced in the forties and his Overlapping Wall on Carreg Wastad was an extraordinary effort which gets two stars in the modern Llanberis guide and is still graded Mild Extremely Severe, 5b. He also did an ascent of Spectre after Lawton's terrible fall from the crux and was fond of visiting the distant mountain cwms and their lonely crags.

John Lawton was already in his mid-forties when the new generation started to find major new climbs in Wales. He was one of the first people to decide that to climb well one should live close to the cliffs. He got a job in a slate quarry so that he would not have the travel problems that all the English climbers faced by living a hundred miles or more from North Wales.

Lawton had an obsession with an unclimbed groove on the Suicide Wall in Ogwen . Even when he top-roped the groove he found it desperately difficult. A second top-roped ascent did little to ease his problem but on March 24th he climbed Suicide Groove. It was a worthy bonus for Lawton who had put so much effort into his climbing.

It was probably Lawton's toughness and manual work in the quarry that saved his life when he fell from near the end of the crux traverse on Spectre. Geoff Pigott, who was seconding him, had slowed down his fall but the rope was sliced in two over a sharp edge causing a hideous fall to the foot of the crag. Peter Harding was very upset by Lawton's fall from Spectre and soloed up the crux pitch and removed Lawton's sling and karabiner from the peg under the overhang. He then soloed Overlapping Wall to prove to himself that he wasn't affected by the accident and also climbed Spectre and thought that it was technically a little easier than Overlapping Wall but was not as sustained.

Clearly Harding was worried about the grading of the harder and more serious routes, which might have led to accidents, and a word of explanation from Harding's guidebook seems appropriate:

'Two more standards have been used to deal with really difficult climbs. Extremely Severe has been reserved for routes of great technical difficulty and Exceptionally Severe for courses 'beyond the pale' or of extreme length and seriousness.'

1948 was the year when Harding started work on the Llanberis guidebook which took in Clogwyn du'r Arddu. During the year two or three significant new routes were to appear. The Old Girdle Traverse of Carreg Wastad which Peter climbed with Peter

Opposite: Trevor Jones bridged out across Brant Direct.   Photo: R.F. Allen.

Hodgkinson took them two days to finish but it was 800 feet long. They thought that the crux pitch under Shadow Wall was Extremely Severe.

Later Harding and Moulam had a fortnight's holiday in North Wales and had the rare use of a car, an M.G. The sport's plan for the holiday was entitled 'Hackit — Attackit' and to make sure they were fully nourished they took with them one and a half hundredweight of food. During the fortnight they consumed 10 gallons of milk, 50 eggs, 9 boxes of Shredded Wheat, 14lbs of jam — it was little wonder with that energy supply that there was to be a surge of new routes. On the other hand it seems astonishing that they got up anything at all after that quantity of food. In fact they did fifty routes in their Hackit-Attackit fortnight, including seven new routes.

The best route was the first ascent of Kaisergebirge Wall which Harding led with John Disley and Tony Moulam following. They light-heartedly recorded the new route description in German in the Stonnis Club log-book.

'New Route. Kaisergebirge Wall. Der Ostwand am links von Mittkamin wir klettern die strengst wand mit sieben hachen (attachen!) zu gipful von *Klein Eric*". Dann wir klettern *"Ledge"* weg zu gipful von *"Clogwyn y Grochan"*. Die ist ein weg *"OO"*. Ho ja! Erste klettern — Les Trois Phoenixiennes. P.R.J.H., J.I.D., A.J.J.M.'

Harding used a lot of aid but one must remember that it was probably the steepest and most continuously difficult pitch so far put up in Wales. The difficult crux moves up the wall still had to be made using tiny fingerholds and where there were no cracks for pitons. It was another major contribution to new steep wall climbing.

1949 was a grand-slam year for Harding: more new routes, the finish of the guidebook and a spectacular new route on the West Buttress of Clogwyn du'r Arddu. Previously in November 1948 Tony Moulam had been knocked down while hitch-hiking and had to go to the Orthopaedic Hospital at Oswestry to recover from his fractures and it was this accident which resulted in his absence from the Christmas Day Grimmett mass ascent. Moulam came out of hospital and worked with Peter on the guidebook to Black Rocks and Cratcliffe, starting his training for Wales by doing all his old favourites at Black Rocks.

Two week's holiday in Wales during April produced in typical Harding fashion thirty-eight climbs including eight first ascents — the best spell of new-route productivity he had ever done. They included: Short Tree Chimney (Difficult) on Craig Ddu, solo; Delphos (Very Severe, 4c) Clogwyn y Grochan; Unicorn (Hard Very Severe with one point of aid) on Carreg Wastad. The latter is still one of the great trade routes of the valley. Two other routes done on the same day were Intermediate Chimney (Very Difficult) in Cwm Glas and Square Gully (Severe) on Clogwyn y Person. Finally two Very Severe girdles on Cyrn Las: the Green Necklace and the Green Caterpillar.

The ascent of Brant Direct resulted from a bizarre set of circumstances. A strong Climbers' Club second eleven had been trying to peg the route for three days and one evening had taunted Harding by saying that when it was completed it would make his routes look like Sunday School picnics. At the end of the third day they were exhausted and still hadn't climbed the route. Peter asked if he might try, then nonchalantly climbed it free to the wide part of the crack near the top where the peggers had run out of equipment. It was a perfect jamming-crack which Harding easily finished before bringing up Gordon Dyke, Peter Hodgkinson and John Disley. While abseiling from the top of

Opposite Top Left: Tony Moulam.
Opposite Top Right: David Cox.
Opposite Bottom Left: Wilfrid Noyce.
Opposite Bottom Right: J.B. Lawton.   Photos: Peter Harding and P.y G. collection.

the route Peter was peed upon from a great height by one of the unsuccessful would-be-first ascensionists. Whether due to malice, envy or an unstoppable call of nature it is now unknown. Brant Direct's continuous difficulty merited its X.S. grading at that time. It was a fine finish to Harding's surge of new routes.

A fortnight later Harding cycled from Shrewsbury to Derby in four hours, had his tea, and then went to Black Rocks with Tony Moulam who had by then fully recovered from his injuries. On that Friday evening Harding made gritstone history by doing Demon Rib which is still E2 5c. He followed this by doing the Hard Very Severe 5a Superstitious Start to Lean Man's. This put him on fine form for the next week-end with Gordon Dyke on Clogwyn du'r Arddu but only after they had acquired sufficient lighter fuel for Peter's Vincent motor-cycle. He had never done Sheaf or Bow-Shaped Slab and set off to do both. He had thought they could climb Sheaf, descend the easy part of Narrow Slab and finish off with Bow-Shaped, thus neatly completing all the climbs for the guidebook.

While they were finishing Sheaf, Harding had the thought that they might complete a Girdle Traverse. Gordon however had sprained his wrist the previous day, but concealed this fact from Peter. This was the critical point. They had intended to reverse the easier bits of Narrow Slab then do the whole of Bow-Shaped, but to do the girdle they had to cross over and join Bow-Shaped at the top of the difficult pitch and reverse the Bow-Shaped crux which had stopped many people including Harding. Even today it is Hard Very Severe 5a, so it must have been an awe-inspiring prospect in 1949.

'It was very exposed and promised a long run-out — a downward traverse, with the most difficult moves at the far end. Some 80 feet altogether. Having carefully weighed things up I was convinced that it was well within the limits. The major difficulty was going to be protection for my second on the traverse.

The slightly downward traverse on the grass line was easy at first until I reached the centre of the slab. I managed to fix a running belay, through which I passed only one of the ropes. I then descended steeply for a few feet until my hands were on the diagonal line. It was becoming difficult. I hesitated. At last I stepped across and up again to reach some small but satisfying finger-holds. The outlook at this point is extremely fierce and exposed. Cautiously I worked across until I was just below a shallow groove and almost directly above the stance which is shared by Great and Bow-Shaped Slabs.

It was possible: but how should I protect Gordon across the traverse? The only solution was to climb up to what appeared to be a small stance at the top of the groove. This was by no means easy and the belays were disappointing to say the least: three doubtful flakes. I belayed to two of the spikes with slings, standing on a small quartz hold.

He traversed to the running belay easily and, leaving it in position, descended to make the lower step across. On this he was well protected by the rope passing through the belay. On the difficult moves in between he was suspended by a triangle of rope — one straight from me to his waist and another by way of the karabiner of the running belay. Everything went according to plan. When he was in a safe position I flicked off the running belay and took him almost directly below me on a single rope. His strained wrists were now beginning to trouble him and there were rather tense moments while I lowered him bodily for a few feet to the stance below, hardly daring to let the full weight come on my doubtful belays.

When he was secured to the stance I prepared to descend from my exposed position. But I had suddenly become very tired, probably because of the nervous strain, and found the short descent to be too difficult. So I decided to abseil from the best of the three spikes.

First I had to be sure that the rope would flick off when I was down for I didn't want to sacrifice a sling. Putting the doubled rope round one of the spikes, I asked Gordon to try and flick it off. It seemed impossible so with time and endurance diminishing I abseiled timidly with the rope scarcely balanced on the extreme tip of one of the spikes. After I had reached the stance the rope came off with the merest of flicks and the worst was over.

That traverse, I think, is the most difficult and exposed part of the route.'

It was a neat solution and initiated the use of double-rope techniques to protect each man in order to complete the route. Dyke, despite his injured wrist, led the 40-foot corner and by the time they reached the Central Rib they had been climbing for seven hours. Their attention faltered as they became more tired, yet on the final stages they moved together, and it was on this last stage that a falling stone neatly cut the rope. By the time they had finished they had produced a 1,000-foot exciting new Girdle Traverse. It was a fitting final reward for Harding for his guidebook work which with those infrequent week-ends denied him many possible new routes.

A month later Harding soloed Overlapping Wall, did Bow-Shaped Slab upwards this time, then followed it next day with Brant prior to soloing up an unclimbed part of Carreg Wastad. He returned the next week-end to produce Lion with Moulam seconding him. Lion has lost its aura of technical difficulty but still stops a few modern leaders at the overhang. This route ended his incredible output of routes in North Wales and it is worth summing up Harding's contribution to the climbing world:

1) The first modern guidebook with the necessary introduction of the X.S. grading which though modified is still in use at the moment. However, it was criticised by some Mandarins (old die-hards) of the time because it contained 'too many Excessively Severes and too few Difficults and Moderates'.

2) Modern hand-jamming techniques for crack-climbing.

3) The first modern hard gritstone climb, Demon Rib, E2 5c.

Looking back at the time Harding spent in Wales during the post-war period it is clear that had he not spent so long in checking routes for the guidebook he would most likely have climbed some of the big lines that had to wait for the Rock and Ice era. He had been so close to a breakthrough on Pinnacle Flake and as Demon Rib had demonstrated that he was capable of leading up to E2 5c standard one can only wonder at what he could have achieved in Wales if the opportunity had arisen.

The Baron and The Villain

Ask people to mention the names of a few well-known climbers and they will probably say, "Joe Brown", pause, "...and Don Whillans." Born in Manchester, the cradle of many top rock-climbers, they became the first climbers from working-class backgrounds to burst through social layers to the top of the climber's pyramid. Together they became the most formidable team ever seen on British rock and in the space of just a few short years in the early nineteen-fifties they changed the face of Welsh climbing. A host of legendary routes were forced up the steep walls and overhangs of the Snowdonia cliffs and the tales and rumours which spread ensured that the climbing world would be intimidated for some years.

Joe was the last of seven children of a closely-knit Catholic family, whose father died when Joe was only eight months old. His mother then had a difficult time rearing her large happy brood of children and had to take in washing to make ends meet. After leaving school Joe became a plumber's apprentice and began to visit Derbyshire regularly where he met Slim Sorrell, a pipe-fitter from Stockport. Slim was older than Joe and knew more about the hills and crags of the Peak District. They soon started to climb together every week-end.

Don Whillans was born three years later than Joe in Salford where his family also had a grim struggle during the depression years. As soon as he left school Don got a job with a firm that cleaned and repaired boilers. It was dirty, heavy work which included manhandling awkward pipework down flights of stairs. Not surprisingly heavy manual work during the week and walking and climbing every week-end set Joe and Don up into muscular teenage climbing machines. The closeness to Derbyshire and abstinence from drink made their life-style similar to the rock stars of four decades later.

Joe and Don were working-class prototypes of 'Arry, of whom C.E. Mathews had spoken so scornfully fifty years earlier, when he predicted that no-one from the working class would ever climb a hill. Joe and Don changed all that because they weren't even aware of the existence of the middle-class climbing world. Joe and Slim met members of the Valkyrie Mountaineering Club from Derby in the summer of 1948. Among the ranks of the Valkyrie was Nat Allen who was destined to become one of the great diplomats of the climbing world.

At Christmas 1948 the Valkyrie went to Ogwen and on Christmas Day Joe did the first winter ascent of Hanging Garden Gully. The following day they then went round to the Llanberis Pass where Joe tried Cenotaph Corner, the big right-angled and unclimbed corner which had been named in advance by Menlove Edwards. Joe had borrowed some pitons from Ernie Phillips as he had none of his own and used these to protect himself as he climbed the corner. During the struggle Joe dropped his piton hammer onto Wilf White's head then after Wilf recovered he encouraged Joe to carry on. Joe got right up to the niche just below the final difficulties but then had to retreat.

The incident provoked Peter Harding to write in his Llanberis Pass guide:

Opposite Top Left: Dennis Gray, Nat Allen, Joe Brown and Derek Carnell.
Opposite Top Right: Jimmie Marshall and Joe Brown.
Opposite Bottom Left: Standing; A.N.O., Ray Greenall, Don Whillans; Sitting; Joe Brown, Fred Ashton, Nat Allen, Ron Moseley.
Opposite Bottom Right: Joe Brown on an early attempt of White Slab.   Photos: Nat Allen and Joe Brown.

'The Cenotaph Corner is still an unclimbed gap, throwing out its challenge. There is no doubt, that with sufficient ironmongery and few scruples this corner could be ascended. The last words are chosen specially. Some day the call will prove too strong and the Cenotaph will lose much of its virtue.'

Perhaps we should bear in mind Harding's first ascent of Kaisergebirge Wall when 'sufficient ironmongery' was needed to overcome its steep wall. It is likely that this early defeat helped to formulate Joe's future rule of only two pitons per pitch on his new routes.

In 1949 just before he was conscripted into the Army and posted to Singapore, Joe climbed with Slim Sorrell on Clogwyn du'r Arddu and did all thirteen routes on the cliff in three days. During his demobilisation leave in August 1950 Joe went back to Clogwyn du'r Arddu with Wilf White, Don Chapman and Nat Allen. Brown then climbed the Drainpipe Crack, not knowing it had been climbed by Arthur Birtwistle, then started on the upper crack which was running with water. After managing to fix a hemp sling of Nat's round a thread, he moved left onto the wall and was not far below the belay ledge when he came off...Nat held him, but the single half-weight hemp rope was half cut through on the left edge of the crack. Undaunted Joe returned next day with Nat and this time climbed onto the ledge below which he had fallen on the previous day. Nat got up to this stance but this time Joe failed on the chimney crux and they had to retreat once more.

After the army Joe returned to Suicide Wall in Ogwen. He remembered an unsuccessful attempt in 1948 when he noticed little spikes on the wall which might grudgingly accept the thinnest possible cord. Joe sat in the chapel porch at Idwal and knotted nylon bootlaces into fragile slings. The conditions were wet again so Joe climbed in socks which rolled onto the tiny spikes of the bubbly-looking rock. As quickly as he put the bootlace slings on the tiny spikes the high damp wind blew them off again; Joe didn't stop on the turf ledge and despite the lack of protection carried on to the top. It was the second ascent but in comparison Preston had top-roped the route before his ascent and had perfect conditions.

It was to be the first of many ascents in bad conditions, when holds were often greasy and made the climbs feel more like winter routes. Brown's attitude on an uncompromising crux was invariably prompted by an aggressive urge from within but this was always tempered by a smooth physical effort. Helped by his almost prehensile limbs Joe could rest in situations where everyone else could barely cling on. In positions of extremis Joe could get his feet higher in a bridging position than almost anyone else. One of his party-pieces in the valley was to fold his feet behind his head, lock them in that position, then walk around on his hands. This extraordinary suppleness and the acquired physical strength from his building work were part of the key to his climbing supremacy.

In April 1951 Joe and his friends went to the Roaches and did the direct start to Peter Harding's magnificent Valkyrie. Slim Sorrell was unable to follow so a small wedge-shaped teenager asked to try it. A few minutes later Don Whillans and Joe Brown sat together on the ledge at the top. Don noticed Joe's banana-shaped strong fingers and a frequent smile which lit up his sherpa-like face. It was also Don's first experience of Joe's conversational charisma, in his flat Mancunian tones with just a hint of self-deprecation,

Opposite Above: Joe Brown on the 1st ascent of Tramgo, Castell Cidwm.   Photo: Edgar Siddall.
Opposite Below: Joe Brown on Suicide Wall, Ogwen.   Photo: J. Brown collection.

but with never a vestige of pomposity or self-elevation. There aren't many people who automatically become the centre of a social gathering when they enter it but Joe still does. His personal magnetism — a trite phrase perhaps best sums it up.

So, the great partnership had started. Just before this Don had had a prolonged period of illness diagnosed as stomach ulcers and ironically was pronounced medically unfit for National Service. Brown and Whillans concentrated most of their early efforts in Wales in the Llanberis Pass and on Cloggy.

There were however other climbers about at that time, not so gifted or strong, who opened up other areas and new cliffs far away from the great surges in the mountains. Tony Moulam, who had been one of Peter Harding's closest climbing friends, did the first climb at Tremadog and dominated the exploration of the cliffs for some years. The cliffs had first been noticed by Dave Thomas who flew close to them in a bomber during the Second World War. Moulam's first invention at Tremadog was Hound's Head Buttress, a striking pinnacle with a superb system of Severe cracks in its front face, which was blown up in 1963 on the mistaken premise that it was about to fall down. Moulam did not confine himself to Tremadog but did some useful climbs on the Llanberis cliffs, such as Ribstone Crack on Carreg Wastad, which he climbed with the Olympic steeplechaser John Disley. The route was a fine steep addition to the cliffs and the name was of course a simple anagram of Crackstone Rib.

The week before Brown's first new route in the Pass, Moulam again turned his attention to the Wastad and put up Bole Way with Geoff Pigott and Tony Hyde. Climbed on May 12 1951 it was an intricate route with its share of loose rock, but it was still a useful addition to that part of the cliff.

Undoubtedly the culmination of Moulam's efforts was his discovery of Mur y Niwl on the lower Amphitheatre Wall of Craig yr Ysfa. A.B. Hargreaves had first noticed the line in the thirties and mentioned the possibility of a route in his article 'More of Arfon', which discussed Welsh climbs and future new areas for innovation. Before the snow had disappeared in April 1952 Moulam and an American, Johnny Churchill, went up to the crag to try the wall. As they approached, the mist was swirling in the gully at the foot of the climb which gave Moulam the idea of the name which means in English 'Wall of the Mists'. Sadly Churchill was killed not long afterwards in the Alps when the Eccles bivouac in which he was staying was swept away.

Moulam concentrated on Tremadog in the years up to 1956 and produced a framework of new routes which instantly became popular. Shadrach, Scratch, Christmas Curry and Merlin all date from that era, and they are still as popular today. By a cruel stroke of luck, another bad accident which was not Moulam's fault put him out of the climbing scene for some years.

While Moulam was beavering away at Tremadog and other areas Joe Brown was getting into top gear in the Pass. In May 1951 Joe climbed his first new route in Wales on Clogwyn y Grochan — Hangover. It took the groove above the start of Slape which Peter Harding had already climbed, but Joe launched out onto the vertical wall on the steep second pitch. Brown had already tried to climb it in nailed boots but one of the holly trees on the wall when sprung by the rope had spiked him in the eye. This time however he was successful and his ascent inaugurated a new era in the Llanberis Pass.

Opposite: Tony Ashton approaching the 'perch' on Mur y Niwl.   Photo: Steve Ashton.

A few weeks later while attempting Diglyph, his first new route on Clogwyn du'r Arddu, he nearly fell off when his peg hammer jammed while he was climbing. Fortunately the peg hammer jerked free and just above he was able to bang in a piton to feel safe again. The incident was sufficiently unnerving to frighten off his second, Eric Price, who refused to follow.

Joe carried on his 1951 surge through Wales in that spring and produced Unicorn Direct with Slim Sorrell. The route has a hard overhanging crack where the sharp rock-leaf at the crux bites into one's arm on the hard move.

Brown and his friends often stayed in Nant Peris at the Cromlech Hut which at that time was just a rough loft above a cowshed at the back of the village. The warmth of the animals took the chill off the room above and they all learned to forget the bovine smells because on sunny days the sun flooded through the south-facing doorway. As rats also inhabited the barn Joe kept his food in a rucksack which he pushed into the bottom of his sleeping bag at night. It didn't matter the following morning when Nat fried up the communal breakfast that Joe's bacon was decorated here and there with the odd feather. It merely added a light relief to the start of the day. When they woke up it was often freezing and Mortimer Smith who was in charge of brewing always emerged first. Condensed milk was the only milk available to put in the tea and it seemed perfectly natural to Mortimer to suck the condensed milk out of the tin...then to spit individual globules into each waiting mug...before passing the tea to the prostrate figures who always emerged at a late hour of the day.

On September 26th, 1951, the Rock and Ice club was formed in Manchester: Joe, Don, Slim Sorrell, Ron Moseley (who was to be the driving force), Nat Allen (the peace-maker, diplomat and nice guy) and eight others. A few years later Don Roscoe was the first Rock and Ice member to apply to join the Climbers' Club. As the profession of a potential candidate had to be stated in the club internal newsletter it went on record that Don was a typewriter mechanic. This prompted one aged member to reply *"Are we to have typewriter mechanics in the Climbers' Club?"* Although some of Peter Harding's more artisan friends had been blackballed the Climbers' Club grudgingly realised that a representative of the new generation was badly needed so Roscoe was elected.

Shortly after its formation the Rock and Ice returned to Wales and Joe and Don went to try a crack in the right wall of Cenotaph Corner. It had repulsed them on their first attempt to climb it and Whillans was very surprised at Joe's keenness to renew the battle while Cenotaph Corner was still unclimbed. This time Joe led up to the holly tree at the top of the first pitch. A ragged crack split the wall above. It was vertical and was strewn with loose rock and tiny pockets. Don launched onto the pitch; it got harder. At one point close to the crux an inviting-looking pocket clustered with razor-sharp little flakes chopped at Don's fingers as he pulled up and cut them badly. He moved on to a tiny ledge where he belayed then Joe came up for an easy pitch on the right to finish the climb. It was their best effort so far. As they were going through Chester on the way home they saw a bus signposted to Cemetery Gates. That was the obvious name for their new route.

Some of the group were not too keen on the formation of a club as it would have to have rules which they would inevitably break. Nevertheless the Rock and Ice was eventually formed and was to become a powerful force in climbing. Both Brown and

Opposite: Ron Moseley as a young teenager.   Photo: Nat Allen collection.

Whillans wore a balaclava helmet which had a capacious rim into which varying sizes of chockstones could be stored as a squirrel hoards its nuts. These could then be easily selected for use in cracks.

Just over two weeks later as the autumn shadows started to lengthen over the Welsh cliffs Joe was drawn back to Vember on Cloggy. Nat Allen had abseiled down and had levered off a large, dangerous block from the crux, but had then to climb back up as his abseil rope was too short to reach a safe ledge.

Joe climbed the first pitch then launched out onto the second pitch gripped with apprehension as he approached his previous highest point. The shallow chimney just allowed the minimum of precarious contact...a tiny ledge...more constrictions...more steepness...It was a chastened Brown who arrived at the tiny stance. Wedge-shaped Whillans however shot up the crux move and pronounced it reasonable. They called the route Vember because it was the Christian name of Mrs Williams' daughter at the Half-Way House, where they always called in on the way up to the crag, either for a sharp lemon drink or occasionally to bivouac in her outbuildings.

Joe was back a fortnight later for his final fling of 1951. On the extreme left-hand side of the West Buttress is a steep, smooth, slabby bastion like an enormous boulder. The first forty feet were simple. Joe had seen an obvious traversing line leading off rightwards into the dripping recesses of the then unclimbed Black Cleft, roofed on its right by an ominously overhanging wall. Joe ran out a full length of rope, then had to ask Ron Moseley, his second man, to tie on another length. After an incredible 200-foot run-out he reached the final difficult overhang. At this point his anorak hood caught on a spike just as he was making the final moves. For the third time on a new route Joe had an epic and the struggle to free himself almost exhausted him. Suddenly the spike was behind and an easy slab above led to another victory.

In 1952 the pre-eminence of Brown and Whillans on the Welsh cliffs was overshadowed briefly by an unknown who dazzled like a dragonfly for the briefest time and then was gone. It was John Streetly. At Cambridge he was persuaded to go to Derbyshire where he polished off some of the hardest routes, then in Wales he led Spectre in a total climbing time of eighteen minutes, including a new variation. He followed this by the second ascent of Mur y Niwl then Harding's Girdle Traverse of the West Buttress of Clogwyn du'r Arddu.

On his second trip to Clogwyn du'r Arddu he made history. On the extreme right-hand end of the West Buttress there is an obvious entry which leads to a rusty-coloured, steep slab, the Bloody Slab. Brown and Moseley had got to the hard moves, made one or two desultory moves to overcome the problem and had then retreated. On 10th June 1952 John Streetly climbed Bloody Slab and with no-one else able to follow he had to unrope when the rope ran out and then finish the route solo. His description of the intricacies of the first ascent are one of the few detailed accounts of a desperate climb of that time.

'From here on the climb became quite thin and now it is difficult to recall how the next thirty feet were managed at all. At one stage the only means of moving up was by reaching at full stretch with the right hand to finger-jam in the bottom of a vertical crack about eighteen inches long and half an inch wide. By pulling up on this and then body-leaning to the left it was possible to swing up to the level of the top of the crack. At this critical point a quick call from an ever-watchful

second pointed to the only possible foothold about two feet away to the left. This allowed a moment's respite in a more or less bridged position which, itself being very tiring and with the previous move being apparently impossible to reverse, left no alternative but to go on up. With the difficult move below and the uncertainty of what was still to come, life at this point seemed to depend more upon faith than friction.

Still, after the second runner, the slab was dry and tiny flakes allowed pleasantly delicate finger-and-toe climbing to lead to a somewhat doubtful flake behind which the placement of the only piton allowed another runner. This was about seventy feet from the start and about a hundred feet from the rake directly below with still no possibility of a stance, belay, or even a resting place. About fifteen feet above was the first large overhang in the middle of the slab and the third runner made for much more confident climbing up to the base of this. At this point the first real handhold of the climb was manufactured by extensive gardening in the crack immediately below the overhang. Here the general dampness and moss made rubbers both useless and dangerous, so they had to be removed quickly and tucked away in case they were necessary later on. The climb was continued in socks, and with the newly found 'Thank God' hold, a stretch round the overhang on the left enabled a small undercut hand-hold to be used by the left hand for a pull round the corner and up to a neat little ledge just to the left and above the bottom of the overhang.

After a rest here, on what was a reasonable stance, it became obvious that there were no belays in the vicinity. However, on the right along the side of the overhang an obvious layback crack of fifteen odd feet led to the possibility of a runner behind a rather shaky flake. On return to the ledge the route became only too obvious! The ledge itself was on top of an overhang; there was an overhanging wall on the right; and directly above were what the guide-book terms 'the obvious overhangs of Bloody Slab'. The only way led diagonally upwards and across the smooth and exposed slab to the left. Fifteen feet away to the left was a thin vertical grassy crack and between this and the ledge the only holds were very tiny vertical ribs; in effect the ideal place for a horizontal rappel. This was done by using the rope through the runner on the shaky flake which allowed a precarious crab-like movement to be made across into the grassy crack.

From this point on the upper slab proper it was possible to climb diagonally up to the left on tiny finger-and-toe-holds with the occasional use of a clump of grass growing in thin vertical cracks. At one stage when embracing such a strip of grass with hands and feet the top portion came away from the crack and started to peel off, rolling down from the top like a thin green carpet. With a seventy-foot lead-out from the last runner — the shaky flake — the situation was critical and the piton-hammer was rapidly brought into use to cut off the detached part of the clump before the whole thing rolled right off. Quick movement off the grass was of course quite impossible owing to the thin and delicate nature of the climb. On the upper portion of the slab there was no trace of any real hold so all movements had to be carefully studied in order to maintain three good points of contact with the rock while looking for, or making, the next move.

Shifting carefully off the grass, movement could again be made diagonally upwards to the left on very tiny rugosities until another large loose flake was reached. This appeared to be resting on a useful little ledge, so bridged on very small toe-holds, it proved quite a surprise when a tentative pull removed the whole issue — all twenty odd pounds of it! This presented an awkward problem, more so in view of the fact that I was holding on to it! One could, of course, hold the flake against the rock, but not for long, and it was too heavy to throw clear without falling off. Throwing would of course also remove two very good hand-holds — and if I dropped it — well my feet were just below. Ted and Brian down below could not have known what was going on until, with a little push to the left, I half dropped, half threw it just clear of my left foot to slither noisily down the slab and over the overhang to crash, after a moment's silence to the screes below.

Opposite: Starting the final pitch of Cemetery Gates, Dinas Cromlech.   Photo: Steve Ashton.

Just to complete the picture, the groove from which the flake had come was rounded top and bottom with no trace of the hoped-for hold. Almost desperate examination of the rock, however, revealed a tiny flake the top of which was knocked off with the hammer to produce a neat little quarter-inch ledge. Using this as a finger-hold a move could again be made across and up to another grassy strip. Proceeding super-carefully up this (a ninety-foot lead-out from the shaky flake runner), it again became possible to move on to the more rugose left edge of the slab which led up to a good grassy ledge...'

Nobody proved able to second this pitch, and John had to unrope and finish the climb on his own.

Brown and Whillans had been proud of the fact that in the early fifties every desperate climb done in Wales was a product of the Rock and Ice. They were staggered by Streetly's solving the intricacies of Bloody Slab. John Streetly was even smaller than the members of the Rock and Ice and even looked like them. He lived in Trinidad and soon returned to the Caribbean where he took up deep-sea fishing. Streetly did reappear a year or so later and climbed with Don Whillans on the Llanberis cliffs. First of all he soloed the first pitch of Ochre Groove which until then had required the use of a piton. Later Don led it and Streetly followed, chattering nonchalantly to his brother at the foot of the crag.

On another occasion Streetly was walking by Harrison's Rocks with his dog. John was in his best Sunday clothes and wearing a pair of crepe-soled shoes. He saw a youth grappling with one of the cliff's hardest problems so he politely asked him to hold the dog's lead while he easily flowed up the overhang, then he thanked the youth for holding the dog and resumed his Sunday walk. Several years later he emerged from the Caribbean again. His first route was the Walker Spur — its third British ascent.

Joe Brown liked the Bloody Slab so much that after making the second ascent he went on to make not only the third but also the fourth ascent.

A few weeks before the Bloody Slab first ascent, Joe and Don had opened up the new route season by plunging into the stinking wet recess of the unclimbed Black Cleft, Joe in tricouni-nailed boots, Don in Vibrams. Nailed boots were a good idea as the holds are permanently running with water and often covered in luxuriant and evil-smelling plants.

Another week-end in June resulted in the completion of Peter Harding's might-have-been Pinnacle Flake, a route that was to be respected by many future leaders. Brown and Whillans also did the intimidating Spillikin just along the front of the Pinnacle. Nat Allen followed them, the first time that one of the non-stars had properly followed a modern new route on the Black Cliff. To his chagrin Nat was omitted from his rightful place in the first ascent list at the back of the guidebook.

Joe and Don kept on and on at the business of producing new routes, the technical standard of which was no harder than the hardest routes which had gone before. In fact Suicide Wall at E2 5c was harder than the Rock and Ice routes of the early fifties. It was the sheer quantity of high-quality routes done by Brown and Whillans which was staggering. The older routes might be harshly described as one-pitch boulder-type test pieces whereas the Rock and Ice stars produced multi-pitch routes of the same standard in more serious places. It was their cunning use of inserted chockstones which made the unclimbed pitches safe. Most of all this team developed crack, wide crack and chimney climbing to a degree not known before.

Opposite: John Streetly on the 1st ascent of Bloody Slab, Clogwyn du'r Arddu.   Photo: Ted Wrangham.

The lure of the new routes was magnetic, but they were poorly paid and found it hard to get to Wales every week-end. Their motor-bike era was still some way off and although their visits were infrequent Brown still kept thinking of Cenotaph Corner, the next great problem.

It had rained every day the very week that Brown went down and the Corner was still streaked with water. Joe got up into the niche and remembered the trauma of his previous attempts. He tried several ways and ended up horizontal, parallel to the ground...there were only seconds left before his strength ran out...and a fall. His socks started to uncurl from their grip. One last lunge for the final holds and his hardest struggle yet finally solved the problem of Cenotaph Corner...but only just.

In 1953 a third man appeared out of the slender ranks of the Rock and Ice. Ron Moseley was to be just as imaginative in his innovative brilliance as the other Rock and Ice stars. In one period of indifferent weather in 1953 on successive days, Moseley led: Spectre, Ribstone Crack, Hangover (which was wet) and Brant Direct. Then in slimy conditions and with a hard struggle he grappled successfully with Gargoyle on the Pinnacle. Unlike the other two however, Ron was a commercial artist and so had to work hard at his fitness.

Moseley was the first unfortunate to be in the shadow of Brown and Whillans, or rather felt that he was being eclipsed. His competitive urge to be as good as the other two drove him on relentlessly, but he never liked to lead Joe or Don up a route in case he did not get the recognition that he felt was his just due. He told them that and they couldn't believe their ears. Brown and Whillans were so close in technique and daring that there was no need for any needle, but clearly Moseley felt it and this introduced the first divisive competitive strand into the Rock and Ice.

Moseley felt the need to distance himself from the official Rock and Ice meets, so if they were in Wales, Ron would go to the Lake District. On the Coronation week-end there was an official Rock and Ice meet in the Lake District. In the YMCA in Manchester during the following week someone asked Ron what he had done. Swelling with pride he said *"A new route on Cloggy, the Left Edge of the Boulder."* The tart reply was *"We didn't do anything either!"*

1953 started off with Brown and Whillans doing the first ascent of Surplomb on Clogwyn y Grochan. This led to an apocryphal story that it was done in nailed boots in a snowstorm. The first ascent details of their new routes often became distorted by a growing public, eager to believe that they were a dual combination of King Kong and Batman. However, even with an aid sling on the first pitch, Surplomb was a step forward in vertical wall climbing.

If anything the quality of the routes in 1953 was better than the previous two years. Joe opened up Cyrn Las with Subsidiary Groove and the 400-foot route, The Grooves — described in the sixties as 'probably the best and most enjoyable route of its kind in Wales'. It was long thought to be the hardest route on the south side of the Pass, and both Don Cowan and Eric Price fell off trying to follow the second pitch.

Brown was soon back on Clogwyn du'r Arddu on the virgin steepness of the East Gully Face of the Pinnacle. A high proud beak of rock can be seen sticking up from the top of the Pinnacle. A series of damp gloomy cracks and grooves leads up to it and Gargoyle seemed a fitting name for Joe's first new route on the Black Cliff in 1953.

Opposite: The formidable Don Whillans in action on Surplomb, Clogwyn y Grochan.   Photo: Joe Brown collection.

In the summer they were tempted back to the East Buttress. The Girdle Traverse had to be started very early as they had to get the 2.30 bus from Llanberis to Bangor in time to catch the Manchester train. At 6.30 the sun was still on the crag lighting up its aretes and walls and putting a glint into its weeping cracks. The light warmed for a while but suddenly it was gone. The team took the traverse of the East Buttress at a rush and to finish climbed The Corner in twenty minutes. Needless to say they caught the bus.

For the big abseil down and across the Great Wall the apocryphal script writers said that Joe had found a tiny blank slot and had rubbed a small chockstone against the rock until it was reduced in size to fit the opening, with just a line sling to hold the abseil rope.

All the Rock and Ice were impressed by the steepness of the walls of the Pinnacle, yet with some timidity Don and Nat went to try the first ascent of East Gully Groove. Joe and Ron Moseley were watching and saw Nat traverse right back into the corner. At any second they expected him to fall off as they were not aware of the enormous jugs which reduced the technical difficulty to sheer enjoyment.

One carefree day Joe realised that the Snowdon Railway offered a quick method of descent from Cloggy and thought of specially-shaped flat stones with a ridge in the middle which would fit in the middle of the cog part of the tracks. Joe reached speeds of up to 30 miles per hour which was even faster than the train. Rumour had it that he had been seen roaring into Llanberis station at 60 m.p.h. Flocks of sheep were put in jeopardy and had to flee for their lives. Perhaps it was fortunate for all concerned that the supply of suitably-shaped slabs ran out before anyone was seriously injured.

There was one hazard in the nineteen-fifties which struck fear into the Rock and Ice in case they had an accident — the thought that they might be taken to the Caernarvon and Anglesey Hospital in Bangor. Ron Moseley had a motor-cycle crash in the Llanberis Pass when the road was in a very gravelly condition. After treatment at the hospital he was driven home in a van and every time they went over a bump he screamed in pain. When he got back to a Manchester hospital they discovered that a large stone was still embedded in his knee-cap under the plaster. On another occasion Mortimer Smith was impaled on the railings at Plas y Brenin when his motor-cycle skidded. He too received treatment for his broken thigh at the Caernarvon and Anglesey...his leg was not properly restored for two years.

The Rock and Ice was a club of scarcely two dozen members but they had already changed the face of Welsh climbing and had by then survived three full years of great achievement: eight routes in 1951, nine in 1952 and seven in 1953. Of these, 11 routes were Extremely Severe, 10 were Hard Very Severe and 3 were Very Severe. Curiously there was a pause in new routes in 1954 from both Don and Joe. Perhaps they felt that they could rest on their laurels for a year.

1954 was Ron Moseley's year, despite the extremely erratic nature of his climbing. One day he would put up a new X.S. route, then the next day he would be unable to lead something quite pedestrian. Tom Waghorn remembers Moseley being quite unable to lead The Crack on Gimmer (an old classic cleft pioneered in the twenties) which Ron should have sauntered up quite easily.

In one week-end in April he did the second ascent of East Gully Wall, then traversed across the upper face to climb a fine corner crack, now known as Moseley's Variation. On the Sunday he climbed the start of The Boulder but carried on up the blunt and poorly protected arete for 130 feet to give Left Edge, his first major contribution to the cliff.

Joe and Don's main thoughts in 1954 were to be nearly a thousand miles from North Wales on the Chamonix Aiguilles. For decades the highest echelons of Alpinism had been empty of British climbers. There were various reasons for this: the depression of the inter-war years and more serious, the introvert attitude of some of the Alpine Club members who stuck their heads firmly in the Victorian sands of tradition. There were exceptions of course such as: Hamish Nicol, Tom Bourdillon, George Band and Roger Chorley, who were the leading Oxbridge Alpinists. But Joe and Don were refreshingly unaware of Alpine Club dogma which anyway was gradually being blown away by fresh winds from Oxbridge.

Their first ascent of the West Face of the Blaitiere was a tremendous climb and immediately put them in the Alpine Club elite. The wide initial crack, the Fissure Brown, repelled team after team of French Chamonix stars and the second complete ascent of the face had to wait until 1958 when Robin Smith and Trevor Jones climbed it. Equally impressive a few days later was Brown and Whillans's third ascent of the West Face of the Petit Dru, taking two days as opposed to a week taken by the first French party. Lionel Terray, probably the finest French guide of his generation, and Louis Lachenal who had just repeated the North Face of the Eiger came to their muddy camp-site to talk to the curious Englishmen who had stormed the Chamonix Aiguilles. Their long career in the Alps and Himalaya had started. 1955 was to produce more surprises. Joe was selected to go on the successful Kanchenjunga expedition — the first working-class climber to enter the exclusive sanctum of Himalayan expeditions. Don's letter-box however never received an invitation to the Himalaya. Perhaps his humorous, abrasive quips were too much for the Establishment.

Even if Don felt rejected in 1955 he buckled down again to climbing and showed the rest of the climbing world that if a route had the stamp of his name on the first ascent, then a ferociously difficult and strenuous battle would probably be in store for anyone who aspired to follow him. The Direct Finish to Erosion Groove was an exposed, vicious and unrelenting pitch of 5c technical standard and it remained a test piece for would-be stars for many years. Countless leaders had to wait for metal nuts to overcome induced cowardice brought on by the uncompromising first few moves.

It was a rare good summer and while Joe was toiling up the snowy slopes of Kanchenjunga with a large load on his back, Don, as if on his powerful motor-cycle, roared up Vember, Boulder, Octo and Left Edge. The West Buttress of Clogwyn du'r Arddu still glittered with unclimbed possibilities but there were no easy entries to them through the continuous overhangs at the bottom of the buttress. Whillans attacked one of the biggest overhangs with uncertain pegs knocked into blind cracks — pegs which bent even under his diminutive weight. Loose rock, dangerous pegs, an enormous overhang...Whillans overcame them with nonchalance and pulled onto an inviting unclimbed slab above. Don was climbing with Vin Betts who got into difficulties on the final moves of the overhang and shouted:

"There's no holds Don."
"Reach up, reach right up for the big jug Vin."
There was a pause while Betts scrabbled about.

The Thing, Dinas Cromlech. *'Possibly the hardest problem in the valley. Difficulty is sustained, protection poor, retreat beyond the crux uninviting and the ground below nasty to land on.'*   Photo: Trevor Jones collection.

"Don, Don, I can only get my finger ends on something."
"That's it Vin, that's the big jug."

Whillans called the route Slanting Slab and it was the first big slab route put up by the Rock and Ice. It was to hold its reputation for some years. At last Whillans had got on to equal terms with Streetly.

Whillans developed into a marvellous lecturer and the Alpine Club invited him to lecture to them. With enormous shoulders and in those days an incredibly tiny waist, he was the joint leader of the Alpine proletariat. In fact Whillans was light years removed from his audience, but after the West Face of the Blaitiere and the West Face of the Dru they could not ignore him. He was politely introduced and soon stood alone on the platform...

"Never before have I lectured to such an old..."

Then he paused...although only seconds it was long enough to cause mental anguish amongst the organisers. Was he going to denigrate them? The seconds of silence ticked away.

"...and venerable club as the Alpine Club."

The thankful gales of laughter were overwhelming with relief. Don's reputation as a raconteur extraordinaire had started.

Joe Brown meanwhile climbed Kanchenjunga with George Band — a tremendous achievement for someone who was still only 24 years of age. Joe seemed to have an Aladdin's lamp — everything that he wanted seemed to come true. Don's great efforts in the Alps after the West Face of the Blaitiere with Joe were the Bonatti and Freney Pillars which put him at the pinnacle of Alpinism. But bad luck, bad weather and sometimes bad or poor companions caused an astonishing series of failures in the Himalaya: Trivor, Masherbrum, Gaurisankar and Huandoy Sur in the Andes. Never was such a talent cruelly denied success. Only on Annapurna in 1970 did Don's luck change and bring a restoration to a rightful place amongst world-class mountaineers.

Woubits was a combined operation. Joe led the damp, loose first pitch and Don led the crux second pitch. This was a pitch through the seriously-forbidding part of the Far East Buttress and was probably the most serious pitch that the Rock and Ice had pioneered up to that time. An ancient photograph shows Whillans capped with the compulsory balaclava peering anxiously up into the final recesses of the pitch. He mantelshelfed the main difficulty — an exposed tiny ledge where the rock seems to push one off. With the completion of Woubits they finished the first route on a hitherto untouched buttress.

Joe tried to make the second ascent of Slanting Slab with Trevor Jones but retreated after the pegs had slipped in the awkwardly-shaped cracks which unsatisfactorily criss-cross the initial friable overhang. Both climbers were only too glad to escape to the more solid Bloody Slab.

During the early fifties Brown and Whillans had done their new routes in a variety of footwear depending on the conditions...nailed boots, socks, and cheap, floppy gym shoes, but in 1956 a revolution occurred in footwear that was to enable them to do even harder climbs. P.A.s were named after the inventor, Pierre Allain, a famous French rock gymnast and Alpinist of the thirties. The boots were constructed like basketball boots, but were much flimsier, yet gave the whole foot much better support helped by tight lacing.

Opposite: 1st ascent of Woubits on Clogwyn du'r Arddu.   Photo: J. Brown collection.

The sole was semi-rigid and so it proved possible to stand on small holds much longer or to use even smaller holds for upward movement. They made a difference of about half a grade, which led to an upsurge in the technical difficulty of new routes; from 5a to 5b or 5b to 5c. Pierre Allain and his Fontainbleu friends the Bleausards had also found an increase in standard in hard French climbing.

1956 was the last year that Joe and Don functioned as a regular new-route team although they did the odd route together later on. The Thing produced by Joe and Don in February 1956 was a typical product from two stars of gritstone cracks. Even in the guidebook of 1974 the preamble was:

'Extremely strenuous. A short vicious climb of high technical difficulty. Difficulty is sustained, retreat beyond the crux uninviting and the ground below nasty to land on.'

The Cromlech Girdle on the other hand was a total contrast to The Thing. It was a masterpiece which took two days to complete and there was even a precarious stance in the middle of Cenotaph Corner. The right wall of the Corner proved difficult and to gain a microscopic foothold required tension from a runner high above the belay in the Corner. A small ledge appeared after a few feet and when it got wider Don suddenly noticed a dead mouse in front of his very eyes. It is not known whether the sudden sight of Whillans caused its demise!

Halfway through the year Joe was again invited to the Himalaya to join the Mustagh Tower expedition, which just beat a French team to the summit. Yet again the luck seemed to be with Joe. The week before Joe went on the expedition turned out to be a fateful one as there was to be a major and somewhat controversial development on one of the big unclimbed lines of Cloggy. White Slab had been known by other names such as the Hour Glass Slab and the Concrete Slab for some years. Dolphin, Harding and Campbell were just three of the greats who had tried it and been repulsed. Brown had tried it twice before. Once he had started at 4.30 in the afternoon and then had to retreat when it went dark. The next time he managed the tricky rope-swing pitch after successfully lassoing the tiny spike, but had to retreat when it started to rain.

Looking back at the week Joe said:

"If anyone in the Rock and Ice wanted to do a route, no-one reserved it as his own. The only time that feelings crept in was over White Slab. I'm fairly sure that Don wasn't 'gripped up' about Moseley doing the first ascent, but with Moseley not mentioning that he was going to do it…"

On Thursday night, April 18th, Don casually mentioned about the following week-end:

"We might have a go at White Slab."

Moseley was galvanised into action and conscripted a reluctant Mortimer Smith to go to Wales the next morning to forestall Don's projected attempt. It was undoubtedly the lead of Moseley's life. Retreat was utterly unthinkable as the relentless Whillans would be on it the very next day, and Moseley finally made it to the top. It was the first major competitive route put up by a Rock and Ice member and it laid the seeds of fierce competition amongst leading climbers.

Brown came back from the Himalaya underweight and weak but was soon back up on Cloggy with Whillans for a fierce open groove on the front of the Pinnacle. Joe tried to lead it, but came to a loose block which prompted him to retreat. Whillans sprang into the lead. He reached the loose block, gave it a contemptuous thump with his fist and

Opposite: An airy position on Shrike wall, Clogwyn du'r Arddu.   Photo: Steve Ashton.

climbed past it to a roof, where he put in a very poor peg. To move left on underpulls and then attack the steep rock above was by any standards Extremely Severe and highly intimidating...The wedge-shaped shoulders vanished upwards to complete Taurus, a route which was to be held in great respect for many years to come — mainly owing to the lack of protection. Seconding the pitch Joe had a fierce struggle and had to have a tight rope.

They probably didn't realise it but their great Welsh partnership on new routes was over. They still climbed together but slowly drifted apart as Don started to climb in other areas such as in 1957 when he went on the expedition to Masherbrum. On that expedition the Cambridge University star Bob Downes unfortunately succumbed to a pulmonary oedema and died:

Don commented on Joe:

> *"Joe was never particularly keen to travel to different places. He always did a tremendous amount on one crag at a time, whereas I went to many different crags and just did the best lines, and then went off somewhere else. Joe was always at home in Wales. For him to go to the Lakes, for instance, was a real event. I realised that he didn't want to do the climbs that I wanted to do and most of the boys tended to do what he did. It got to the stage where they were going to Cornwall for their holidays and going fishing. Well, holidays meant the Alps for me; you can go to Cornwall any time. So I started climbing with different people, blokes such as Bonington, Paul Ross and Peter Greenwood."*

Soon Joe and his immediate friends became known as 'The Fishermen' but this really does not do Joe complete justice. By 1957 he had climbed Kanchenjunga and the Mustagh Tower and it would be perfectly reasonable after two successive Himalayan expeditions to have a sabbatical holiday in Cornwall.

1957 was a sparse year for new routes but The Mostest and November were climbed by Brown while Whillans was away on the traumatic Masherbrum expedition. The Mostest was to be the second route on the extremely forbidding Far East Buttress. The crag is cut off at the bottom by another line of rather unsatisfactory cliffs. Access from the top down slippery grooves, unstable grass and small scree-chutes all added to the air of inaccessibility. In early April Joe and Nat went to have a look at the right-hand side of the buttress.

The Mostest proved to be a big four-pitch three-hundred-foot route and was Joe's first big serious crux pitch on the Far East. Nat was unable to make the move round the hard bulge on the second pitch and had to retreat. In fact he still hadn't regained full use of his knee which had been broken in a bad motor-cycle accident. At this point Joe still had the crux pitch in front of him — a corner with a fierce roof at the top.

> 'I put a peg in the back of the overhang and got a runner in the roof on a poor chockstone. I moved onto the arete on the left of the overhang and laybacked the arete so that my head and shoulders were right above the overhang, but I couldn't get into a position to leave go to get hold of anything above. So I had to layback down under the overhangs to the peg. I did this three times and eventually thought, *"Well I'm not going to get any better at doing this"*. So I stuck a peg in my mouth and laybacked up the arete again. I jabbed the peg into a fault and moved back down. I came back up, hit it with the hammer and just got hold of it like a jug, without clipping in. Then I looked down at the peg. It wasn't in a crack at all — it was just resting on a hold with the end biting into the texture of the rock. I lifted it off.'

Opposite: Trevor Jones using sticky tape to hold down a runner on East Gully Wall, Cloggy.   Photo: R.F. Allen.

Trevor Jones confesses to naming the climb 'Mostest' because it was the climb with the most difficulty, exposure and inaccessibility. Jones also propagated with tongue-in-cheek that Joe had had to spend three days in a darkened room after the ascent to recover from the experience. The story was soon forgotten but the name remained.

Next month Joe had some difficulty persuading Morty to go on the unclimbed cracks of November. Joe was twenty feet up the big pitch before Morty told him that Moseley had abseiled down it and inserted all the chockstones. There was no great row with Moseley after Joe completed the route but it seems strange that Moseley did no more new routes and gave up both climbing and the Rock and Ice next year.

New routes from them were getting more sparse and people outside the Rock and Ice were repeating their routes and putting up their own. In 1958 Brown did his last great route on the gully face of the Pinnacle. Apart from the faithful Morty the third member was Harry Smith of the Birmingham Cave and Crag Club, who had pioneered many new routes at Tremadog. Harry tried to lead the final unclimbed wall of Shrike but had to use several slings for aid before retreating, and Joe led it.

During the great years of the early fifties a dual revolution took place in Wales. While the heavy guns of the Rock and Ice pounded away in the mountains the small-arms blazed away on the more amenable Tremadog cliffs. Tony Moulam had started the exploration of the buttresses of Bwlch y Moch, Pant Ifan, Castell and Gesail but others soon took over. Roughly at the same time as Moulam's efforts were being brought to an untimely end, another group appeared on the scene, the Birmingham Cave and Crag Club. They acquired a hut on the plateau above the Pant Ifan cliffs, which was only two-hundred yards from the Hound's Head Pinnacle. For the first time for twenty years a group of innovators appeared who had not had their initial teenage training on gritstone. It was as easy for them to go to North Wales where their hut was, as it was for them to go to Derbyshire. The main innovators of the Cave and Crag were an immensely-strong plasterer Harry Smith and a cheerful extrovert Trevor Jones.

There were very few people on the cliffs then, but the views over Tremadog were just as beautiful. The Portmadog soccer club dashed about like multi-coloured ants and whenever they scored the faintest of cheers drifted up to the crag.

From 1956 Harry Smith did half a dozen new routes at Tremadog, his two best being Stromboli and Grim Wall. The latter, up a steep section of rock, was a fine effort as Harry had previously injured his hand badly in a serious accident. Trevor Jones did about sixteen routes in the South Snowdon area, such as The Brothers, Great Western, Kestrel Crack and Barbarian. On the latter it is recorded that many pegs were used, but one must remember that in the fifties a great deal of pegging was done in gritstone quarries and the Tremadog cliffs were not regarded as more than minor outcrops. Routes were often festooned with vegetation and being led on sight were far different from the clean rock of today. Before criticising such routes, one must remember that in the sixties huge numbers of pegs were used on the Gogarth cliffs before the routes were properly gardened.

Perhaps the best of Jones's routes was One Step in the Clouds, a highly popular route which found a way up the edge of the Vector buttress in an exposed position. Amazingly it was one of Ron Fawcett's favourite climbs. Also done in 1958 The Maelstrom proved to be an alarming experience on pumice-like rock. At the end of the traverse was a tree

Opposite: Joe Brown approaching the groove of The Steep Band, Clogwyn du'r Arddu, in June 1960.
Photo: Rosemary Soper.

with long roots which came away with a plate of earth. The leader's alarming arboreal descent consequently lessened his faith in the stability of all Nant Gwynant trees.

The greatest event of 1958 however had nothing to do with new routes — it was the break-up of the Rock and Ice. There was an indifference to normal club discipline and subscriptions had not been paid. Finally Ron Moseley and Doug Belshaw decided to wind up the club without in fact consulting anyone else.

Was there a possibility that Moseley was still piqued over November? He had certainly raced desperately in front of Whillans to snatch the glittering prize of White Slab. His great route, Phoenix, on Scafell, done in 1957 did not appease him and it is doubtful if he realised its significance. The guidebook later pointed out:

'Although not generally realised at the time this climb was a full grade harder than anything else on the crag.'

The Rock and Ice had dominated new routes since 1951 but determined and able new stars such as Hugh Banner were already beginning to appear. It would be perfectly reasonable for Moseley to think that he had missed the boat. Certainly his feelings, that his climbing years were 'five wasted years', don't suggest that he looks back with any nostalgia or camaraderie to the fifties which the original old-timers still remember nostalgically at the annual Rock and Ice dinners. However we must remember Moseley's great contributions in Wales: Left Edge, White Slab, Moss Groove and his 'Meccano-nut' solution to the Left Wall of Cenotaph Corner.'

And yet there were other reasons for the demise of the Rock and Ice — summed up perfectly by Whillans:

'...the longer he continues to climb, the less he'll see of his original mates. They'll get married or lose interest. This is really because they are just not very keen. I think in any field you really have to want to do something if you want to do it well.'

Ron Moseley was the Secretary, Doug Belshaw was the Treasurer and they had both recently got married, which tends to buttress Whillans's remarks about marriage and climbing. Some of the wives too disliked camping in the incessant Welsh downpours and as the club had no hut, camping was another contributory factor.

One of Whillans's last great efforts was Grond — hard and uncompromising like its author. The second, Morty, led it immediately afterwards. It seems a good finale to the Rock and Ice club.

1959 was also to be a memorable year in that it saw the last major new route on Clogwyn du'r Arddu put up by Brown. A flood of new climbers from the next generation began to repeat some of the desperate new routes and break through into the front ranks of climbing. But it was the weather that was to be the key factor; and all through that brilliant hot summer which lasted late into October the young generation continued to flourish all over the crags of North Wales.

Brown started to climb with the Cromlech Club climbers who were particularly addicted to the cliffs in the Nant Gwynant and at Tremadog. One warm day in February 1959 a large party of Cromlech Club stalwarts lazed in the sun at the foot of Clogwyn y Wenallt in the Nant Gwynant. Joe espied a crack in a wall on the left-hand side of the crag — a fierce 80-foot crack in the Brown tradition with only Trevor Jones able to follow. The crux caused Jones such exhaustion that when he pulled over the top he was unable to

speak for at least five minutes, a phenomenon not known either before or since. The route was called Ferdinand.

The real significance was that Joe had by then for the first time moved away from the Llanberis Pass-Clogwyn du'r Arddu axis and Ferdinand was the first of dozens of highly-technical new routes on both lowland and sea cliffs.

Cloggy was to see two new routes from Brown; Boomerang was a slab climb Brown did with Doug Verity in the spring, but by autumn Brown was drawn back to the Far East Buttress in a bid to complete a magnificent trilogy with the awe-inspiring Woubits Left Hand. The most interesting thing is that the second man happened to appear at the foot of the crag just at the right time. Martin Boysen, who was the sandstone expert trained at Harrison's Rocks, was one of the young Turks, a group which included Barry Ingle and Peter Crew. This group with several other leading climbers was to sweep away most of the legend and mumbo-jumbo which had surrounded the Rock and Ice and their routes for so many years.

Brown struggled hard on Woubits Left Hand but eventually made it to the top where he was able to watch with interest the ease with which Boysen followed the pitch. Looking back at the crux Joe was able to reflect:

'I was only a move away from the top. If I could get myself onto the wall on the left I could get over the top. I kept going up to this position and back down to the peg. I must have done this three times before I got really exasperated. I was certain it could be done without a peg if only I could stay there long enough to work out the move. But I was bridged across the groove in a really strange position. So I thought *"To hell with it"* and got out a peg, and it was all over. When Martin came up, the first thing he said was:

"I'm sure that top peg wasn't necessary."

I thought that if I had offered him the lead, he would have got up without the peg and I was certain I could have, if I had been more patient.'

It was an uncanny moment, Joe's last major climb on the Black Cliff, done with the young climber who was to be a major force in the next generation.

Until then, whenever a new generation arrived, the old guard would retire with dignity, was outclassed, or like old soldiers just faded away. Joe would have none of that. He started a new career on the small cliffs where he vied with the young Turks and often outclassed them in his spectacular solution to improbable lines. He acquired a new entourage mainly drawn from the Cromlech Club and even moved back into their barn above the cowshed where the Rock and Ice used to stay in their early days.

Early in Brown's Cromlech Club days Trevor Jones recalls one of Joe's masterly uses of the verbal putdown for which he is so famous:

'Once I managed to do a boulder problem which Joe had been unable to do, by extensive use of the knees. The entourage was aghast; the Master had failed them. Joe thought intensively for a few seconds, then said *"Trevor, you're probably the finest knee climber in the country"*.

Often he teased the entourage with enigmatic remarks. One wet day on gritstone a silence descended on the group sheltering in a cave. Suddenly Joe said:

"Even in dry conditions, there's more people can't get up Oblongata than can."

Joe was still working hard in the building trade during the week. He was working on a roof one wet day when he suddenly started to slide off. He grabbed at the guttering as he fell, but crashed onto an outhouse roof. The lady of the house heard the noise and came out.

"Oh, Joe, I didn't know you were working on the roof. Would you like a cup of tea?"

Surprisingly Joe found the work mentally stressful, developed a stomach ulcer and for some years had to go on a strict diet with plenty of milk. To compound his internal problems, Joe broke his leg running down the scree from Clogwyn y Grochan and that curtailed his climbing for some time. He returned for this brief period to his old love of fishing, which necessitated standing in shallow water. The hospital was not very pleased when he returned for a check-up as the bottom of his plaster cast had dissolved away and the ragged ends had water plants entwined among the gauze fronds.

When the leg knitted Joe carried on with climbing but the Rock and Ice, which had been reformed in the winter of 1958/1959, did not have the same dominant position it had had previously. Moseley had gone to live abroad and Whillans began to climb with other people; but the Rock and Ice still held the memory of eight marvellous years when its members towered over Welsh climbing.

Almost at the end of the Rock and Ice era another climber arrived on the scene to challenge their dominance. Hugh Banner came from Merseyside, the birthplace of many hard climbers, but he had an uphill task ahead of him. While at Bristol University he climbed in the Avon Gorge during term time and then at Helsby while he was at home. While still in his teens his first new Welsh route was Cornix on Carreg Wastad, done in July 1953. Although this was only two years after the Rock and Ice had started their Welsh charge, he was still a long way behind; it took him some years of apprenticeship to bring the top routes within his grasp.

In the mid-fifties Banner repeated all Harding's routes as well as some of the easier Rock and Ice lines. He even encroached onto the Tremdog cliffs for a couple of new routes but soon turned his back to do grander things. Amongst Banner's many achievements were his feats of soloing and there were few climbers in the late fifties who were quite as daring. Even in the nineteen-eighties when he was fifty, Banner nonchalantly soloed Delstree, a Hard V.S. on Hen Cloud, which reserves its 5a crux for the top moves. Certainly he was one of few Helsby climbers to reach a hundred miles an hour on his Vincent motor cycle, on the big straight past Helsby Grammar School while en route to the Golden Lion in Frodsham. In the pub he would outline his next plan, spoken in a slow nasal drawl...fingers delicately gripping the top of his pint pot while he slowly ran them round the smooth rim.

In the same deliberate way, so Banner climbed, with agonisingly long appraisals of a difficult sequence; he gained height by careful movements with one shoulder bent inwards and a positive caressing of the holds. No other climber had ever concentrated so intensively on the hardest routes. Eventually, just as he reached the pinnacle of his ability when he was certainly climbing as well as Brown, he faltered...and fell into the trap of repeating route after route of the Rock and Ice. Unconsciously he thought that in that way he would show that he was the only climber with the nerve and ability to surpass Brown. In retrospect Banner feels that he lost two vital years in doing repetitions when instead he could have put up so many of his own new routes. One route however was to attract and intimidate the climbers of the next generation.

Opposite: Joe Brown high on the Great Wall, Clogwyn du'r Arddu, during the historic attempt.

Photo: Joe Brown collection.

Troach was a great step forward in that it encroached onto a blank wall which required a new approach. Brown was certainly intrigued by the competitive edge of Banner's defiance, and was clearly worried about one of his own lines. As Banner approached for his second attempt at the Troach wall, Brown sprinted up to the foot of the unclimbed Great Wall which was his big ambition. He was clearly worried lest Banner should be after his line and was forced into a determined attack. He gained about sixty feet on the big wall but eventually had to abseil off.

Whillans who was almost at the foot of Banner's line casually said that he might be interested in the wall to the right of Curving Crack. Banner was instantly galvanised into action and went back up. At that time Troach was very poorly protected and one of the pegs driven in under an overhang only went in a few grudging centimetres. There is no doubt that Banner realised that his ascent would be significant so he didn't move the peg or knock in another replacement. As he finished the long and serious pitch it became the first modern wall climb. During Banner's epic ascent he had been closely watched by Brown and Whillans as well as two unknown youngsters — Peter Crew and Jack Soper. Troach was the last big new route of 1959 before climbing was brought to a halt when banks of dark cloud rolled in to herald the start of the torrential autumn rains.

Opposite: Dave Alcock working out the next move on the White Slab of Clogwyn du'r Arddu.

The Young Turks

In the golden year of 1959 when the hot weather lasted right up until October, Jack Soper and Dave Gregory were just two of the younger generation who broke through a mental barrier to repeat the big routes of Brown and Whillans. Brown was still at work on the cliff producing the odd new route here and there but he was aware of the rising tide of the new generation climbers who were beavering away doing his hardest routes. Soper and Gregory were on the fringe of the Alpha influence as the Alpha was much more loosely knit than the Rock and Ice had been. They had a much greater reservoir to tap and their members were drawn mainly from the northern universities, with only the odd one such as Peter Crew who was briefly at Oxford.

The change was basically red-brick — although the Rock and Ice involvement with red brick was mainly on the building site. During the 1960s the restless teenagers joined flourishing climbing clubs at the red-brick universities. Sheffield in particular unleashed its storm-troopers most week-ends to Wales. There they scaled the battlements of increasing climbing difficulty to the top of the keep where Brown was pacing uneasily — realising that the young hordes would not be repelled by him alone. The outer defences of the Rock and Ice, of half-truths, innuendoes, appalling sycophancy and conversational one-to-one batterings by the Baron had already been overwhelmed.

The Alpha had three leading lights: Peter Crew, Barry Ingle and Martin Boysen — all were to play a prominent part in the events to come. Crew was born in a mining village in Yorkshire in 1942 and in 1960 went to Oxford to study Mathematics with a County Major Scholarship, State Scholarship and an Exhibition in Mathematics. As he did not fit into Oxford life he left after a term to run a climbing shop in Manchester where he began to prepare himself to break down the prevalent hero-worship of Joe Brown. Crew climbed confidently and very fast and as an explanation commented:

"I have to climb fast. I haven't the strength to hang around."

His climbing gave an impression of tremendous nervous energy, conquered anxiety and unstoppable drive. *"He's got a neck as long as a giraffe"*, was Hugh Banner's telling comment, although this was in no way meant to be disrespectful.

Barry Ingle on the other hand was shorter, dark and abruptly monosyllabic compared with Crew's staccato bursts of animated conversation. Born in Nottingham in 1941, Ingle was at university studying for an engineering degree. His smooth climbing technique gave an impression of neatness that would be equal to any situation.

Martin Boysen had a German father and an English mother and was born in Aachen, Germany in 1942. During his early teens he lived in the South of England and became an expert on the sandstone outcrops around Harrison's Rocks — where he had already pioneered a 5c route which became known as Boysen's Arete. His attitude and superb ability were once summed up by the phrase 'languid genius'. One windy day in the Pass he reached the crux of a route, stopped...and combed his hair...to reassure the second man who had mistakenly assumed that there must be large holds. When the second arrived at the same spot he was unable to remove either hand except to lurch up for the next diminutive hold.

Opposite: Martin Taylor making his way along The Hand Traverse on Cloggy.   Photo: Mike Browell.

Above: Dave Gregory and Jack Soper making a breakthrough on Lithrig, Cloggy, in 1959. Photo: Rosemary Soper.
P. 139: Traversing out on to Llithrig from Sunset Crack, Clogwyn du'r Arddu. Photo: Steve Ashton.

Boysen studied biology at Manchester University and as a botanist he takes a keen interest in the protection of the mountain environment. In Ken Wilson's Idwal guidebook he contributed a section to help protect the rare Alpine flora of the calcareous cliffs:

'Any gardening on the Kitchen cliffs or on Clogwyn Du must be strictly avoided. What to the layman may be a grass sod, could contain a number of exquisite plants of great rarity. Once the reservoir of these breeding plants has been removed from these crags they will quickly become extinct. In climbing terms this is the equivalent of blowing up Cloggy.

The safest practice is to avoid gardening at all costs. Far too much pointless cleaning of routes takes place. Climbers as a group profess to love the wild beauty of the crags. Part of their beauty is the plant life. Already too many crags have been stripped to the bare bones of rock — deserts — disfigured by fag packets, broken bottles and discarded socks.'

In 'Still More of Arfon' Jack Soper wrote what is undoubtedly one of the best accounts of the struggle to topple the legend of the Rock and Ice:

'We were sitting in the shepherd's hut at Montenvers after several infuriating repetitions of the sequence: walk to hut; weather breaks; return to valley; weather improves. Half-seriously someone suggested *"Cloggy may be dry"*. Sixty hours later we were roping up for Sheaf, our last outstanding *"old"* route. After that there was nothing for it but to try one of the new climbs. We selected The Corner because the description indicated good protection...

...I felt that it was time for a push. In those days Llithrig, Diglyph and Vember were the legendary big three. Vember was wet still; we thought Diglyph went up a series of grooves which looked impossible and was in fact unclimbed (now Daurigol): Llithrig it must be. Dave greeted the suggestion in the non-committal manner which signified that he was prepared to do his share and more if necessary...

...I remember scrambling down repeating ridiculously *"We've done Llithrig!"* Next day Dave led Cenotaph. By then we had so impressed ourselves that we went home to think about it. A great deal has been made of the *"mental barrier"* to the harder climbs but something of the kind did exist at the time...

...At the next opportunity we returned to the Big Cliff, intent on White Slab. Why we thought of trying White as our second major route I cannot conceive. It had been climbed less than half a dozen times and had a tremendous reputation. But having watched Banner's ten-hour epic ascent we perhaps surmised correctly that there were holds. For the first and last time Rosemary said, *"You won't get up"*. Allan Austin, on the West Girdle, gave us a pitying look but provided his black book of descriptions...Our ascent diminished the climb's reputation and within a couple of months the number of ascents had doubled.

Next day a defeat on Red Slab served to maintain our sense of proportion. The following Saturday it was Octo and then The Boulder from which I had a grandstand view of Austin on the crux of Black Cleft, an impressive sight. On Sunday, instead of attempting the Cleft, which has never subsequently been drier, we tried Diglyph and Dave created a precedent by falling off and bloodying my head. To restore confidence we thought to climb Pinnacle Flake, graded easier than Octo: an unfortunate error. Joe and Mortimer were just ahead and surprisingly, Joe seemed hesitant. When my turn came I balked at a horribly exposed mantelshelf. The advice which floated down was unhelpful...

...As people returned from the Alps more and more of the major climbs were repeated. The spell of good weather engendered a general desire to climb the big routes and the effect of the successes of other parties was cumulative...Peter Crew made his effort on Vember and entered a period of falling off White Slab. The season closed on October 11. That day Paul Nunn, then still at school, climbed Vember in the first rainstorm...

Opposite. Looking down on The Left Wall of Dinas Cromlech. .   Photo: Chris Jackson.

...Next year we returned to Cloggy armed with cryptic duplicated descriptions ("*...climb the groove, hard at 90 feet...*")...'

As there was less information about The Mostest they scrapped their plans and went into Woubits the day after Peter Crew's ascent:

'Dave nearly came off the first moves and I had a gruelling time on the second pitch in spite of Crew's new piton glinting encouragement and I had a mental picture of a square man in his ratting-hat bridged on the same inadequate holds and perhaps also experiencing some difficulty...

...It was Saturday around Midsummer's day. We had a bivouac beside the llyn. The hills circling round to Moel Eilio were assuming their characteristic velvety appearance in the evening light as we paused below the wall to observe for the twentieth time Banner's sling which had hung for almost a year from the upper peg. I suggested an exploration of the first moves...Feeling rather committed, I placed a sling and progressed by long reaches on flat holds. The sling fell off so I pressed on to the first peg. This seemed poor so I continued with difficulty now, to the second which was in vertically below a little ceiling, and wobbled. Ninety feet of rope were out, hanging free...'

On the successful second ascent of Troach:

'Dave led the traverse to the arete in gathering gloom and later the exultant party ate rabbit stew below the moonlit crags...'

Soper, who was one of the first climbers to use threaded nuts for protection, was a master in the art and used nuts to fiddle his way cunningly up Scorpio. In fairness, whatever aid was used was vital to clean mud and lichen from the holds, while Crew sitting at the foot of the crag, became blue with cold. Immediately after the first slightly tarnished ascent they repeated the route in a legitimate style. Looking back Soper recalled:

'...Next year saw changes. The partnership dissolved and I teamed up with Peter Crew who had also fallen under the spell of the place. Between us we had repeated nearly all the existing climbs and begun to think of new ones, which is the proper order of things.

  Came the blustery morning when Peter and I scrambled up the first pitch of Pedestal Crack and I pointed out a hold high up to the right...A hand traverse led to several juniper tufts and a large spike. Above was a groove, apparently holdless, furnished with a cap of overhanging turf. Two hours later I had scraped every accessible inch with my wire threader and the groove was still holdless, a new phenomenon. It was necessary to cheat. Base Camp forwarded our supply of very small nuts threaded on line loops and the back of the groove took two of these. Standing precariously in the uppermost, which settled several times, and braced on a knob to the left, I was able to remove the turf.'

One of the nuts from the first ascent of Scorpio is still in place close to the layback flake. It is covered in encrustations of rust after its twenty-five years of service and its nylon sling has been reduced to a dark green slimy thread. At that time redundant coach-nuts from the Snowdon Railway were much in demand owing to their chunky size but other shapes and sizes were commonly adapted from household equipment. Before threading the nylon it was first necessary to ream out the thread on the inside of the nut. Looking back it is amazing to realise the ingenuity of climbers long before commercially produced nuts were available.

A route that was to carry a big reputation for some years was Slanting Slab. Not only was there the prospect of running out of rope on one pitch but even the start was to blow

the minds of many leaders. It was not long before the route went to the top of the hit list as Soper remembered:

'Slanting Slab, unrepeated since Harry Smith and Joe Brown had made the second ascent in 1958 was surprisingly climbed three times within a week. The climb starts with a loose overhang on pitons then, immediately, a slab thinner than anything else on Cloggy followed by a traverse between overhangs to a point where 150-foot ropes hang free. The second pitch involves a 180-foot run-out up a crack in the slanting slab proper, ending with two overhangs separated by another vicious little slab. Crew and Ingle had just returned from their ascent and when we arrived at Ynys, Crew had recovered and was breaking the hut rules as usual, but a pale shadow of the former robust Ingle crouched silent in a corner and could only take soft food. His darts game suffered too. Barry Webb and I climbed the Slanting Slab a few days later and were duly impressed. On seconding the first pitch I was horrified to find I could easily tap the pegs out with a karabiner, the leader having our only hammer.'

The Girdle Traverse of the Pinnacle started to inflame a lot of people's ambitions and in 1960 Ron James and Trevor Jones tried to go from left to right. After a couple of pitches they took a stance in East Gully Groove. Jones tried to do a very long shallow diagonal abseil into Gargoyle, but it wasn't possible, so he started a series of ever-increasing pendules. On the maximum amplitude of the greatest one he managed to hook a foot onto a tiny grass ledge on the very edge of Gargoyle. A problem was solved. Suddenly Newton's law inexorably took effect as his heel was dragged off the turf despite desperate efforts to dig it in...A series of swings over the emptiness of the East Gully brought a shriek of fear...as Jones realised that the rope might not reach the dank slippery rushes far below. James in East Gully Groove was silent...Happily the stretch of the hawser-laid rope allowed just one tremulous foot to reach the tips of the rushes.

After this escapade Brown thoughtfully pronounced with a flinty grin in mid-sentence:

"...goin' from left to right...All you've got to do is a little bit of climbing, then an abseil, another bit o' climbing, then another abseil...it's downhill all the way!"

After the last grin of finality it was like having a last appeal turned down by the House of Lords. The Master of the Rolls had spoken. No further attempts were made until Banner and Jones tried to go from right to left. Banner in extremis decided to stand in a sling, while Jones, who had dropped his jersey behind the pinnacle flake, was trying to hook it out with a chockstone-threading wire. Jones was however holding Banner's rope with the other hand and behaving in that rather disturbing way that seconds often do when their leader is having a bad time. It was a difficult visual job for Jones keeping one eye on Banner and the other on the jersey which had been knitted by an admiring girlfriend. At that point Banner's sling broke and Jones was promptly snatched from his perch by his falling leader. Thus ended both the exploration and jersey recovery.

Solely with the jersey in mind, Jones returned to the Pinnacle again and realised that there was a big gap between the precarious Pinnacle Flake and Spillikin. As he stepped round onto the front face, Jones noticed a faint line up to the left-hand side of the flake. It was delicate and not his normal territory but the jersey spurred him on. When he breathlessly reached the flake he triumphantly lunged head first down the back of the flake — only to discover that the jersey had slid further down in the previous weeks and was still tantalisingly out of reach. Miserably Jones brought up Pete Hatton to finish Guinevere.

Opposite: Trevor Jones on the Girdle Traverse of Carreg Hyll Drem.   Photo: R.F. Allen.

Trevor Jones on the top pitch of Lavaredo, Carreg Alltrem.

An early ascent of Clapton's Crack, Craig Bwlch y Moch.

Banner and Jones went back yet again, and discovered a delightful but vicious finger-traversing crack which gave the spectacular Hand Traverse. The 1976 guide-book observed it to be:

'A short and sensationally exposed climb...Strong fingers make it straightforward, otherwise it can be very intimidating.'

It was Banner's most spectacular climb on the cliff and it spurred on the young up-and-coming stars. Crew and Soper felt that if they solved the problem of the Girdle they would be one up on the old Master. Soper wrote:

'The following morning we were soon across the front face and up Taurus. On the belay ledge Peter lifted a suspiciously withered piece of turf to reveal a new piton, sure evidence that the Master had passed this way. The rest of the day was spent in reaching the arete which, after much heart-searching, required a piton. On the morrow Peter led the Hand Traverse, Banner's harrowingly-exposed pitch across a smooth vertical facet of the gully face.'

The route had taken them three days and the nine-pitch climb included a sensational diagonal abseil into East Gully Groove. As a joke they fitted a piece of rope round a spike leaving the ends unknotted in the hope that someone might pass that way and want to use it for aid. At the end of the route Soper commented:

'That night nature celebrated our success with a violent electrical storm and I saw a blue fire-ball but nobody believed me.'

1960 was an astonishing year as it ushered in the first of the new generation after the demise of the Rock and Ice. The activist who stole the limelight for some time was in fact Joe Brown. Somehow he did a mental somersault and turned his new-route genius to the sunnier rocks of southern Snowdonia. Undoubtedly he had grown tired of the old scene, and became rejuvenated when he realised the enormous new-route potential of the south Snowdon crags with which the Cromlech Club had been familiar since the early fifties. Joe joined the small Cromlech Club which had only a few activists such as Claude Davies and Trevor Jones. As a present for joining, the club gave Brown the ugly crag, Carreg Hyll Drem. Brown made good use of it while the club basked in the reflected glory of his new routes. The crag overhangs alarmingly and it required all Brown's route-finding skill to produce its first route. Primus was the hardest route in the area and it was still only February! On Hardd a tricky diagonal abseil in the middle of the overhangs solved the problem of how to escape from the face. Brown decided that finishing direct would require too much aid and left it for Martin Boysen who needed three aid points the following year.

In just over a month Brown put up four significant climbs that were to become classics: Primus E2 5c, First Slip E1 5c, Hardd E2 5c and Vector E2 5c. It was not so much an increase in technical standard but rather the intricate solution to uncompromising overhanging rock which had not been tackled before. Brown also did three new routes on Castell Cidwm in the Quellyn Valley. Although not as hard as his other routes of 1960 they were on a beautiful crag set in the hillside of Mynydd Mawr on the flanks of a stream which splashes over boulders into Llyn Cwellyn. In the far distance were the lower slopes of Snowdon and the grassy top of Clogwyn du'r Arddu. It didn't take the climbing fraternity long to realise that the whole area around Cidwm was inhabited by unfriendly farmers who took an instant dislike to climbers and came in hot pursuit whenever they saw them. Some time later near Rhyd Ddu, Martin Boysen was even struck with a stick brandished by an irate farmer. Boysen being a placid character responded by breaking the stick in half. But despite unfortunate incidents such as this the new routes still tumbled thick and fast.

The greatest route of 1960 was undoubtedly Vector at Tremadog which was described twenty years later as, 'steep and intricate climbing through impressive overhangs — a tremendous climb, one of the best at Tremadog'. To set the first attempt record straight; Brown arrived late at the foot of the buttress on March 24th and got to the first stance in the failing light. Joe tried to go left while Trevor Jones held his foot in place as he prospected. In fact Brown was prospecting the line of what is now The Weaver. He came down and the pair abseiled off. Next week Brown completed the route with Claude Davies. It was a masterpiece of route-finding through the upper band of brooding overhangs and the route feels every bit as serious as those on high mountain crags. Although the Ochre Slab turns back some leaders, the main cause for panic was the awkward layback crack right at the top. Over the next few years this caused many spectacular falls until the crack was fully gardened.

Brown had put himself into E2 overdrive, a full grade harder than most of his routes of the fifties. Claude Davies who has climbed with Joe for nearly thirty years says:

"Joe has the ability to look at a piece of rock and work out a sequence of moves like a good chess player."

Ten routes in 1960 and eight more the year after; Nimbus proved a worthy companion to Vector while The Neb concealed two short vicious overhanging 5c cracks, just right for Brown's gritstone fingers.

While Brown was turning the Tremadog cliffs into a forcing ground for hard climbers, Cloggy was not left in peace. After the ascent of the Pinnacle Girdle there was some comment about the time the route had taken and the fact that some aid was used. Crew contemptuously brushed aside the criticism by storming up Serth a superb E2. While Crew and Ingle were breaking through to climb pitches of 5c in impressive situations, Brown was doing the same, twenty miles away at Tremadog. Except for the Great Wall, Brown had run out of steam on Cloggy, but the roadside crags intrigued him and surprisingly his technical standard increased. It was not surpassed by the younger generation for some years. Nut protection opened up many new routes which would have been unthinkable two or three years before, and in 1961 and 1962 Brown churned out lots of new routes. The Alpha stars who plugged away elsewhere had a very different social scene to that of the fifties. Football, fags, fast driving, darts and great ambitions were all interwoven between rock 'n roll music. They were the most inspired group of hard climbers ever and put up routes all over Snowdonia.

Allan Austin one of the leading Lake District climbers of that time and also a member of the Climbers' Club, wrote in the 1963 C.C. Journal:

'Competition which was virtually killed under the sway of the Rock and Ice has returned in a virulent form.'

Clearly he meant the Alpha Club and in 1962 they produced another cluster of important new routes on Cloggy. Crew and Ingle started in April with The Shadow on the blunt arete to the right of The Corner. Done with one peg it was a precarious Extreme and not well-protected even by today's standards. With tongue in cheek they

graded it Hard V.S. Next day on the 28th Ingle joined forces with Martin Boysen to force the slim twin-grooved Daurigol, the second pitch of which required several points of aid before Boysen could overcome it. On the third day Soper joined up with Crew again to launch the first successful Alpha assault on the West Buttress, to do Bow Right-Hand, a route which one climber likened to climbing up the outside of a huge egg. Sharp's guide-book was a bit more basic:

'A fine route in a very exposed position. The crux pitch builds up slowly in difficulty to a very hard move at 60 feet and then the climbing relents, with the third pitch in a tremendous position above the overhangs.'

Three major routes in three days not only inspired maximum effort but also ensured a fair share for all. There was a big corner to the right of Bloody Slab and it was obvious to the Alpha that it would be climbed soon, so they tried it three days after Bow Right-Hand. Ingle got a long way up the first pitch then fell from a difficult layback corner, but still carried on before being stopped by water seepage. Later he returned to his high point but was again stopped by the damp. Crew took over the lead and climbed past the wet bit and reached a stance. On the next pitch the crack was full of grass and had to be gardened to reach a tension traverse, but the route was soon in the bag. Brown was furious with himself over Haemogoblin as he had been thinking of trying the route for some time.

Between Diglyph and the Drainpipe Crack of Vember is one of the smoothest sheets of rock in the British Isles. Brown had tried the faintest of crack lines in the left-hand side but after several attempts he eventually placed two pegs to reach a point just over seventy feet from the ground. It came to be known as Master's Wall in deference to his efforts. Soper and Crew became interested and abseiled down the route pulling off a large grass sod which revealed a huge hold just above Joe's last peg. Sharp's guide-book stated correctly that Brown had previously climbed what is now the first pitch. He had done the pitch and shrewdly assessed that the difficult crack would take more than his normal frugal two points of aid per pitch.

Crew abseiled down and put in half a dozen chockstones in the final difficult crack on what is now the second pitch. On his successful ascent he finally used the chocks for aid to reach the top. By the time he was belayed it started to rain and Ingle was unable to follow the pitch. In his keenness to beat Brown, Crew had made an error of judgement on what he finally called Great Wall. Almost certainly Brown could have completed the route if he had been prepared to use the same amount of aid.

A week later Crew restored his image with one of the most popular climbs that he and Ingle had pioneered. West Buttress Eliminate is slabby and superb, with a 5c crux and three 5b pitches. Incorporated into its three stars is Walsh's Groove right at the top of the crag. Pat Walsh was one of the legendary Creag Dhu club from Glasgow. He had immense strength and talent but was incredibly short-sighted and often wandered onto unclimbed ground owing to his inability to see anything more than a few feet away. Half-way up the groove, which he mistook for Sheaf, he remarked:

"Och, the old-timers could certainly climb!"

West Buttress Eliminate was the best route done by the Alpha up to that time and Crew was clearly at the top of the heap after his fine series of new routes. The virulent

Above: Claude Davies, Dennis Grey, Joe Brown, Trevor Jones and M. Tweed taken about 1960.
Photo: Trevor Jones collection.
Below: Al Alvarez (poetry critic), Frank Davies (shop owner) and Joe Brown cooking something up.   Photo: Claude Davies.

competition which prevailed at that time was neatly summed up in an article 'The Llanberis Movement' by John Cleare and Robin Collomb.

'Open competition flourished between climbers on these cliffs. Subterfuge in passing on information, laying false trails, inventing non-existent routes on horrible pieces of rock, were common ploys pressed into service by rival parties. One contestant held a pack at bay by clinging to the first pitch of a potential new route for three hours moving slowly up and down 30 feet of rock...until an overdue companion arrived to take up the lead.'

The Alpha climbers were also fond of the Lakes and less than a fortnight later Crew snatched a real plum route with Central Pillar on Esk Buttress. Arthur Dolphin had sniffed at it and the route was on the list of every hard man in the Lake District. Allan Austin intended to try it on the same day as Crew but to his chagrin he did not know of Crew's dawn start. When Austin arrived at the foot of the crag, Crew was well up the route. Austin's grim humour labelled his own new route that he put up that day — Black Sunday.

Hiraeth, or a 'longing for Wales', was another new route that the Crew/Ingle team put up on Dove Crag a week before the ascent of Central Pillar. They wrote impishly in the C.C. Journal:

'It rained so we went to Keswick and they were all dead sick because we had swiped their routes, but they bought us some beer and we bought plenty more for a party.'

Another interesting quote from the same article sums up their itchy Welsh competition:

'Now whenever I see a line I get really nervous and jittery in case someone else should swipe it and so we expected Geoff Oliver and Les Brown, or Paul Ross, to come rushing round in the night to steal a march. Even though they didn't appear we got up early just in case they crept over from Dunmail.'

On June 17th, the very day that Crew was storming the Central Pillar, Boysen was hard at work on the Cloggy Pinnacle to solve the much-tried Pinnacle Arete, high above the evil slopes of the East Gully. Boysen had been ill for some time and his second, Colin Mortlock, was alarmed at Martin being violently sick at a critical point. He recovered however and made the crux moves then a blind swing round the arete from one vertical wall to another so that he could finish the route.

Boysen had his detractors. Certainly his collection of new routes was fewer than that of Crew and Ingle, and it was even said that he had an outcrop mentality. Perhaps his laid-back approach is the reason why he still climbs at a very high standard twenty years later and can even now put up new routes with technical 6a cruxes. As a brilliant mountaineer he can take all in his stride while his critics have long since given up climbing.

The same driving force that Peter Crew put into his climbing resulted in the production of the first independent guide to Clogwyn du'r Arddu, which was written in conjunction with Hugh Banner. It contained an original and imaginative technical grading of pitches and a refinement of the O.G. Jones adjectival gradings which were starting to creak at their ancient hinges:

'The numerical grade can be said to be a measure of the technical difficulty of each pitch (as if it were a boulder problem) while the adjectival grade can be used to assess the overall atmosphere and seriousness of a climb.'

Further extracts show a prophetic vision, almost approximating to the present-day scene:

Dave Potts attempting to lasso the spike on Troach, East Buttress of Clogwyn du'r Arddu.   Photo: John Cleare.

'Obviously, in ten years' time climbs like Llithrig and Vember will be regarded as Hard Very Severe; but they will retain the same numerical grade, and the hardest climb of the day will probably be graded Extremely Severe (6b or 7a)...

...No method of grading can be absolutely accurate; nor do we want it to be, since the resulting controversies are an interesting and essential part of climbing.'

The accuracy of Crew and Rodney Wilson's analysis can be easily verified by comparing his gradings with those of a modern guide. They are virtually the same and only the hardest routes are now thought to be technically easier. Crew's guide-book was also different in that it had neither padding nor humorous ramblings. They were even more severe when describing the Alpha routes:

'The Great Wall   200 feet   Extremely Severe
This is the central wall of the East Buttress, between Diglyph and Vember. It is split at its left-hand side by a thin crack line. Start just to the right of this.'

The Rock and Ice routes were described in almost amiable terms; Shrike was a fine steep route on good holds and East Gully Wall became a pleasant route, steep and well protected.

Cyrn Las was an obvious big crag worthy of attention and, in a pause between football matches in the broad meadow in front of Ynys Ettws, Crew and Ingle saw the black frowning overhangs. They soon split the crag in two with their joint lead of The Great Buttress, a series of overhanging grooves which were impressively positioned below the great beak. Shortly after this Bas Ingle went up to Cwm Silyn with Rodney Wilson to snatch Crucible one of the outstanding last great problems. There was then a pause before the Crew/Ingle machine transferred to the bubbly rock of Suicide Wall in Ogwen. Their route which they called Route II was slightly easier than Preston's line and needed a peg to make them feel safe. It put Crew in fine form and a week later he was back on the Black Cliff for his last major new route on the crag.

Crew and Ingle always had one 'last great problem' but on Cloggy it was to be rather special — a fierce-looking groove just to the left of The Black Cleft. It was September and word went round that Crew was going to try a new route on which Ingle had already failed. Crew got to the overhang at the top of the groove and knocked in an ice peg which only went in halfway.

'The moves across the top of the groove seemed desperate — friction for the feet and undercut hand-holds, so as soon as I could stand on a small ledge to the left of the overhang I tried to put another peg in but this was hopeless so I had to press on. After each move I became progressively more depressed as I realised I couldn't get down. After about 30 feet I could rest again. With the last runner 40 feet below I was getting scared. I moved across to a flake on the right and tried to fix a peg. It only went in half an inch so I moved across to a flake on the right and found I could stand in balance. This solved the problem immediately, and I put the bolt in...'

Soper, who was among the watching crowd, recalled:

'Even after Pete got the bolt in, his position looked critical. It could not have held much of a fall. Suddenly he shot up and simultaneously a flake of rock came flying down. It looked as though it came off as he was pulling on it, but he just kept moving up.'

Crew again:

'Eventually I plucked up courage to move from the bolt. There was a long reach for a small

Opposite: Pete Crew on The Great Wall in May 1962.   Photo: Rosemary Soper.
Over: Martin Boysen near the foot of East Gully, Clogwyn du'r Arddu, April 1962.   Photo: Rosemary Soper.

ledge covered in grass but I had to knock a flake off it first. From the gasp that came up from below, the crowd thought I was off. In a few feet I was on the Boulder traverse and it was all over.'

The Boldest was a 150-foot pitch, giving superb and sustained climbing; it was dangerous too as despite the bolt it was not well protected. There was an overall feeling of grudging approval by his friends who were watching him, but in a way they were all implicated in the placing of the bolt. The very fact that the bolt had been brought to the cliff in the first place suggests a premeditated act, as has happened several times in climbing history. Although some of the leading climbers tried to justify the bolt at the time, the offending metal would only last until a bolder climber came along a decade later. Whatever the verdict of future generations the deed was done and The Boldest stamped the seal on three great years of Alpha exploration. The stage was set for the discovery of one of the biggest and most exciting cliffs in the country.

The Old Order Changeth

Rock climbing in Wales had for many years followed the established pattern of escaping from the cities to climb in the mountains. As the search for new rock continued the net was spread to encompass low-level climbing areas, such as the cliffs at Tremadog, where one could still climb when the weather in the hills had deteriorated. It was at this stage that a discovery was made which was not only to divert the leading activists away from the mountains but was also to inject a new interest into the search for new routes. At first the discovery of Gogarth's sea cliffs in 1964 made little impact despite the fact that Crew, Ingle and Boysen were all aware of their existence and had all done new routes there. By 1966 however the secret went further than just a few close friends and a whisper spread round the climbing world that there was an amazing new secret cliff complex just waiting to be snapped up. On the other hand there were also rumours of huge loose blocks and climbing only by the use of pressure holds to keep the fragile rock in place. It would not be long before climbers would flock in from afar, but many were intimidated by the place and departed...

Perhaps a better name for Gogarth might have been Cloggy-on-Sea. Rising out of the restless waves of the Irish Sea the cliff was a serious proposition for those who wished to get a closer look. There were new factors to contend with that were not normally encountered in the mountains. The Anglesey cliffs had swirling sea below them, difficult and often complicated access, a great deal of loose rock and not least masses of screaming sea-birds which nested on the ledges and the steep finishing slopes. All these factors combined to induce an uneasy nervousness amongst those attempting first ascents. When the sea was angry the inexorable foam smashed into the rock walls and threw spray hundreds of feet up the crag. At such times the prudent climber faded from the scene. There are other sea cliffs, Chair Ladder, Swanage, Bosigran...but nothing quite so uncompromisingly majestic as the grey and orange-red cliffs of Gogarth which rise a full 300 feet above the water on a calm day.

The first proper exploration in April 1964 was by Martin Boysen and Bas Ingle when they ventured onto the edge of the Main Cliff to produce Gogarth, a fine Hard V.S. with a 5b pitch right at the top. Ingle went back the following week with Crew and encroached even further towards the centre of the crag. The black traverse line at sea level was the only chink in Gogarth's armour but the turbulent sea was ready to trap the unwary and retreat has been cut off for many parties. Although it was not hard for its grade Pentathol (Pentothal!) was an intricate introduction for two gripped climbers and Crew was impressed:

'My main memories of that climb are of being absolutely bloody frightened by the sea. I've got a morbid fear of water anyway, and I can remember going along that traverse, thinking, "God, we're going to die if we're not careful", and then struggling on that first pitch of Pentathol, watching the tide coming in and wondering if we were going to drown.'

The Alpha climbed on the Upper Tier too and produced a clutch of easier routes. They had difficulty working out the lines as Crew remembered:

Opposite: Peter Crew sorting gear at the foot of the crag.   Photo: John Cleare.

'I looked at The Ramp for week after week, trying to work out whether it was a slab or an overhanging wall with jugs. Until we went on it I had no idea at all, and I literally had bad dreams about it. The main crag we just regarded as ridiculous: it's a psychological problem, just a massive blockage — steepness, water and loose rock.'

They did nine routes and then considered that the cliff was worked out — an incredible judgement. Crew then went to live in London and spent his time worrying about girls, jobs and guide-books. Gogarth was then left for a while to the sea-birds.

Another determined university climber filled the new-route vacuum during a temporary lull of inactivity by Brown and the Alpha stars. John Clements was as dedicated as Crew and had already turned his attention to crags which had been ignored by the Alpha teams. He only had a few months on the new-route scene before he was killed in January 1966, winter climbing in Glencoe. Clements waved a magic new-route wand over North Wales and selected three particular crags. On Castell Cidwm's steep ramparts, Glwm, Central Wall, The Erg and the Cidwm Girdle were all exciting new additions to the beautiful Quellyn Valley. Another clutch of routes: Elliw, Endor and the superb Great Corner brought Llech Ddu to a more mature stage after extensive gardening.

Clements was aware of the ruthless Alpha competition and was ultra-secretive about the location of his potential new routes. It seems strange that the two main innovators in the Carneddau, John Clements and Lawrie Holliwell should both be killed while climbing. The last great climber killed in Scotland had been Maurice Linnell, thirty years earlier.

In London Crew met a young photographer, Ken Wilson. Whiz as he was known to his friends was fanatically keen on climbing although his own abilities on the crag were modest. Climbing history was being made and Wilson was in a position to record it — particularly as Editor of first Mountain Craft and then Mountain magazine. Wilson paid £5 to hire a boat from a Holyhead pilot to take pictures of Gogarth; and Crew and Brown accompanied him to spy out new lines. When the boat came close to Castell Helen, Wilson saw a team climbing on the cliff and asked them to look gripped for his camera. They willingly obliged...Wilson spread the word with his first-class photographs, his infectious enthusiasm and a furious rate of conversation. For a while he became the Pied Piper of the climbing world, producing photographs of fabulous new crags for the Padarn Lake bar on Saturday night.

The social scene had changed from the Pen y Gwryd Hotel where climbers had gone for eighty years to the more earthy Padarn Lake bar in Llanberis village. At 'the Pad' darts was the big challenge and for a little time there was enough room for everyone to foregather to look at Wilson's pictures and to tantalise each other with snippets of information about the extraordinary new route they had worked out, then silence. Interested onlookers were always hovering in the hope that they might learn the location so that they could rush in next day to forestall the opposition. In time the Pad became overcrowded and on Saturday nights the bar became a seething mass ofhumanity.

Several keen climbers went to live in Wales and formed a tight climbers' commune isolated from the local community by the Welsh language and insularity. The cheer leader of this group for many years, until his untimely death in a car accident, was Al Harris, a good climber in his own right. The commune became even more insular until

their habitat was rather unkindly described as a psychiatrist's paradise.

Crew's lack of ability on boulder problems led Harris to say that anything that Pete could do he would follow in winkle-pickers. He was as good as his word on the first ascent of Zukator wearing a cow gown and the appropriate long-pointed shoes of the early sixties. Unfortunately Crew used seven points of aid to complete Zukator which rather flawed the route. In fact Crew didn't like Tremadog one little bit and condemned the crags out of hand with the derogatory suggestion:

'Dismantle Vector Buttress stone by stone and rebuild it in the Pass and they could then blow up the rest of Tremadog for all the good it is.'

For a time Crew beavered away on guide-book work and first produced the 1966 Llanberis South guide (for which Ken Wilson provided the photographs) before completing his 1967 Cloggy guide. On Dinas Mot, Crew climbed M.P.P. (which stands for Micro Precision Product) to indicate the plate camera which John Cleare used to record the first ascent. Martin Boysen found it hard to enthuse over Gogarth and he too started to comb the south side of the Pass where he found a host of good routes in 1965. Black Spring, Plexus, Sexus and Plexus Girdle were a good start to maturing the wings of Dinas Mot.

By 1966 the Welsh scene was set for a big change and Rowland Edwards, who had started off with Spectrum and Perygl on the Grochan the previous year, showed a strong sense of tradition by concentrating his initial attack on Cloggy. Seemingly every inch a Lancastrian with a fine Bolton accent he was in fact born in Llanberis. Having lived in Bolton for most of his life he eventually returned to live in Llanberis though his accent excluded him from becoming a born-again Welshman. Edwards was not part of any one particular group and developed his skill on Wilton gritstone quarries where he did the first recorded route in 1959 as well as many others. When he returned to Wales he developed new routes all over Snowdonia including its coastal crags.

Edwards evolved a master plan for the West Buttress of Clogwyn du'r Arddu — a series of new routes which would culminate in an attempt on a harder girdle than Harding's line. He made a preliminary attempt in November but retreated. In April he returned with a full head of steam, a big bag of pitons, and playboy Harris who was to provide light relief. The overhang grudgingly accepted just enough of each piton but there was still sufficient sticking out to set Rowland's heart thumping. A fall might have unzipped the whole sequence and when it was Harris's turn he plucked out the pegs with ease. Shallow grassy grooves in the upper part required gardening and in the process Edwards dropped a large sod studded with rocks onto Harris's head and knocked him out for a few minutes. After he had recovered they finished the route and called it Spartacus; but poor rock and doubtful pitonage make it an unpopular route.

A line even more uncompromising than Spartacus seemed possible but unlikely. A tantalising spike was spotted on the very lip of the overhangs. Could it be lassoed? Everyone talked about it but equally everyone had carefully and sensibly avoided doing anything about it. Edwards tried to interest Harris, who was neither interested in new routes nor in enduring more personal pain. After several attempts Edwards lassoed the spike to the cheers of a watching crowd. The prussik was absolutely frightening as the spike might easily have broken off. As soon as Edwards reached rock he promptly

Opposite: High on The Great Corner of the sombre Llech Ddu in Cwm Llafar.   Photo: Chris Jackson.

knocked in two pegs much to the surprise of those watching. He resumed next day to finish what was to be a fine route, Mynedd, which now merits an E3 grade.

Edwards also put up a third route, Fibrin, which linked Slanting and Bloody Slab. It was October before he could try the girdle traverse. It took several attempts to link it all together as the route was 1,500 feet long but it was controversial as three bolts and two pegs were used to cross the bounding wall of The Black Cleft. On the section moving out of Mynedd, Edwards had a traumatic time:

'One of the small foot-holds I was bridging on broke off. I went with it, but incredibly I just slipped back onto a flake; by a great feat of balancing I was able to stay in contact with the rock...a fall from here would have been really serious. I had no protection...'

Edwards still found that he had a tiny section left to do and although he had broken his neck doing pull-ups and was in plaster he abseiled down complete with plaster and finished the route alone. It is a sustained E3 with some good climbing along its considerable length.

At the same time as Edwards was exerting himself on Cloggy, Martin Boysen spotted an amazing line in Cwm Glas. It was seven years since his ascent of Woubits Left Hand and Boysen still felt more at home on the big mountain crags. On May Day a major new route was done on Cyrn Las and although The Skull needed five points of aid it was a tremendous achievement. While Boysen was at work the old fox, Joe Brown, arrived at the foot of the cliff to try the same line. Brown climbed another line, a harder start to the Great Buttress, and called it The Prune, a dried up plum — it nicely summed up his feelings at being beaten to the big line. Eighteen years later Brown led The Skull in its clean E4 6a condition when he was 54.

Not to be outdone by others, Crew did ten new routes in three months and was clearly getting better technically, just as Brown had done in 1960. When Crew was gardening Central Park while climbing with Jancis Baldock, Dave Alcock and Dave Potts were trying another groove over to the left. They had got up to the crucial overhang but ran out of steam and retired, so they passed the ropes to Crew, who arrived at the overhang in a fresh condition, made two or three hard moves then finished the route. It was the classic case of a leader's dream — a friend fails to finish a hard section, has it well protected and then utters the magic words, *"Would you like to have a go?"*

Central Park still needed further gardening sessions but eventually Crew and Alcock completed their big clean up:

'It took three or four days to garden. The first pitch was just literally a green field and, once it had been gardened, it was just a narrow band of clean rock going up through the green field. We gardened it entirely from the bottom, partly because it wouldn't have been easy to rig up an abseil rope due to the big grass run-off. I think we used the odd sling to stand in for cleaning, but it was led free. I thought it was a hard route, but that's the problem with new routes — often the psychological and physical effort of pioneering is out of all proportion to the eventual route, and of course Central Park soon came to be regarded as a very reasonable climb.'

High up on the right-hand end of the Upper Tier is a series of unconnected cracks only an inch wide at first, then widening as they escalate, to finish in a vicious hanging chimney crack at the top. Brown said that every time he passed it the route winked at him. It winked once too often and Joe was tempted. He had to sprinkle it with six pegs to reach the final crack which didn't yield without a fight. The winking leer didn't succumb

Opposite: Rowland Edwards and Al Harris on the 1st ascent of Spartacus, West Buttress of Clogwyn du'r Arddu.
Photo: R. Edwards collection.

to an easy technique such as a hand-jam, but gave awkward arm-locks. Brown's crack technique, honed on Right Eliminate and Elder Crack, made sure that the unprotected crux would go. Winking Crack gave Gogarth its first real 5c crack pitch and later it defeated several top leaders including Geoff Cram who slid precariously all the way down.

One week-end a large party, including Crew and Brown walked to the Main Cliff at Gogarth and while Crew went down the normal descent gully, Brown carried on along the top of the cliff with Martin Boysen. Suddenly Brown saw the top of a piece of rock:

'All you could see was about forty feet of slab sticking out above the grass. We walked round and were pop-eyed when we saw the thing. We only had a little bit of gear with us so we borrowed odd karabiners and slings that odd people had got and went and did it.'

They called it Wen, the most beautiful slab on Gogarth. What Brown didn't say was that it required a difficult diagonal abseil and was the most serious approach on Gogarth. Crew enviously commented:

'You wouldn't believe it but until that day no-one had ever seen it. That's the funny thing about the old man, he's got a nose for rock — he can smell a new route from two miles away.'

After Brown's thrutching triumph on Winking Crack, Crew was galvanised into action and went for an unclimbed plum in the centre of the Main Cliff. Three other parties were interested and there was an exciting race along the sea-level traverse; Crew won. Later Crew wrote with some degree of hilarity:

'When we arrived there was an extra complication in the form of Doug Scott, who was already half-way up the groove of Syringe, pegging his heart out. One of the funniest things I've ever seen happened that day. I was belayed in the middle of Jaborandi, when Scott's head appeared round the corner, his hair plastered all over his face with sweat. *"Can I come over there?"* he said. *"No,"* I said, *"Piss off! Your route goes up round the corner."'*

Scott put in nine pegs to force Syringe and although some were used for belays the number wasn't very well received in the bar of the Padarn Lake. Before criticising one must remember that between 1964 and 1977 over 250 declared points of aid were used on the Gogarth cliffs. Scott did other aid routes such as the horrendous Big Overhang at North Stack, but became better known as one of the luckiest and most durable top Himalayan mountaineers.

While on Jaborandi, Crew had noticed a large left-facing corner which was then unclimbed. Big Groove was to be the best pitch on the cliff done by Crew and it fully deserves its cluster of stars and popularity as a top E2 route. That evening Crew could have rested on his laurels for the week-end but he had been intrigued while watching Brown attempting and failing on another big route up the great overhanging central wall of Gogarth's Main Cliff. Crew had already named the route Dinosaur because it would need a long neck and no brains:

'That day we did Big Groove the old man was trying Dinosaur, and he'd got up to the first overhang and left a sling in place. We'd never climbed together, and in fact we'd never even conversed, except at a distinctly cold distance. I went to him that night at Dave Alcock's prompting, because Dave and the old man were quite friendly. The approach was: *"You've been trying Dinosaur today and I'm going to do it tomorrow, so why don't we team up to save burning each other off?"* At that time the old man was definitely short of a good partner, but that was the only route on which I ever really burned him off, or climbed better than he...Every time since, he's definitely been boss — I don't mind admitting it. On the first pitch, he had got the

runner on the end of the overhang, and it took a lot of courage to launch up the short wall above. He tried it several times and I tried it several times, until eventually I managed it. The second pitch was extremely loose and I frigged my way up it, using several points of aid. It's one of those routes that's now done more or less free, but at the time every bit of aid was justified. It took a lot of doing, that climb. We were out there early in the morning and didn't get back until nearly ten o'clock at night.'

Brown's account of the first pitch of Dinosaur differs considerably from Crew's:

'I tried the first pitch and got round the overhang and up to the final wall which leads up to the stance. The only protection I had was those two pegs driven upside-down under that flake, and I thought, *"Bugger that!"* So I went down and Pete went up and, at the point where I'd been standing, he found a hole in the rock into which he put this peg. It was an absolutely perfect peg, and it made a very safe lead then. When I got up to the stance and looked up, I thought, *"I don't like it at all"* — it might have been something to do with seconding. Pete said, *"Right, off you go,"* but I said, *"No, I don't want to do that."* Pete led it and I was still absolutely bloody gripped seconding. I felt more frightened of coming off that seconding than I would have done leading, because I don't normally think I'm going to come off. But that time, even though I was seconding, I felt I was going to swing off with a big piece of rock in my hand.'

Brown was less experienced on the cliff than Crew but with so much aid it is not surprising that Crew triumphed over Joe. Despite the looseness ten pegs to force the climb was undoubtedly excessive.

Even while these heroic deeds were taking place Malcolm Howells was battling away at Rat Race. Almost up to the standard of the leading lights Howells was making a big effort to get on to equal terms. When the going got tough Malcolm started to cough. As the technical standard or danger increased, so Malcolm's bronchial spasm would become louder and more prolonged, causing extreme anxiety amongst his seconds who prayed for the coughing to stop — which meant that Malcolm had reached easier ground. Howells was keen to make his name and while on Rat Race was urged on by the top team working away just next to him.

Howells got across the initial traverse which had been attempted by Geoff Birtles and Chris Jackson. On the next attempt he got farther but was stopped by a hard section. In contrast to Brown and Crew he decided not to use a peg and retreated. Shortly afterwards Brown climbed the whole pitch using a peg for aid but on both occasions the seconds could not or would not follow — a scenario Brown was ruefully used to by then. The attack was renewed by Howells and on the main pitch he was assisted by the slings left by Brown. He then climbed the overhanging chimney above which completed the main problem. Crew and Brown added the upper pitches whereupon Crew credited the route to himself and Brown with a footnote about Howells. Now it is felt that Howells deserves the main credit for the route.

Later in the year Crew wrote an interim guide with thirty-nine routes which had nearly all been done in a space of four months. The new-route activity on the Main Cliff then abated for a while and the action moved to the cliffs near the South Stack Lighthouse. Deep zawns, contorted rock and no apparent lines were all perplexing to the climbers of twenty years ago. The rock seemed strange, being red or yellow — unusual colours for an unclimbed cliff. Brown told the story:

'While we were doing the television programme, I noticed the line of Wendigo, which I though might be a two-inch crack all the way up the cliff, and I thought, *"Well...that's what I've been looking for all my life.*" So, later, I went back to the wall with Pete, intending to do Wendigo. When we actually got on the wall, we saw how broken the rock was in comparison with what it looked like from the top, so we did Red Wall instead, which I thought was fantastic...Doing something like Red Wall you snapped some of the holds off. You could see that they weren't loose, they were just so thin and big that they snapped off like biscuits, and you very quickly got the hang of just smashing them off, so that what was left was thicker and stronger.'

Surprisingly they had missed Castell Helen, a superb grey crag in front of the little turreted keep of Helen's Cottage. Two abseils led down unknown ground, the first to a big ledge, and the second to wave level where they could look up to untouched walls of the soundest rock on Gogarth. Blanco, the first route, was sheer entertainment before the slightly harder Atlantis. Two weeks later a day of frenzied activity gave four more routes: Pel, Rap, Lighthouse Arete and the Girdle Traverse.

Still farther right was the Yellow Wall, an evil place, where Brown and Crew eventually accepted the challenge. They dithered at first and did a steep little route on the right-hand side, called Pterodactyl. Birtles had been with them on their first attempt but he was not able to leapfrog them on this occasion and a romantic moonlight escape was necessary. In fact several attempts were needed before the old master triumphed, but not easily; Crew thought that it was the hardest thing he'd done:

'It was one of the only two routes on which I've seen the old man in trouble. When we did it the whole of the wide crack on the left of the slab was full of yellow dust, and we both had bad guts for months afterwards because of all the dust we'd taken in.'

They called it The Sind because the dust from the crag was just like sand.

The sea-level traverse of the Main Cliff carried on past all the glories of previous months then suddenly the rock became smooth until it proved impossible to traverse any further. Tantalisingly the water lapped right up against the steep cliff and prevented any further exploration. The crag photographs showed that there was a whole new section of unexplored cliff round the corner just waiting for someone. Brown had become rejuvenated by all the excitement and got a tremendous boost; again he felt that he had captured the enthusiasm of his early days. He prospected and found an appallingly steep and vegetated gully which roughly led down to what he hoped would be the promised land. With a considerable amount of timidity he and Dave Alcock lowered themselves down the gully to a ledge where they did a long abseil into an intriguing zawn. Superb routes began to flow from the Easter Island Gully crags, which were so named because the strange rock formations had a likeness to the brooding figures perched on that remote Pacific island.

Two newcomers to the Welsh new route scene considerably increased the speed and spread of new routes, and in just over a month the Holliwell brothers produced four impressive Extremes: Itch at Tremadog, Eureka on Cwm Silyn, Venom on Llech Ddu and Poker on Carreg Hyll Drem. Of them, Poker and Venom eventually became modern E3s. The Holliwells were to become the most effective new-route team since Crew and Ingle and despite their unique apprenticeship they rapidly absorbed the complexities of climbing and had repeated many hard routes including The Skull (second ascent), Great Wall (4th ascent) and Dinosaur (3rd ascent).

The brothers, Lawrie and Les, were a phenomenon hitherto unknown in the climbing world. Machine-gun burst patois, curses, and in-jokes were all wrapped in barely

Opposite: Bob Berzins pulling up on Spectrum, Clogwyn y Grochan, 1979.   Photo: Mike Browell.

Above: Lawrie Holliwell commencing the layback up Park Lane on the Upper Tier at Gogarth.   Photo: Leo Dickinson.
Opposite: Marjorie Allen on Wen Slab, Gogarth.   Photo: R.F. Allen.

intelligible Cockney accents. They came from Ilford and catapulted forth every Friday night to North Wales at breath-taking and law-breaking speeds. Not content with getting to their destination they roared around looking for new crags. On one occasion Les even found a drivable route onto the top of the Carneddau plateau before his multi-coloured G.T. Cortina developed engine trouble. It was not long before they were at grips with new rock:

'I reached the roof. Confidently I pulled up until the lip of the overhang was at waist level. Alas, no jugs. Instructions from above were explicit but the mere thought of their execution was repulsive. My strength was deserting me. I jammed my arm into a crack too wide for comfort and moved up — the world spun. I was now suspended beneath the overhang and gripped, the mist that had enveloped the cliff now served to enhance my unenviable position. A trail of abuse suddenly shattered the silence of the cwm. It was apparent that my dear brother was dissatisfied with my efforts and wished to encourage me to repair my deficiencies with expedition. A frantic struggle and it was all over. My derisive companion coolly enquired, *"Do you think it was Extreme?"* My agonised expression was apparently sufficient confirmation. I was impressed with Venom.'

The Holliwells also made sure that everyone knew about their routes. They wrote them up after each week-end and also circulated duplicate copies to all and sundry whom they thought might be interested. While prospecting a potential new route on Red Wall the Holliwells had a rather frightening scare. Lawrie was at the top of the pitch belayed to a peg while Les was rushing up the pitch anxious to finish and get to the Padarn Lake. He grabbed a spike when:

'Suddenly the cliff started wheeling away and I started falling. I fell ten feet and thought *"that's a long way for a second"* and then I just kept on going. I thought, *"Shit! That's curtains!"* I was completely convinced I was going to die, when suddenly I stopped — I must have gone seventy or eighty feet...'

The spike that he had grabbed had broken off, and with it the sling that was draped over it. The combined weight of the spike and Les had caused a huge strain to come on to Lawrie who was turned upside down and eventually was just able to hold Les after his fall.

Alcock with his own cronies had been unearthing secret routes in the Wen Zawn area very early in 1967. Smug smiles and innocent leading questions from the arch advocate, Brown, elicited the fact that the Wen Zawn gold mine still had rock nuggets to be discovered. Brown and Crew consequently went for Concrete Chimney which Crew described:

'Concrete Chimney was definitely a big psychological problem, because we had no idea how steep the wall was — it's supposed to be a slab, but it becomes much steeper. We didn't do it the way it's described in the book, and we had all kinds of epics on it. For instance, when I led the first pitch, I did a tension traverse down into the chimney for some reason — I actually belayed to pegs hammered into the crap in the chimney. We had no idea how long it was, and we didn't even know if we'd be able to get to stances or anything, but once we'd got on to that section of the cliff, it was obvious that there were routes there...'

Brown had been developing the seemingly preposterous idea of climbing out of the arch of the bridge that spanned the entry to Wen Zawn. On the first attempt he had quite an epic:

'This was the first proper attempt on Spider's Web. It was a nice day, very calm and with no wind. We had traversed across from Genuflex and Fred had taken a stance in Archway. I had climbed the first pitch of Spider's Web and I was messing about on the second pitch when I realised that we couldn't communicate — the noise was too great. I started to traverse back and, when I reached the arete, the first of a whole lot of big waves was just coming in — God knows what caused them, there was no wind. Anyway, this one completely buried Fred the Ted. I almost fell off laughing, saying, *"Never mind, Fred, I'll probably get wet next,"* not for one minute thinking that I would. The traverse back to the ledges by Genuflex was being buried by the waves so we went up Archway for fifty feet. The plan was to abseil down to above the waves and then rush across the traverse when there was a lull. I started to do this, but, when I was quite a long way above the traverse, about thirty feet, I saw a big wave coming in. By the time I had realised just how big it was, it was too late to do anything. It came sailing into the zawn, right over the top of me — I was completely soaked. I went back up the chimney to Fred, who'd been hit by the spray from the wave. I said, *"We'll have to go straight up and try to climb out. I'll just put pegs in wherever I can."* I started off and couldn't put anything in. I laybacked round three little overlaps, then got a good runner and went round the corner to start bringing Fred up. He took absolutely ages, and was three times under water — yet he must have been fifty or sixty feet above sea level. I couldn't understand how he managed to take so long on a layback, but what he'd done was fiddle little nuts in and come all the way up on those, and I couldn't get a bloody runner in!'

Brown did not complete Spider's Web until August 1968 when he did it with Crew. They took a stance right in the arch then Brown swung into etriers. Fortunately huge holds led to a straightforward pitch above.

Out of the 105 new routes put up in North Wales in 1966 an astonishing 49 were on Gogarth, and Tremadog yielded a healthy 21. The Pass had 9, Ogwen 8, Cwm Silyn 6, Cloggy 6 and the Carneddau 6.

Crew had been responsible with his climbing friends for introducing the new alloy chocks which were manufactured to replace the old assortment of household nuts so beloved by the Alpha. Crew recalls:

'When we did Great Wall, nuts had only been out for a few months. At first we'd reacted against them, but then we started to use them. On that climb, though, we only used one brass nut. The thing that's of relevance here to Anglesey is that when we first started climbing there we didn't have nuts. I can remember doing Pentathol with a little bag full of limestone chocks — we used to go to limestone and get bits that could easily be chipped to size on the route. That was the height of technical achievement at that time. Now Anglesey is the ideal nut cliff, in the sense that it's bloody awful for chockstones, which don't work effectively in those pockets, and I suppose Anglesey could have been the making of nuts. The more sophisticated development of nuts, making use of hexagons and tapered ends, was probably as much a response to Anglesey climbing as anything else, and no doubt helped to overcome the practical difficulties of climbing there.'

There was a pause from the avalanche of new routes in 1967, but another star soon appeared. Ed Drummond had wound himself up to a high standard on the Avon Gorge limestone, then became a student at Bangor. Drummond recognised Crew's pre-eminence and made up his mind to topple him from his perch in the same way that Crew had reasoned about Brown. Drummond decided on a war of attrition by climbing with Crew. He first took Crew to the Avon Gorge for a hard day's climbing then they went back to Wales where Drummond was pointed at Crew's Great Wall at Easter. Not only

Opposite: The bizarre and corrugated rock of Mousetrap, South Stack.   Photo: Alan Hinkes.

Rowland Edwards on the 2nd winter ascent of The Black Cleft, Clogwyn du'r Arddu.　　　Photo: R. Edwards collection.

Pete Crew in action on the second ascent of Aries, Clogwyn du'r Arddu.

Photo: John Cleare.

was it a cold day but it had rained a lot the previous week and climbing in shorts Drummond felt the cold. At a critical point as he moved up Crew shouted up to him, *"Clements fell off that way"* — clearly Crew had learnt about deflationary quips from Brown. Drummond however kept his head and eventually completed the route, but it was late so Crew abseiled down to remove the runners. By doing Great Wall, Drummond had passed the entrance exam to Welsh climbing and he followed this up emphatically by making the second ascent of The Boldest.

Crew let Drummond have a go at the next route which they did together but impatiently called him down and climbed the pitch himself to produce Mammoth. The important thing was that Crew had well and truly beaten Drummond by his psychological tactics, but it was Crew's last major route as a leader and his dynamic drive was sadly not felt any more.

The week after Mammoth was climbed, Brown did four new routes in two days: Primate, Wrangler, Hombre and Praetor. It looked as if it was in retaliation but Brown later wrote:

'Pete thought I was really gripped up about his getting Mammoth. I probably had some feelings, but they weren't very strong ones. It was the weekend afterwards that I did those four routes with Mac in two days, and Pete thought this was my way of getting my own back, but it wasn't.'

After his baptism of fire introduction, Drummond went on to make his own stormy niche in Welsh climbing. Controversial from the start, he trained hard and was careful with his diet and drinking. Crew and his cronies on the other hand drank hard, smoked a lot, and certainly never trained. This asceticism isolated Drummond to such an extent that he was not accepted on the social scene and his routes were greeted with a great amount of derision.

In 1967 Drummond made his mark on a superb sweep of unclimbed wall to the left of Central Park on Gogarth. A faint crack line gave an intriguing possibility; so on a cold October day Drummond in shorts climbed The Strand, pronounced it X.S. 6b and proclaimed it wouldn't be climbed for another twenty years. It was a fine achievement, but his arrogant statement infuriated the Welsh establishment and they were suspicious that he had used more aid than was necessary. Alan McHardy, better known as Richard did it with only one aid point a few weeks later and the Establishment sat back with some smugness. Seven years later The Strand had its first solo ascent by the American star Henry Barber who had been urged on to it by Al Harris — the object being to record the ascent for American television.

On the same day that The Strand was first climbed the talking-machines, Lawrie and Les Holliwell, started the first of their fine series of new routes on the cliff. One of these lines was U.F.O. which they climbed the day after they had smashed their car up by skidding off the road on some black ice.

The pace of exploration which had been so frenzied in 1966 and 1967 slowed to a relative crawl in 1968 and Gogarth was the only crag where anything significant happened. Tom Proctor the limestone ace from Derbyshire went down with Geoff Birtles to make a determined onslaught to produce Deygo. Crew had already been put off the route as it was clearly a very intimidating bit of rock. The hard pitches were done on separate days and the route needed four points of aid as well as a pendulum from a stake which had to be placed by abseil — exciting stuff, and it was a fine effort.

Opposite: Brian Molyneux on the Girdle Traverse of the Lower Amphitheatre Wall, Craig yr Ysfa.   Photo: Leo Dickinson.
P. 186: Ed Drummond and Dave Pearce traversing out on A Dream of White Horses just above the spray. Perhaps one of the most satisfying of all climbing photographs ever taken.   Photo: Leo Dickinson.

Another attack on the Main Cliff came from the Holliwells who were still as animated as ever — and in possession of another car by then. The route was to be Hypodermic:

'We did it on a paralysingly hot day and after one pitch we were both ready to abseil off, we felt so horrible. We sat there for about two hours, because the tide was against us and we didn't want to get wet. When the sun started to go down we felt a bit better, and decided to get the hell out. Lawrie was still for going down, but I went up and had a try and put that peg in. Then Lawrie tried the pitch and carried on, because we both felt much better. We didn't think it was all that good a route, but people now tend to say that it's very good.'

Drummond then made two more fine efforts on Gogarth. The first route was to have probably the most inspired name of any route in the British Isles — it was of course A Dream of White Horses, a meandering but spectacular line roughly girdling the the Wen Slabs. Drummond graded it Hard V.S., then Crew magnanimously uprated it to Extreme for his own guide. Now the dust has settled it is Hard V.S. but if a wind is blowing along the crag or the weather is poor it can seem a far more serious proposition. Teams do have epics on it and escape is by no means easy. Royal Robbins liked it so much that he enthused about it to the American media to such an extent that the route is now a tourist attraction.

There was still an intriguing possibility on the main part of the cliff and its ascent was going to be a major prize. Crew had already tried it but had failed:

'Just looking at Citadel used to frighten us — thinking about hanging from one of those overhanging flakes. I tried it once with Mac. It was in the middle of one summer, and we set off for Gogarth on an incredibly hot day, carrying sacks full of pegging gear. We were literally going to peg our way up the wall. I remember going about ten feet up the climb and getting no further, thinking, *"Hell! we must be absolutely bonkers".'*

Jack Street abseiled down the line and hammered etrier rungs into the crack — an amazing affair really for such a talented climber. He then completed the climb using quite a lot of aid. The general feeling was that it didn't amount to an ascent at all, and that Street had stolen a prize that did not belong to him.

An even bigger sensation occurred that year. A climber from the Midlands reported four new routes on the Upper Tier with seconds who could not be identified by the man's club mates. Mr X had not even been seen to lead anything particularly hard. X emphatically claimed that his routes had been done mid-week and kept churning out bogus route descriptions. He even published an interim guide-book which included his spurious routes. His club then published a disclaimer in Mountain magazine which tended to confirm that at the very least a great hoax had occurred. During the ensuing uproar some of the lines were inspected by abseil and pronounced as being far beyond X's abilities. The climbing world was so outraged that eventually The Sunday Times published the story. Thankfully, X retired into the shadows and Welsh climbers breathed again.

Brown in one of his last great efforts of that era on the cliff produced Spider's Web which conquered an overhanging arch above the sea. In a position of frightening exposure it required tension, a prussik down the rope at a crazy angle and more aid. Just the type of acrobatic which amused Joe and terrified most other people. Some time later a dreadful accident took place on this very serious route when two inexperienced teenagers, Robert Brown and Arnis Strapcans, made a fatal route-finding error.

P. 187: Maria Cranor powering up The Strand, Gogarth.   Photo: Steve Ashton.
Opposite: A study in concentration on the short wall on Gogarth.   Photo: Bob Allen.

Strapcans fell off and pulled Brown from his dubious belay pitons, which resulted in a fall into the turbulent sea. After getting tired trying to swim while encumbered by climbing gear and heavy winter clothing Strapcans was fortunately washed onto a rock. Brown on the other hand eventually failed to surface...Strapcans tried desperately to pull him out, but the ropes were badly tangled under-water. After half an hour Strapcans soloed out to safety with great difficulty, but tragically Brown's body was not found until several weeks later. Strapcans wrote:

'It stands as a stern warning in this age of climbing walls when one can gain a disproportionate level of technical ability without the accompanying rock sense that is so essential for big routes.

Technical ability must be accompanied by a commensurate degree of real climbing experience, particularly if one is to tackle serious sea cliffs such as Gogarth. Fitness and technical ability alone are insufficient when one is faced with loose rock situations and the problem of runner placement, safe belaying and complex route-finding.'

Sadly Strapcans disappeared during an Alpine holiday in the Mont Blanc area.

One of the big efforts of 1969 was Lawrie Holliwell's ascent of Wonderwall. His second, Dave Potts, was stunned by the performance:

'As I recall, the recent wave of desperate routes hadn't started then, and Lawrie was undeniably one of the best climbers around. He pissed up to the roof, and then, before resorting to aid in the overhanging groove, he moved about six to ten feet right and simply tried to climb the thing free. It looked preposterous to me: it wasn't as though he was making for anything, just more overhanging rock. I was very impressed: he got right out to the lip before jacking it in. The point of this is that he was quite prepared to try anything. That doesn't sound much now, but it astonished me then.'

In the climbing world life doesn't begin at forty and sadly 1969 saw the end of an era. Joe Brown was then thirty-nine and had been at the top for twenty years, but that year he slipped from the top rung of the ladder. Happily he finished with Red Haze an impressive line which he did with Crew. Brown remembered the occasion:

'We abseiled down Red Haze to get rid of some of the loose rock and look for runner placements. Coming up again, we climbed to within about 40 feet of the top, where there was a really good place for a peg. I was thinking, *"I don't really need that, but there's no other good runner, so I'll put the bugger in"*, so I put this peg in. The climbing's all right at that point, so I climbed up about 15 feet, and was just swinging from one big side-pull to another, when my last hold fell off. It wasn't a flake, it was the corner of an arete. Luckily the rope-drag through the peg behind stopped me swinging off; if I hadn't put it in, I'd have just gone flying through the air.'

Brown had done 48 first ascents on Gogarth and Crew almost the same number. They had dominated Welsh climbing, and had stormed many unclimbed ramparts together. The first ascent lists are thick with their names and their considerable achievements.

Again in 1969 it was Drummond who sparked off interest in a line at the back of Wen Zawn, which captured everyone's imagination. T. Rex was to become one of the great routes of Wales. Although Drummond didn't advance technical standards, he showed extraordinary tenacity on lines that he believed in. He was certainly a great route-finder but was before his time. One of his habits was to hammer his alloy protection nuts so that they were permanently intruded into the cracks. It seemed to others however little different from knocking in a piton. Despite this drawback Drummond produced some

Opposite: The 1st ascent of T Rex, Direct.   Photo: Rowland Edwards.

great routes although controversy surrounded many of them...controversy on which he seemed to thrive. For T. Rex, Drummond assembled a strong team including Lawrie Holliwell, Janet Rogers (one of the leading women climbers of that time) and Dave Pearce. One wonders whether it was a shrewd P.R. move on Drummond's part, to draw respected Welsh establishment climbers in order to lend credibility to his efforts.

Drummond climbed the first pitch using two aid slings then Holliwell led the hand-traverse of the second pitch — after which he became very excited about the route. They returned next day with a full team and abseiled down to the end of the hand-traverse. It was later to be the scene of a television spectacular. While in front of the cameras Les Holliwell fell off when a hold broke but to the chagrin of his friends was not televised. The guide-book gave the route three stars and referred to it as 'Magnificent...beautiful and varied climbing...one of the finest and most enjoyable routes in Wales'.

Autumn saw Drummond venture into the happy hunting-ground of the Holliwells — Llech Ddu. There he did The Great Arete, an alarmingly overhanging line. The third pitch took several days to do — a groove cut out of an overhanging arete. Unfortunately too much aid was used for it be a respectable ascent. It was another superb line grabbed as a result of Drummond's tenacity but once again he was under scrutiny in the Padarn Lake.

1969 saw the swan-song of Trevor Jones who was the same age as Brown. He managed to force the vicious right-hand side of the Pinnacle Wall on Craig yr Ysfa to give Pinnaclissima which is now thought to be E3 5c without the peg. Jones had done several minor routes on Craig y Llyn which had slumbered in its hunch-back form for some time. There was an untouched buttress on the extreme right of the crag with an alarming Vember-like shallow chimney which gave The Thirty Nine Steps — which seemed an appropriate name considering his age.

1970 was almost a non-event apart from Jim Perrin's lead of Resurrection on the little visited Llechog and 1971 was to be the next year when there was any significant activity. Lawrie Holliwell realised two last ambitions on Gogarth before he died; first Ziggurat then Hysteresis, a testing E3, which follows the impressive wall to the left of the Mousetrap Zawn. The second, Barry Whybrow, described some of the problems:

'The climbing on the first pitch was quite technical and steep, and we used a rather loose peg to surmount a final overhang to gain the horizontal break. We returned a few weeks later and abseiled to the stance. Lawrie began to make a number of sallies at the next pitch, all of which failed.

We never consciously decided to use alien means to insert a peg, but it seemed clear at the time that we wouldn't get on to the wall without a peg, and we couldn't find a suitable place to put one. On our next attempt, we again abseiled down the wall, this time carrying a star drill. Lawrie again tried to climb the overhang free, but with little success. He then attempted to place a peg, but couldn't. Eventually, we decided to drill a hole and insert a small angle peg, but even this was easier said than done. I had to lasso the abseil rope, which was hanging 10 feet out, and pull it in to allow Lawrie to clip a prussik in and so drill a hole and place a peg. The rest of the pitch, though sensational, had no extreme difficulties...'

Shortly before his death (by abseil accident on Craig yr Ysfa) Lawrie repeated Hysteresis free and chopped the peg. We had made a mistake, and Lawrie corrected it, or almost.'

The obituary of Lawrie written by Malcolm Howells sums up his excellent qualities:

'He was a climber of rare talent who created a formidable array of climbs which alone will ensure him lasting recognition. However he also had something much rarer than a high level of climbing skill. He was a man of unbending honesty in everything he did. He never cheated, he saw no point in it. He understood very well that British climbing is based on arbitrary, almost pointless rules but he always kept the rules.'

Howells made an important point about Lawrie's honesty. Some of his contemporaries showed shameless lapses of memory recording the number of points of aid used to overcome difficulties. Lawrie Holliwell did not advance standards but he had a superb eye for a line, a relentless urge to do new routes, and was a credit both to himself and to Welsh climbing.

A new star appeared, Alan Rouse, a Cambridge University undergraduate. From the start he showed superb soloing capability and an ascent of Beatnik at Helsby was followed by an even more impressive solo of The Boldest on Cloggy. The locals stood back admiringly at this Cambridge meteor and it was soon generally felt that Rouse was the best climber in the country and that nothing could stop him. He was about to take on one of the greatest challenges at Gogarth. First he tried to climb the large corner between Dinosaur and Rat Race, but retreated when he couldn't find adequate protection. He was aiming for a section of rock of awe-inspiring steepness and started up the steep wall immediately to the left of Rat Race. He fell off the second pitch while his foot was still in a sling, then after finishing it he discovered that the third pitch was even more alarming. At one point Rouse found himself unable to take either hand off, either to put in a nut or even to reach for one...Calmly he fell off...

An evening in the Padarn and much Dutch courage with alcohol spurred him on. Next day he enlisted another playboy of the Welsh world, Pete Minx, who resourcefully armed himself with a miniature transistor radio. Rouse had thoughtfully memorised the size of the right nut to go in a critical placement and gripped the sling between his teeth for quick use — hoping that he wouldn't sneeze or cough. This time he placed it correctly and quickly, then used it for aid, and was able to join Dinosaur. The first E4 in Wales was born. The irreverent Minx followed the crux pitch of Positron with the dangling transistor sacrilegiously blaring out pop music at full blast.

1971 was to be a good vintage year with quite outstanding performances from several top stars. One in particular was Ray Evans who showed a studied nonchalance to normal gear by putting up new routes on Cwm Silyn in a pair of old R.A.F. boots — probably the only person to put up Extreme routes in such footwear. Evans showed his true class by climbing the long-standing problem of Curving Arete on Cloggy, which Crew had dismissed as needing too many pegs to protect it adequately. Crew had said:

"Can't be done. Only two jugs. It would need at least four pegs."

It is still one of the more serious problems on the cliff and a fall from it would probably be fatal.

Evans was immensely talented, withdrawn and not part of the noisy Padarn Lake scene. While on the dole he lived in Wales for three years and was usually motivated by Chris Rogers, a Manchester University student who had considerable drive and ability. After Curving Arete they moved to Gogarth where Evans's first new route was a superb line to the left of the Gogarth pinnacle. Considering the proximity to the waves, the cliff, and the sky the route was well named and Rogers seconded up with his transistor

blasting out the theme of Bubbly Situation Blues.

A life of leisure in Wales did not induce any laxity in Evans's moral climbing standards and he was an example to many cheating stars. If he couldn't do a move or a pitch, he would retreat and desist from knocking in surreptitious pitons which might conveniently be forgotten later on. The only thing that he couldn't, or wouldn't do, was grade routes correctly. People soon got wary when they couldn't get up Evans's routes, which were nearly all graded as Hard V.S. Later guide-book writers often had the painful experience of discovering that H.V.S. might mean anything up to E3. Another Evans route on Cloggy was Jelly Roll which traverses out from November onto the Great Wall, giving the leader a feeling of both exposure and insecurity, until fingers unexpectedly curl into the most satisfying of cracks.

Martin Boysen carried on with his general policy of detaching himself from the Gogarth scene though that year he did an E3 on the Upper Tier. Determined to give it the longest name in Wales he called it Fifteen Men on a Dead Man's Chest...etc, etc. Fortunately he turned to more serious matters when, with Dave Alcock, he added three new routes on Suicide Wall during one week-end in September 1971. Ogwen's reputation has always been increased by top climbers of each generation who have felt a magnetic urge to visit Suicide Wall. Following in the steps of Preston, Lawton, and Crew, Boysen added his own major contributions: Capital Punishment, an intimidating line to the left of Route II, was fingery and tiring work in order to solve the complex mysteries. They needed to put in several pegs of dubious safety in order to lower off so that the other man could have a try.

1971 wouldn't be complete without another act in the Drummond command performance. He solved the horrendous central part of Yellow Wall to give a three-star E3 which rates superlatives such as 'powerful', 'strenuous', 'sustained' and 'fine positions'. Like blood out of a stone the praise for Drummond started to increase, particularly after his fine effort on The Moon which was a tribute to his eye for a line on a route which he described as 'The situations are strictly space-walking'. The route was freed several years later by John Allen and Steve Bancroft.

The following year, 1972, very little happened, although Jim Perrin produced a clutch of difficult routes including the powerful pitches of Samson on Gallt yr Ogof and The Green Wall, E3 5c, on Craig yr Wrysgan. In 1973 however a super-route was to appear on Gogarth. Pat Littlejohn was a newcomer to North Wales and had started climbing at the age of thirteen at Chudleigh near to his home town of Exeter. One of the first modern great climbers not trained on gritstone or limestone, he led his first Extreme within eight months. During his teens he climbed with Peter Biven, then Frank Cannings, who were the leading climbers in the South-West. Littlejohn, a short slightly-built climber, soon overtook them both and started on his own career. When he went to Gogarth he did the first free ascent of T. Rex then soloed Hombre in the Easter Island Gully area. With comparatively little experience on the complex system of cliffs Littlejohn picked out an impossible-looking line up the steep, smooth wall between Left-Hand Red Wall and Deygo:

'Several months previously I abseiled down the upper part of the face to look around and to clean out the big flake crack at the top of pitch two. From the end of the abseil rope, which ran out at the flake, I got only a vague impression of the terrain below...

Opposite: Leigh McGinley and Phil Davidson, high above the waves on the legendary Positron, Gogarth.
Photo: Paul Williams.

A couple of years before I had made an ascent of Deygo and, though I really enjoyed it, I didn't like the way the route had originated — a day for each pitch, considerable aid and prolific protection pegs, despite abseil preparation. I wanted Pagan to be a complete contrast, and this mode of thinking nearly got me into trouble on the main pitch. Above the stance of Deygo, you climb 25 feet, with one poor spike runner, to gain a sort of shelf where you can rest. I got a small wire runner in above my head then made some quite hard moves up onto a wall. I carried on for a while, before realising that the difficulties weren't going to end so soon, and that I should have got better protection. I reversed, until I was just above the wire, which seemed to be lifting out, then found that I hadn't the strength to reverse any further. I yelled to my second to pull, then stepped down onto the climbing rope, in the dip formed between my waist and the runner. The runner held, and the technique has got me out of trouble since, but if the runner had pulled out it would have meant a hell of a fall. Back at the shelf, I walloped in a thick chromolly peg, and things went more smoothly afterwards.'

Three stars and magnificent was the verdict of the guide-book of that time. A good E3 start, but only a taste of what Littlejohn was to do in time for Wales — north, south and west. On balance it was Littlejohn's year, just on the evidence of one new route.

Having brightened his image with the ascent of The Moon, Drummond went up to the Great Wall of Cloggy. Would he wave a magic wand on the Great Wall? Would asceticism, dieting, and great ability forge a new path for the future? Would he slot himself into immortality alongside Pigott, Kirkus, Brown and Harding? Alas it was not to be. Every hard man in the last twenty-five years has looked on the Great Wall of the East Buttress of Clogwyn du'r Arddu and lusted after a new route. In August 1973 Drummond made an attempt on a new route on the wall via a left-slanting weakness, mid-way between Great Wall and Vember. He top-roped it first, then placed four pitons and a bolt. It was an unacceptable ascent, caused widespread irritation and condemnation and, despite his other good efforts on new routes, this was to tarnish his reputation for years to come.

In what seemed like a few short months the scene had changed dramatically. Evergreen Joe Brown who had seemed at times as if he would stay at the top for ever, was suddenly gone from the top ranks just before he could get into his stride in his fortieth year. Peter Crew initially his deadly rival had become a friend and rope mate. Lawrie Holliwell the Cockney meteor fell among his favourite crags of the Carneddau and was killed while abseiling, as was Joe's other friend Dr. Tom Patey. The three stars had in some ways been like the three colourful musketeers and after their demise climbing was not quite the same for some time.

Opposite: Al Rouse poised above a big drop on Erebus, Craig Pant Ifan.   Photo: Leo Dickinson.

Up Against The Walls

For nearly a century mountaineering philosophy had remained nearly the same but in 1974 it was about to be changed considerably by a climber who was to have a profound effect on the future of the sport. Peter Livesey at the age of 31 was by no means young as far as hard climbing was concerned and he didn't even look like a climber. Born in Huddersfield, Yorkshire, in 1943 he was to develop into a bespectacled colossus who was to reign for just a few short years, but who was to change the status quo for ever. Not only was he a brilliant climber but also a successful Olympic-style rock athlete who was to shatter the idea that a top climber should ideally be in his teens.

Before Livesey came on the scene people climbed in Great Britain for most of the year, went to the Alps in the summer, and later if they were good enough went on Himalayan expeditions. Livesey changed all that. He could have introduced athleticism into rock-climbing, done his stint at the top, and then been superseded by the next generation. Rock-climbing and mountaineering as a closed loop was opened then closed by him to the exclusion of the mountaineering component.

Livesey advocated climbing in T-shirts and shorts on the limestone cliffs of the sunny South of France and the Yosemite Valley in California. This delightful concept was eagerly embraced by young climbers in search of a change from boring traditions. Livesey then wrote a guide-book to French rock climbs, which was hugely popular and caused further demolition of the summer traditions of Alpinism.

From an early age Livesey had athletic ability and became a junior international cross-country runner before he took up caving and climbing. He trained intensively on a local climbing wall and like all good Yorkshiremen he honed up his technique on both Yorkshire limestone and gritstone. A technical taste of what was to come was the first 6b move on limestone, on his desperate new route Pumpwater at Malham Cove. After this he developed the horrific Langcliffe Quarry in the Ribble valley near Settle. There he did the hardest route on the crag, The Sickler, E3, in 1970. It was described in the 1985 guide as 'very bold and impressive' and in the introduction to the guide, which is a tribute to Livesey's steadiness under fire while using loose limestone holds, it says rather grimly:

'One wonders if the crag is just a vertical extension of the tip at the bottom.'

Even in the graded list at the back of the guide-book the writer's black humour referred to all climbs at Langcliffe Quarry as being E8 and above (a grade above our present system).

Relentless training gave Livesey hidden reserves of finger strength which prompted him to write about:

'Having the strength not just to climb the route, but to hang around long enough to select and place your running belays and then have the strength to go on climbing.'

This was a new approach, compared to that of some previous stars who had used aid then had a memory lapse. Livesey summed up his own cavalier attitude to protection:

'I always climb better with no protection...although you'd take a long fall if you fell off.'

Opposite: Wild seas boiling below the Wen Slab, Gogarth. The climbers are on A Dream of White Horses.
Photo: Chris Jackson.

Even on climbing walls he developed training with a difference; instead of continuously doing hard problems he did long traverses at a slightly easier standard to increase his stamina, thus anticipating the damage that would be caused to tendons and joints by continual hard problems.

In 1974 Pete Livesey aimed a double-edged swipe at climbing standards in both the Lake District and North Wales, with two super-routes that were to intimidate and inspire the climbing world. In Borrowdale during April he made a supreme effort and climbed Footless Crow, an E5, which was by far the hardest route in the Lake District at that time. He followed this up with a stunning ascent of the Right Wall of Dinas Cromlech in North Wales — also graded as E5. These two routes were the first of their grade and more importantly they had an almost complete lack of the necessary protection which everyone would have thought necessary for such a step forward. With a lack of modesty which was justified Livesey said:

"I was doing routes that were more sustained and bolder than any routes that had been done before."

His ascent of Right Wall in June overshadowed everything else done in Wales that year and indeed for some years to come. The climbing world was staggered and Welsh climbers were both piqued and envious that a Yorkshire climber could descend on their cliffs and raise the standard of Welsh climbing on a seemingly bare wall.

Livesey had approached his ascent of Right Wall in a thoroughly modern manner by first abseiling down it twice to prise off loose rock and inspect the few meagre holds. On his first attempt he got up the unprotected first section and reached the ledge on the girdle traverse in a tremendous burst. There he tied off the ropes and soloed up the last easy pitch of Cemetery Gates. Clearly still worried he decided on another abseil inspection of the unclimbed top part of the route, just to make sure of the difficulty. He also practised some of the alternatives on the rope before he pulled down the ropes tocomplete his ascent.

In retrospect he thought the route not so much technical, as fierce, with difficult route-finding, poor protection and few resting places. He advised anyone who wanted to do it, to abseil down first for a close preview. Obviously on-sight repeats can be much harder, especially if the first ascent details are not available.

Livesey's words about soloing are worth quoting:

'When I first started climbing I soloed everything. Although I had a rope, I didn't put in any protection at all. I never had any equipment either and virtually everything I climbed I was prepared to solo.'

It is interesting that some of his contemporaries, who were not quite as able, had some tremendous falls while soloing. One such incredible experience had already happened in 1970:

'At the beginning of May, Cliff Phillips had a narrow escape when he took a long fall during one of his bold soloing exploits. A slip on the third pitch of Black Foot, on the right wing of Dinas Mot, resulted in a fall of at least two hundred feet to the scree below, His injuries were numerous, the most painful being two cracks in his pelvis, but despite these he inched his way down to the road and drove himself to Nant Peris where he collapsed over the wheel, unconscious. He was found around midnight. An impressive display of will-power!'

It it interesting to examine some of the soloing exploits from earlier times until more

recently:

1927	Ivan Waller	Belle Vue Bastion
1931	Colin Kirkus	Pinnacle Wall
1932	Maurice Linnell	Curving Crack, pitch 1
1938	David Cox	Spiral Route
1942	Wilf Noyce	Curving Crack
1947	Peter Harding	Spectre
1948	Mervyn Hughes	Overlapping Wall
1957	John Streetly	Ochre Groove
c1965	Joe Griffin	Diagonal
1969	Richard McHardy	Vector and Overhanging Arete
1969	Eric Jones	Grasper, Fang, Hardd, Cemetery Gates and The Thing
1969	Cliff Phillips	White Slab
1970	Richard McHardy	Woubits
1970	Alan Rouse	Suicide Wall and The Boldest
1970	Cliff Phillips	Pellagra
1971	Pete Minks	Mangoletsi
1972	Jim Perrin	Cenotaph Corner and Hangover
1975	Pete Livesey	The Groove
1976	Alec Sharp	Hand Traverse and The Troach
1976	Henry Barber	A Dream of White Horses
		The Strand
1978	Ron Fawcett	November and The Shadow
		Big Groove
1980	Phil Burke	The Mongoose
1981	Steve Haston	The Weirpig
1982	Andy Pollitt	Great Wall (Forwyn), Quickstep
1982	Phil Davidson	Right Wall
1983	Jerry Moffatt	Cenotaph Corner, Memory Lane, Foil, Left Wall, Right Wall (all five routes in an afternoon) Curving Arete and Great Wall
1984	Andy Pollitt	Firefly, Price of Gold, Solid Gold, After the Goldrush, Clear White Light, Excursion (descended), Silver Surfer (on sight), Prospectors (2nd ascent, on-sight). All routes done in one afternoon.
1984	Martin Atkinson	Fingerlicker (pitch 1)
1984	Phil Davidson	Cockblock

Climbers have always felt an inner urge to solo routes in order to experience a freedom of movement not normally known — without the usual encumbrances of ropes, harnesses, slings etc. It is only incredible that more people have not died during such exploits. All that is needed is for a key hold to break off suddenly and even the world's best climber could be gone in an instant. As climbers push soloing to the top technical level the inevitable will happen one day.

Returning to Livesey it is interesting to note his analysis of the problems of climbing a crack in his article 'I Feel Rock'.

Opposite: Pete Livesey soloing on Sickle, Clogwyn y Grochan.   Photo: John Sheard.

'From bottom to top a crack demands unending attention to movement, that is at the same time delicate yet strenuous, dynamic yet slow and balanced. Every foot requires something different of a climber. Every movement is deliberate and worthwhile. A knee or arm too far out and the layback doesn't work, or balance is lost. Too far in and you begin to swing outwards slowly but irrevocably: in three or four seconds, finger friction will be lost and you'll be away.'

As a true Yorkshireman living in his home county Livesey preferred to spend most of his leisure hours on his home crags and only occasionally went to Wales. Nevertheless, high ambition, ability and strong nerves made him the top climber in Wales whenever he cared to visit, and during his descent of Llanberis Pass he could always look up at the Right Wall of Dinas Cromlech, the scene of his greatest triumph where he broke through to new standards of difficulty.

Livesey's total number of new routes was very small compared with that of anyone before him, and whereas there had been dozens or even hundreds of new routes from people such as Joe Brown, the contribution made by Livesey centred on quality rather than quantity — just like Whillans before him. Just as remarkable was the fact that Livesey was not part of an established group such as the Rock and Ice or Alpha. By his sheer drive and determination he had forced himself to the top of the heap rather like rhubarb shoots under a bucket or in a dark shed.

On one occasion the Yorkshire hard men were attracted to Craig y Llyn, a disjointed crag above the lake in Nant Gwynant. The crag looks as if it has been assembled in a hurry and keeps on turning at right angles to itself in a distinctly perturbing manner. Most people tend to be put off but there were gems in wait for those with the ability. Gomersall and Livesey eyed the possibilities and promptly attacked the bold first pitch of Sybilla the Pun which gives access via a quartz break to a square-cut roof and an impressive crack. This was to be the first new route since several lines by Trevor Jones in the sixties.

It was left to Livesey to produce one of the longest pitches in Wales, not quite the hardest, but typical of the man. It was to be a thin bold pitch up the main unclimbed part of the crag. It was the sort of place to which Livesey naturally gravitated and after some long stretches Wailing Wall, E4 6a, provided a two-star route as a counterblast to the Gogarth entertainment. The Yorkshiremen also had a Chance Encounter on Craig y Llyn to give a poorly protected pitch with excellent climbing and the ascent was nicely rounded off by Bonny Masson, the third member of the team. John Sheard, a close climbing friend of Livesey, summed up the great man's technique rather aptly:

'His completely free solo of Tensor at Tremadog in Hush Puppies (suede shoes) will take some beating. The thing was typical of Livesey — of his ability, his humour, his competitiveness. He was supposed to be seconding me — a rare occurrence — and I took the rope in ever faster, until the free unattached end appeared at my feet, to be followed shortly afterwards by Pete...

...With this sort of confidence plus the ability to press forward, move after committing move, on very hard and unknown ground...

Not that he has the sort of style which attracts attention. At first acquaintance his stance on steep rock seems to be dictated primarily by knobbly three-inch knee-caps and a permanent awareness of a rear end thrust out as far as possible...

He is not an exceptional exponent of thrutchy crack climbing; his talents really come to the fore in steep face climbing with very small hand and footholds. This is where his well-developed finger and arm strength pays dividends, while his footwork is always so confident and positive that the moves often appear far easier than they really are.'

Opposite: Nigel Riddington alone on The Right Wall, Dinas Cromlech.   Photo: Paul Williams.

It would be wrong to leave 1975 without mentioning the ubiquitous Rowland Edwards. Single-handedly he started to develop the limestone cliffs which encrusted the Great and Little Orme where a frightening big overhang at its base had been formed by millions of years of sea washing. Not put off by dense vegetation and guano he enthusiastically set to work gardening potential new routes on an abseil rope. One of them was Detritus which gave a six-hundred-foot route on the enormous wall of the Little Orme. He dug out Detritus over an extended period of time with five separate companions: Leo Dickinson, Pete Minks, Nigel Horne, Brian Molyneux and Cliff Phillips. Eventually as if he couldn't wait any longer he returned to solo the route.

After spending long hours abseiling and jumaring up his rope afterwards, Edwards was unaware that the serrated cams on his jumars had been worn down as a consequence of the sliding action of the rope which had abraded the soft aluminium. On one typical gardening day he started using his jumar clamps, but they failed almost immediately, though they were still attached to the rope. Rowland slid faster and faster down the rope, luckily stopping at the knotted end which prevented him from plunging into the sea which was waiting below.

From 1969 to 1978 Edwards produced at least fifty-five new routes on the Ormes and Craig y Forwyn — thus developing a whole new climbing area almost single-handed. It is hard to believe that at that time the rest of the Welsh climbing fraternity was almost totally unaware of what was going on, and those who did know casually dismissed what they had heard as not being very important. Today the area merits a guide-book all to itself.

One cold winter's day in December, Edwards took two future Presidents of the Climbers' Club up Tartarean in the Great Zawn. Derek Walker, who was in no fit state to climb, having been in bed with influenza until that morning, was persuaded by Trevor Jones to go to the Little Orme solely for health reasons. Suddenly Walker found himself tied onto the end of the rope with Jones ensconced as middle man. After six freezing hours of climbing, darkness came, just as Walker was about to start the unprotected and scary traverse to reach Jones and Edwards who were belayed safely to a fat piton. Walker managed to do the traverse but relations between himself and Jones were somewhat frosty for several weeks.

In 1975 and 1976 Edwards put up his best and most spectacular route, New Dimensions. This brilliant E3 needed some aid when he first did it, but he soon returned to remove the metallic intrusions to give one of the best climbs on North Wales limestone at that time.

During the years 1974 and 1975 one of Edwards old haunts, Craig Cwm Trwsgl, had been extensively developed by Jim Perrin, who discovered several excellent climbs, including the classic three-star slab of The Exterminating Angel. On the E3 5c crux he found himself committed and faced with the prospect of a ground-fall when it started to rain. From a wrong-footed position he jumped for the only hold in sight — a side-pull — and went on to complete the pitch.

Although 1974 had been Livesey's great year, Alec Sharp, an undergraduate from Bangor University began to make some impressive inroads on the climbing scene. On Dinas Mot he bagged two new routes, The Windmill and Ten Degrees North — an obvious line which many climbers had had their eyes on. It was not long before his interest turned to Gogarth where he was not only to make several useful contributions

Opposite Above: Vector Buttress, Bwlch y Moch, Tremadog.   Photo: Alan Hinkes.
Opposite Below: 1st ascent of Void on the Ochre Slab.   Photo: Rowland Edwards.

Opposite: Rowland Edwards making the 1st ascent of Void, Vector Buttress.
Above: Paul Williams and Jim Moran on the headwall of Void.

Photo: P. Kershaw.
Photo: Steve Ashton.

but he also wrote a guide to the cliff after doing the Cloggy guide. He started off with The Camel, a strenuous and steep route, so called because it was near The Needle (a biblical reference to the impossibility of getting a camel through the eye of a needle). With fellow maths student, Steve Humphries, he tried a route through the impressive and unclimbed overhangs of Yellow Wall. On the long initial pitch they eventually had to retreat because it got dark.

When they returned to make a start on the second pitch a complete slab, on which Sharp was standing, started to break away just as he stepped off it. It was instantly dislodged from the cliff and crashed into the sea far below. Shortly afterwards, a loose hold that Sharp had needed to use on the crux moves snapped off suddenly when Humphries tried to use it. The rock was unpredictable and the tension must have been high — they retreated again. Perhaps not surprisingly, when they returned a week later, they placed two protection pegs by abseil before completing a superb climb called Creeping Lemma. When thoroughly cleaned it proved to be surprisingly reasonable with only two very short hard sections.

1975 saw an upsurge again, and it was Sharp's turn to fight back for Welsh climbers. In an exceptional leap in his standard he eliminated all five points of aid that Alan Rouse had used on the first ascent of Positron four years earlier. Sharp's free ascent thus gave Wales its second true E5.

Just to show that Right Wall was not a flash in the pan and that he was still in contention, Livesey produced Fingerlicker, an E4 at Tremadog. It was exceptionally strenuous and eventually even Livesey's strong fingers gave out. As a way out of the problem he had to resort to yo-yo tactics and lowered to the ground from his runners. After resting he made another effort but it took two yo-yos to force the crux pitch. Although at that time there was much criticism of this ascent Livesey did give a degree of respectability to the yo-yo technique which has come more and more to the fore for desperate routes. As technical standards have increased, the margin of safety during desperate moves has become wafer-thin and the yo-yo enables leaders to make calculated and precarious moves to finish off a difficult sequence.

It was the year of Sharp's finals at university and he celebrated with another E4 on his Gogarth home ground. It was fittingly named Graduation Ceremony but this was not the end. Later in the year Sharp added a fine twin route to his free ascent of Positron with the sensational Ordinary Route, another E5. It was a tongue-in-cheek name given after the easy route of the same name on the Milestone Buttress in Ogwen. The route involved a very hard traverse across the most impressively steep part of the Main Cliff. That made two E5s from Sharp and although the protection on them had been adequate, the same could not be said of Right Wall when it was done.

Rowland Edwards, who was close to the end of his tremendous contributions to Welsh climbing, ascended Groove of Horror, an E5 on Craig Pant Ifan at Tremadog. It is extremely strenuous and not often repeated, but it was typical of the audacious Edwards and to be expected from a man who finished off his West Buttress Girdle Traverse on the Black Cliff when he was still in plaster.

It was a restless but fruitful year for Edwards as, not content with limestone triumphs, he beavered away at routes on Clogwyn du'r Arddu and in the Pass. Something about his new-route construction often gave the lines an immediate classic status. In particular, the

Opposite: The strength-sapping crack of Fingerlicker, Craig Pant Ifan. Mike Owen climbing.   Photo: Gavin Peat.

Above: Pete Livesey taking a breather below Zukator.
Opposite: Pete Livesey making the 1st free ascent of Zukator, Craig Bwlch y Moch.

Photo: John Sheard.
Photo: John Sheard.

overhanging Vector Buttress had not had a proper new free route for some ten years. Edwards saw a potential direttissima on it and he constructed a superb three-pitch route which opened up the head-wall to give Void. Even though a point of aid was used on the crux, which was eliminated by Ron Fawcett the next year, Void was undoubtedly the best effort by Edwards at Tremadog. The route immediately became classic and as popular with young hard climbers as Vector had been fifteen years before.

Edwards returned to the Pass and turned his attention to the left wall of Cenotaph Corner which was just waiting for a breakthrough. The brilliant Left Wall was free-climbed by Adrian Garlick from Glossop in 1970, pre-dating the well-known free ascent of the American climbers Steve Wunsch by two years. It was then left for Edwards to snatch the companion route, Resurrection. Although it needed a small amount of aid to do it at the time Resurrection is one of the three-star routes of the Pass. When Peter Livesey freed the route later, in 1975, it put another E4 route into the record books.

Dave Pearce who had taken part in routes such as A Dream of White Horses and T Rex then added Lungfish on Craig y Rhaeadr with Nick Estcourt in 1974 prior to teaming up with Paul Trower for The Cow a powerful companion route to The Moon in 1976.

A very young Yorkshire climber appeared on the scene in 1976 and it was not very long before Ron Fawcett surfaced at the top of the Welsh pyramid, a position he still occupies. He started climbing when he was only fourteen in 1969, and almost immediately he began to lead Very Severes which was still quite respectable in those days — and even more so for one so young. He was hungry to get to the top and in the impatience of extreme youth he fell off while trying a new route at Malham Cove. It was a sixty-foot frightener, but fortunately he landed in a tree and escaped with a cut hand. When it had healed, after a lengthy break from climbing, he returned to produce Mulatto Wall — an impressive E3.

He left school at sixteen and went to work for a roofing firm in Skipton, but after a few months he fell through a roof and fractured his skull and shoulder. After recovery he found that he had lost some mobility in his left arm, although this did not seem to deter him in the least. Like Livesey he trained intensively from the start and can do two hundred press-ups straight off and endeavours to climb hundreds of feet of rock every day of the year.

Even before his entry onto the Welsh scene he went to the Vercors and soloed the Livanos route on the Rochers d'Archaine, a 1,600-foot route that had pitches of VI, VI superior as well as artificial pitches. Fawcett did the whole climb before a French party, who had started at the same time, had even finished the first pitch.

When Fawcett made the long-awaited second ascent of Right Wall he had really arrived in Wales. He went on to free Void of its piton in 1976 and increased the hardest grade on the Vector head-wall to E3. On Mayday Peter Livesey teamed up with Fawcett to share leads on Cream, the first E4 on Vector Buttress — thus raising the standard another notch.

Livesey and Fawcett climbed two very hard new routes in Wen Zawn on the same day. Broken Mirror takes the centre of the Uhuru Wall while High Pressure follows the slab between Wen and Quartz Icicle. Livesey, who was never one to miss a chance of adding to his reputation, wrote:

'We did an extremely brief cleaning abseil down both routes, then climbed them. Both required further cleaning en route, together with modifications in the original concept of the line. I was shit-scared leading the first half of mine, and Ron was shit-scared leading the first half of his. I was really annoyed seconding Ron's because it was hard and he couldn't possibly have led it unless he'd got really good, and Ron was really annoyed seconding mine, because it was so hard that nobody would lead it without runners.'

Livesey had already arrived but Ron was still climbing his way up, but neither of them at that time was a slavish devotee of the crag in the way that previous pioneers had been. Gogarth has a peculiar aura about it brought about by a combination of the sea and the seeming looseness of the holds. It is not surprising that they had qualms. Considering this, the fact that they did the two new routes in the same day, one of them called High Pressure, perhaps gives some idea of the competitive edge that was urging them both on for their individual and joint reputations on this major sea cliff. As in the case of Brown and Whillans two leading climbers were combining to make the maximum use of their talents.

Livesey soloed a lot of routes of the highest standard so it is not surprising that his great friend and rival Ron Fawcett also carried the concept of solo climbing as far as he dared, causing him to write later:

'To me it is the prime method of climbing, to be free of the snagging rope, rack of runners and the weight of both. I soloed bigger and better things including November and The Shadow on Clog., both E3. We had done Great Wall, Silhouette and Medi — and Gibby wanted a doss in the sun. As I hadn't done either Vember or November I plodded up the Drainpipe Crack to where the routes divide. Tom Jones had just strolled up November so I went for that. I find the worst situation to be in is where you have to totally commit yourself on a series of moves that you couldn't reverse. Luckily November was nowhere near like that, it was just very satisfying.

On another occasion I happened to be at Gogarth on my own, so I wandered along the sea-level traverse wondering if I dared solo Big Groove. I had only done the route once before and I remember finding it desperate with the top peg for aid. The thin little corner above was where I had my last grip so I knew that it did go in that direction, right foot in the groove, left foot out on nothing. I was sure that there must be a good crack in the back because there was no peg in now. I could hardly get my finger-tips in. I kept trying to bridge up, gain a little ground, but my foot was slipping or so I had convinced myself. Luckily my left hand groped out onto the rib, a super little finger-hold appeared, a quick pull and I was on the ledge.'

To prove his point on a wet week-end on Gogarth he did seventeen Hard Very Severes and Extremes, including Mammoth and Left-Hand Red Wall. On another occasion while soloing over twenty routes he even got up the first two pitches of Positron, then not surprisingly felt slightly tired and came down again!

Livesey dropped in to have a look at Craig y Forwyn, a limestone cliff in Rowland Edwards's bailiwick. Just after he had done Cream at Tremadog, Livesey freed Great Wall to give one of the finest pitches on Welsh limestone. One can only wonder what Edwards thought when he turned up at the crag to discover that Livesey was already half-way up this magnificent route. In all the major new routes better protection meant less risk and consequently this was then counterbalanced by a rise in standards to keep the risk level to roughly what it was before.

The most ubiquitous climber on the Welsh scene, Pat Littlejohn, returned to Gogarth to put up a companion route to Pagan with Redshift. Unfortunately this happened during

Opposite: An airy belay on The Appian Way, Castell y Gwynt.   Photo: Rowland Edwards.

the normal voluntary ban on Red Wall during the nesting season and Littlejohn was met at the top of the crag by an enraged ornithologist. Littlejohn politely suggested that the signs should be made clearer and left the birds and the red-faced ornithologist to ponder his new route.

Although chalk started to be used in 1975 and the criticism inevitably began the issue did not blow up straight away. Geoff Milburn recalled:

'It was the hottest June for over 50 years and Moran was determined to go to the Roaches. I literally had to drag him to Wales to get to Cloggy. Coming down from The Mostest we ran into two young climbers, John Allen and Chris Addy, who had just freed Great Wall — but with chalk. Nevertheless it was a tremendous achievement and they were so casual that we did not learn of the event for some time.'

1976 however was the year of the great chalk controversy and opinions polarised round younger climbers who favoured it and predictably the older generation who rejected it. Geographically the Lake District and the Peak District were sympathetic to its use, Wales was firmly against it, whereas the South-West and of course Scotland remained neutral. However, the use of chalk was here to stay, despite all the rumblings from the Establishment, the has-beens and the old campaigners.

Only three years after Pete Livesey broke through into the rarified atmosphere of an E5 grading, Clogwyn du'r Arddu was lifted into the modern era with another route on the Great Wall of the East Buttress. This awe-inspiring route, Midsummer Night's Dream, E6 6b, was solved by Lakeland climbers, Pete Whillance and Dave Armstrong. Whillance originally came from Manchester and started climbing on gritstone, but eventually went to live in the Lake District in 1974. He was immediately aware of the shattering blow that Livesey had dealt to established Lakeland traditions by his ascent of Footless Crow. Whillance then stepped forward to steady everyone. Perhaps it seems fitting that his near-namesake Whillans had occupied a similar leading position when he had increased technical standards twenty years earlier. There is no doubt that Whillance learnt from Livesey's techniques and soon put up a route on Deer Bield Crag, neatly summing up his competitive attitude by calling it Take it to the Limit. This cool-headed and daring Lakeland climber picked Clogwyn du'r Arddu for his immortal contribution to Welsh climbing.

The first pitch of Midsummer Night's Dream goes up the increasingly steep smoothness on the right of Great Wall. On ripples and the tiniest of rugosities one of the steadiest minds in the climbing world was needed to put it all together for the big lead. Fortunately there was a 'bolt' in one of the most precarious places on the first pitch, put in by Drummond on his aided ascent of this section which received so much justified derision when it was done. Whillance fell some sixty to seventy feet during some desperate moves and eventually fell on the bolt. Luckily the rope stopped him near the ground, but the snatch bounced him back up causing him to hit his head under a small overhang so that he bit his tongue badly and lacerated his hands at the same time.

After resting from his injuries he again attacked the unclimbed pitch and yet again he fell off, but fortunately this time with no further injuries. After another rest it was third time lucky and he completed the big 6b pitch. Although he had to return later to finish the climb, the tremendous first pitch was a great step forward in Welsh wall-climbing in its own right. Again it was an outsider who set a new standard — just as Livesey had done.

In the summer Whillance often gave up his job as a scaffolder in order to devote time to training and climbing, often training every night mid-week in the summer. It is of interest to note the rather telling words that Whillance had to say about the contribution that Livesey had made to climbing:

'Quite a few in the Lakes say that Livesey never instigated any new move in the 70s and there was no real increase in the grade...But I was there and I know differently. He's done so much and he brought a new approach...he was going to push standards...go for the hard lines and he stood on his own and went for them.'

By 1977 Geoff Milburn's Llanberis Pass guide was at an advanced stage and the Pass cliffs started to rear their heads again as teams began to see that if Livesey could grab gems such as Memory Lane and Foil on the Cromlech then there must be far more possibilities just waiting. Although far-away cliffs were often the scene of frenzied activity and excessive adulation it was never for any great length of time. Tremadog, Gogarth, Llech Ddu...all of them had their day, but the Llanberis Pass always returned with another route and another hard man who would inch up the standards on another piece of blank-looking rock previously thought of as being impossible.

One of the most gifted climbers of 1977 was Dave Roberts, unusual in that he was a Welsh climber from Wrexham. It was the time of maximum work on the Dinorwic Dam project on which Dave was an employee; there was good money too. However, it was the elite employees, the Swedish drillers at the rock face deep inside Elidyr Fawr, who would make £15,000 a year. That was a lot of money in 1977, and they were made very welcome in the pubs of Llanberis.

Dave Roberts started at the beginning of 1977 as a very modest climber who could lead E2 comfortably, but during the long winter nights he climbed continually on the Llangefni climbing-wall. It had spectacularly beneficial effects and he increased his leading grade by a dramatic three E notches in about six weeks. In July he made the fourth ascent of Right Wall then half an hour later nonchalantly led Memory Lane without putting runners in Left Wall which was the common practice for protecting the route at that time. Roberts's rather laid-back approach was typified by an evening's climbing in the Pass after a day's work on the dam project.

After doing most of Nexus he decided to have a look at Nexus Direct which had only been done previously with the aid of several pitons. It had already been cleaned by Jim Moran, who paused before trying it because of the lack of protection and the blankness of the groove which rather bafflingly refused to indicate where Crew's original aid pegs had been. Roberts made a completely free ascent of the route which is now considered to be E5 6b, and it was probably the first major route ever to be done in the evening after a day's work. There is no doubt that at that time Roberts was one of the most gifted and elegant leaders who was capable of doing routes of the highest calibre.

Jim Moran a tough gritstone climber from the Peak District began to have a pronounced effect on the Welsh climbing scene in 1977. Stocky in appearance, with round steel-framed spectacles and an infectious grin, he was to become one of the most enthusiastic of rock-climbers. When the conversation turns to hard climbing Jim's blink rate goes to zero like a housewife hypnotised by supermarket bargains. His face flushes with a glow of enthusiasm at the very mention of a hard route, a desperate climb, or

P. 224: Phil Davidson soloing the Great Wall, Craig y Forwyn.   Photo: Mike Owen.
P. 225: Strenuous moves to overcome the roof of Gritstone Gorilla, Great Orme. This route by Paul Williams did much to make the Ormes a popular climbing area.   Photo: Paul Williams.
Opposite: Dave Lee going strongly on A Midsummer Night's Dream, Clogwyn du'r Arddu.   Photo: Paul Williams.

someone else's keenness.

He had come to the forefront in 1976 when, with Simon Horrox and Geoff Milburn, he ticked off a host of hard routes including what was at the time believed to be the first complete lead of The Skull in its free form, but Ray Evans and Hark Pasquil had shared leads to free the route in 1975. Moran teamed up with Al Evans that summer and impressed everyone by his spectacular fortnight on Cloggy during a perfect summer. Crags magazine recorded:

'A young Manchester climber Jim Moran had an amazing fortnight recently when he achieved an almost complete wipe-out of Cloggy. He made ascents in pure style of Great Wall, Woubits Left-Hand, Curving Arete, The Boldest, Jelly Roll, Silhouette, West Buttress Eliminate and several more. Considering that some of the routes Moran climbed were among the highest-rated in Wales it is interesting to note that his rampage stopped on his return to Derbyshire.'

Moran began a determined campaign of seeking new routes in 1977 with lines such as Quasar, The Molehill and Curfew. Quasar was a brilliant E3 crack-line just right of Hangover on the Grochan. On these routes Moran was just beginning to find his feet and this was merely a beginning. He was a rock athlete like Fawcett and Livesey, not quite up to their standards, but nevertheless he was still a superb and prolific innovator. Although already firmly bracketed as a rock gymnast he was on one occasion seen on the Devil's Kitchen cliffs on a superb winter's day when the ice was in a magnificent condition. All round dozens of teams were enjoying themselves. Moran came down from his ice route, looked up at the cliff which was decorated with chandeliers of beautiful blue and white ice, and said with some feeling:

"You can keep all this stuff, I'm going back to gritstone right now."

Above: Jim Moran seconding the big pitch on Freebird, Castell Helen.
Opposite: John Codling in an impressive position on Stroll On, Clogwyn y Grochan.

Photo: Al Evans.
Photo: C. Griffiths.

Years Of The Big Men

1978 was the year of the big bang when North Wales exploded into new galaxies of starred routes on both the sea cliffs and in the mountains. It was undoubtedly Jim Moran's year as out of seventy-eight new routes on Gogarth Jim was on 35 of them, usually in the lead. When he was only 17, with Gabe Regan, he had done the first free ascent of Spectrum on Clogwyn y Grochan, the first of many routes that he was to free of steel. As an apprentice tool-maker from Glossop, Derbyshire, he habitually climbed on the factory wall where he worked during his lunch breaks, making sure he took his chalk bag to work every day.

Geoff Milburn, climbing historian, organiser and guide-writer, Jim's close climbing friend in Glossop, had introduced Jim to most of the Welsh crags over a four-year period and together they ticked off many of the standard hard Welsh routes. Moran had his sights firmly fixed on only the top routes and while discussing which crag to go to, he would inevitably raise every possible objection until eventually they went to the crag he really wanted to visit for his latest big route.

With a forthcoming guide in mind Milburn started the purge of aid from the cliffs in the Llanberis Pass and with good publicity in a very short time it reduced from 90 to 18 points of aid. Moran, an enthusiastic convert, got a real gem on Cyrn Las when with Dave Hollows he freed the heavily-aided route Black Mamba which was controversially renamed Times Past to reflect a changing attitude.

Moran conceived an ambition to do fifty new routes a year and for some time Wales was to be his happy hunting ground, until on his return to Derbyshire he was brought to an abrupt halt when up against the top talent. Like Littlejohn, he too was mocked and laughed at for not being quite equal to the top stars, but Wales showed him to be a big cliff man. As he said:

"On the big cliffs you need experience and brains to get you and your mate off when things go wrong. To have credibility for your own new routes you've got to repeat the big routes first — a sort of entrance exam — Positron, Midsummer Night's Dream, Hall of Warriors...People such as Livesey you look up to, like everyone used to with Brown and Whillans. You've got to have determination and interest in what you're doing, it's no good having new route megalomania, you've got to be inspired by your peers, the big men."

With an eye to getting a few good lines Milburn had collected together some large photographs of Gogarth from Ken Wilson and these proved invaluable to work out whole clusters of potential new routes. On Barbarossa, Moran's best new route, which is on the Upper Tier of Gogarth, Al Evans had had the initial inspiration to abseil down to clean it thoroughly of loose rock and vegetation so that it was in a condition for Moran to lead it. Initially Moran had thought that the route was impossible, so Evans placed a protection peg in the middle of the first hard section which prompted Moran to try it after a closer abseil inspection. He first tried it on a searingly hot day when everyone else was on Cloggy, and the sun reflected off the dazzling white rock in a similar way to the Verdon cliffs, in the South of France. The line had been tried many years before when

Dave Pearce saw someone who was stoically trying to bolt his way up. Dave's increasingly enraged shouts eventually persuaded the mechanical monster to give up his unwelcome intrusion onto Gogarth. On Moran's first unsuccessful attempt on Barbarossa, to quote Geoff Milburn:

'Chalk cascaded down in handfuls and Jim got really angry as the heat sapped his energy slowly but surely. After a whole series of short falls he finally had to admit defeat and was lowered off bruised and bloody. The runners were all removed by abseil, but next day he was back in the cool of the morning.'

Moran had had to dislodge several large blocks during cleaning, some of them into the neighbouring Bloody Chimney, where a leader who was already at work thought that his time had come, but fortunately the blocks missed him. On the successful lead there were no such problems and Barbarossa, which is perhaps Moran's greatest effort, has been described as bringing boulder problem techniques to Gogarth.

On a day when Joe Brown and Ben Wintringham were discovering Smurf Zawn at the southern end of the cliffs Geoff Milburn persuaded Moran and Evans to have a look at the prominent wall which sticks out into the sea to the left of Parliament House Cave. It turned out to be almost virgin and Geoff later described their reaction in his article 'The Gold Rush'.

'Sitting on the old cannons in the zawn we just couldn't believe our luck. Why hadn't Joe been there long before? Even the coastguard was pleased to see us and provided ace brews to keep us going. Nice 'n Sleazy, Talking Heads, South Sea Bubble...the routes kept coming one after the other.'

Rather optimistically Al Evans cleared a 10-foot swathe of rock by brushing away the lichen and the team top-roped it in some awe. With much hilarity Evans and Milburn hatched a plot to casually leak the news that this was the biggest and most serious unclimbed pitch in Wales. Little did they imagine then the events that would in time follow. The news filtered through the grapevine quickly and both Ron Fawcett and Pete Whillance, having heard the whisper, turned up at the same time to have a look at the wall.

After the initial brushing by Evans, two holds had been chipped on the route, but the culprit could not be traced despite much speculation and some acrimony. If that was not bad enough Fawcett made the decision to place two protection bolts by abseil before leading the pitch. It was almost a similar situation to Crew's bolt placement on The Boldest fourteen years before and it provoked almost as much controversial discussion in the pubs and cafes of Llanberis. Fawcett called his route The Cad which seemed an appropriate name.

Perhaps the bolts gnawed at Fawcett overnight for next day he put up a necky 6b pitch next to Barbarossa and the serious nature of the route tends to diminish the two-bolt indiscretion on The Cad. Certainly Blackleg was a route to command great respect from leaders but it was only given a grudging star in the guide. Later John Redhead wrote in his article on North Stack:

'Fawcett placed two bolts on his route The Cad, E5 6a, behind the back of his main competitor Whillance. The latter finding himself outrageously burnt off, repeated the route chopping the first bolt and finding the rock palatable, forged his own line leftwards from The Cad's start to give The Long Run, E5 6a.'

Opposite: Forcing the intimidating wall of Barbarossa during the 1st ascent.   Photo: Al Evans.

Just after the ascent of Barbarossa, Jim Moran went to Castell Cidwm to attempt to free Tramgo. Jim had read with awe the account that after the first ascent Joe brown had been unable to raise his hands above his head on account of the exhausting and demanding nature of the climb. Edgar Siddall's picture of Joe on the overhanging section gave Jim visual inspiration and he managed a free ascent of Tramgo just in time, as a tremendous thunderstorm burst shortly after he had reached the top. During the storm communication became impossible and Horrox battled upwards while Milburn froze in a thin T-shirt on top. Moran, who had descended, sheltered warmly under the overhangs below the route and idly noticed an inviting crack just to the right of Tramgo which he stored away in his new-route memory bank.

Pat Littlejohn returned to Gogarth in 1978 to attend an International Meet at Plas y Brenin where all the stars were gathered. He discovered that climbers such as Livesey, Fawcett and Gomersall were doing routes two grades harder than he himself was doing. Livesey had also been free-climbing routes which had previously been aided, some of which were Pat's. Livesey delivered a lecture on training, the importance of finger strength, and the proper racking of gear so that in positions of extremis valuable seconds would not be lost in searching for the right sort of nut. Instead of being blown away by the star-spangled opposition Pat went back home to Cardiff and started to train on rock walls. His standard increased a grade and a half in two months and he too then began to repeat his own new routes without aid. Littlejohn gradually got better and his new routes became more impressive. Not surprisingly the mocking comments about him died away.

The elfin Littlejohn made one of his lightning visits to Gogarth to tackle the most impressive wall which already housed Mammoth. He produced a mind-bending E5 route through the roofs with two more pitches after that to give a three-hundred-foot, three-star route called Hunger. Littlejohn rightly took his place amongst the great ones such as Livesey and Fawcett. Livesey subsequently tried Hunger and failed on it. It was right that Pat should have the last laugh. As Littlejohn neither inspected routes nor practised moves prior to an ascent — new routes were much harder for him. An on-sight lead of a hard route where there has been no prior knowledge is much harder mentally as one neither knows where the protection is likely to be nor how long a difficult sequence of moves is likely to last. Hunger had to wait some time for Jim Moran to repeat it.

Al Evans must take most of the credit for developing the beautiful reddish-coloured head-wall to the right of the solid part of Castell Helen which contains Blanco, Rap and Pel. The first new route was Freebird, a long diagonal line which took Evans two days to clean. On May Day, Evans and Siddiqui joined forces with Moran and Milburn for North West Passage which was an instant three-star classic on account of the superb position of its steep top pitch of 140 feet.

One of Al Evans's other fine routes, and certainly his hardest at Gogarth, was Aardvark which was so called because he wanted it to be the first route in the guide-book index. It took a line up a big wall at the very start of the main cliff and Evans failed several times on the 6a crux. Moran politely declined to have a go wishing to leave it for his friend but as Ben Wintringham was just itching to try it Evans went back to the attack. This time he found the solution and overcame the fingery problem to leave a route which is very popular when it is impossible to get along the sea-level traverse.

Opposite: John Redhead making a difficult sequence of moves on The Cad, North Stack, Gogarth.   Photo: Paul Airey.

Several other climbers played a prominent role in the scramble for new routes on Gogarth. Ben Wintringham clocked up a hefty tally on the cliff, climbing mainly with his wife, Marion. Some of his best new routes were Anarchist, Stimulator, Mayfair and on Red Wall, Infidel and the fine Fantasia. Pete Whillance and Dave Armstrong also found choice lines with Energy Crisis and Blue Peter while Dave Knighton concentrated more on the Upper Tier with a series of fine lines such as Run Fast Run Free, The Emotionary and Street Survivor.

1978 cannot be passed by without mentioning Mick Fowler, a hard character with a bizarre sense of humour, who revels in loose rock and ice. His dedication to ice climbing is shown by an astonishing period during one winter when out of twelve week-ends he went from London on eleven of them to the North of Scotland in search of good ice — round trips of a thousand miles each week-end. This restless all-rounder also developed the crumbling white cliffs of Dover using double ice-axes and front-pointing crampon techniques.

Fowler stamped a firm imprint on 1978 with first the horrific Ludwig, then Heart of Gold on the Left-Hand Red Wall of Gogarth. Prior to this Moran and Pete Whillance had met and discovered that they were both after the same line on Red Wall. They agreed on a compromise by which Moran agreed to leave the route for Whillance to attempt, while Moran made a start on another mutual line elsewhere on the cliffs. Their plans were foiled when Fowler stepped in before Whillance could have a go, and produced Heart of Gold which seems to suggest that Fowler may have felt just a touch of irony when naming the route.

Thirty miles away in Llanberis Pass, the Cromlech boulders came under attack. Having originally tumbled from Dinas Cromlech, to reveal the two superb walls of Cenotaph Corner, they came under the scrutiny of a pagan council who wished to blow them up in a senseless road-widening scheme. During the year a fierce campaign was waged by environmentalists to save the boulders but the time came when workmen had actually arrived to perform the desecration. Fortunately fierce opposition was immediately aroused and the Cromlech boulders which have given so much bouldering pleasure and which have been such a scenic delight have remained in their resting place.

Another fierce debate blew up after Jim Moran trundled a few tons of loose rock from Red Wall in order to make a free ascent of Television Route. Geoff Milburn wanted to rename it Land of the Blind to show contempt for the steel desecration of previously untouched rock solely for commercial reasons to pander to the media. Eventually the calm logical arguments of Joe Brown persuaded them that the name Television Route was sensible for identification purposes and so the name was retained.

It is not right to leave 1978 by without looking at that tried and tested crag Tremadog. The flaxen-haired whirlwind Peter Crew had said more than a decade before that apart from the Vector Buttress the rest of the crag should be blown up. Since the early fifties Tremadog has been contemptuously written off as either 'not a proper mountain crag' or merely as 'a heap of choss'. Happily more reasonable younger activists have felt the attraction of this cliff which was once washed by the sea before William Maddocks closed off the water with his embankment in 1807. The crag is still the home of the buzzard, the white-tailed owl and even adders, which can unexpectedly and alarmingly be found asleep on ledges, providing there is some sort of access from the ground.

Opposite: Jim Moran below the bulge on the second ascent of Hunger, Gogarth.   Photo: Paul Williams.

As late as 1978 there was still the odd crack, faint groove and tantalising arete which was left to tempt the climbing entrepreneur who explored the Tremadog area which incorporates all the South Snowdon crags including: Craig y Llyn and Clogwyn y Wenallt in the water-studded Gwynant, as well as Carreg Hyll Drem — the ugly crag, which causes a hiccup in a road from nowhere to nowhere. Despite the great deeds on Gogarth forty miles away the low-lying crags struck back and yielded thirty-four new routes innovated by connoisseurs such as Pete Livesey, Pete Gomersall, Ben Wintringham and Rowland Edwards.

The seventy-eight new-route explosion on Gogarth in 1978 crystallised the minds of the first ascensionists regarding their ethics. In the Climbers' Club Journal Jim Perrin made the comments:

> 'You cannot trust the route descriptions of many of our major pioneers because they provide an account which is conceptual rather than actual; they describe the route not as they have done it, but as they would like it to have been done.'

Strong words, but it typified the opposing forces of the new generation and those who had been the climbers of a few years before. The war raged for some time, but inevitably the old order changed and the new methods slowly and reluctantly became the norm, whereas the older methods of doing first ascents slowly faded away. The people of the fifttes and sixties who had used aid to get up vertical rock with hazardous rock and vegetation were in a curious way vindicated because they too could have done their routes in a similar manner to the modern generation.

Not often is there a development in equipment which revolutionises climbing. The P.A. in the mid-fifties was one such advance. Another was the transition from the inserted chockstone to the metal nut. One unique invention that changed the whole concept of crack-climbing came on the scene in 1978. An American, Ray Jardine, invented Friends, an ugly looking assembly of four spring-loaded serrated cams made from aluminium. The curve on each cam had been worked out by computer analysis so that when the device was placed in a crack a load caused by a falling leader made the cams grip together onto the walls of the crack. Adjustability was not the main advantage; it was the speed with which they could be placed in a desperate crux situation which was the main benefit to hard-pressed leaders. Friends are indispensible for roof cracks or flared cracks which are so prevalent in the Yosemite valley in California — there is no alternative protection. A perfectly straight-sided crack which will not accept an aluminium wedge is also ideal for the placement of Friends. The exhausting pitch of Grond on Dinas Cromlech is a perfect example of this. If a climber were rich enough there would be a safe placement for a Friend every two feet — that is if he had the strength to pause to put them in place. As to historic importance, Friends made the greatest difference to small-width cracks and although there was some initial reluctance, the resistance to them collapsed when it was realised that they could stop a forty-foot fall, and there was a rush to the shops to buy them.

1979 saw nothing like the number of new routes that there had been the previous year but one new route caused a storm of controversy which spilled onto the pages of all the climbing magazines. Amazingly the route was not even in the mainstream of hard climbing and being a mere ninety feet in length hardly seemed a likely candidate for such an explosion.

Opposite Top Left: Al Evans.
Opposite Top Right: Jim Moran aged 17 on Castell Helen.   Photo: Dave Jordan.
Opposite Bottom Left: Pete Whillance gearing up.   Photo: P. Whillance.
Opposite Bottom Right: Geoff Milburn thinking of Clogov in Africa.   Photo: Anon.

The component parts of the controversy were intriguing and involved Martin Boysen —
a mature rock star, and John Redhead, who was to become probably the most daring
rock genius of his day in the British isles. A route put up by Boysen made copious use of
a solitary and beautiful oak tree, which grew out of a faint but possible line on the historic
upper part of the Milestone Buttress. Subsequently two vandals, lesser men than
Boysen, tried to gain a few extra miserable feet of unclimbed Ogwen rock by sawing
down the tree which up to that time had been safe from the voracious incisors of Ogwen
sheep.

Boysen's route was a hard and good climb and he enthused about it to a few friends,
including the guide-book author of Ogwen, but typically he made no attempt to write up
a description. Eight months later, in 1980, a hornet's nest of controversy was stirred up
by the tree-felling. The tree-felling vandals did not know that Boysen had already
climbed the line, using the tree to gain a lodgement on the lower reaches of the crack.
They were unable to climb the new start and so they enlisted John Redhead.

Redhead certainly had no part in cutting down one of Ogwen's few oak trees but the
other two people involved closed ranks with Redhead to conceal which of the two of
them had taken part in this act of desecration. Redhead did the route after the
desecration, climbed it at a higher standard and named it The Wrinkled Retainer, E5.
There is no evidence to suggest that he was the instigator of the felling and although he
climbed the route with one of the culprits, it was the crime of the lesser men in every
respect.

Jim Perrin in the historical section of the Ogwen guide-book wrote:

'At the beginning of April in 1980 two young climbers spotted the line Boysen had climbed, and
decided to *"improve"* it by cutting down the tree at its foot. They took a saw up to the crag and
did so, thus adding a few feet to the climb. Then, laughably, they failed to get up it. They
enlisted another leader, John Redhead, who succeeded and saw fit to give it a crudely
humorous name...

...The younger generation of active Welsh climbers, rather than disown a shabby action of the
grossest stupidity, appeared to condone it...protecting the identit₁ of the lumberjacks...

...This guide makes the Climbers' Club view of the incident one of appalled outrage...but the
route and name are unequivocally Boysen's and the action of the later vandals should be
universally condemned and deplored.'

Andy Newton wrote in reply to this and other comments:

'No-one condones the cutting down of the tree, but to besmirch Redhead for climbing and
naming the route is silly and childish. Neither is it up to Leppert (the guide-book writer) to
rename the climb completely differently from the previous two versions. Ask any climber and
they'll tell you what it's called.'

In the interim period before the true identity of the tree cutters was known, Martin
Boysen wrote a letter to Crags magazine:

'Dear Mr Blockhead (I think I have got that wrong), I congratulate you on *"creating the
variation start to Desecration Crack — a fine little route I did with John Yates last year on
the Milestone Buttress...A pity you thought it necessary to cut it down — it provided a
pleasant not to say amusing start to the route...Carry on the good work, there must be
many a fifteen-foot of unclimbed rock obscured by thoughtless trees. Perhaps chain saws
will soon be as small and convenient as a large Friend. Think of the scope then; Verdon,
Yosemite, even North Crag Eliminate."*

Signed Martin Boysen, Altrincham

Opposite: John Redhead and Chris Shorter with the remains of the oak tree on Wrinkled Retainer, Ogwen, 1982.
Photo: Andy Newton.

The editor added below:

'The above was written before it transpired that John Redhead is not the Mad Axeman of Idwal. Boysen's views are therefore directed to those responsible.

In the interim guide to Gogarth Geoff Milburn wrote of the new route explosion in his introduction:

'One thing is certain, there are still plenty of lines left and some of them will be hard...very hard.'

In 1979 there were only eleven new routes done on Gogarth but typically Jim Moran again appeared on the new-route scene as soon as the temperature increased and the rain clouds rolled away. Both Moran and Paul Williams with whom he teamed up were just missing the level of top ability to which they aspired. Paul was to be involved in nearly a hundred major new routes in North Wales and, like Rowland Edwards he had an eye for a classic line. Twice in May, Moran and Williams walked down the Gogarth descent path through the luxuriant plants to the natural black high-water marks on the Gogarth pinnacle at the foot of the Main Cliff, to see whether or not it was safe for the sea level traverse.

Moran had his eye on two routes which eventually gave over seven-hundred feet of new climbing between them. The Tet Offensive followed a sensational hanging arete which overlooked Big Groove and gave two 6a pitches to start with. Sebastopol near to the latter was yet another impressive route on Gogarth's big walls and nudged a junction with Sharp's Graduation Ceremony at one point. But it was to the Red Walls that Moran was most keen to return to finish off his 1979 blitzkrieg. Paul Williams caught the atmosphere and lure of the place:

'The Red Walls offer some of the most committing, serious and exciting climbing in the whole of Wales; with a maximum height of 350 feet exposure is guaranteed. Dubious rock and occasionally inadequate protection make each route a real experience...Red Wall itself has a proliferation of fault lines, chimneys, grooves and cracks...When viewed from the side, Left Hand Red Wall seems a vast expanse of blank orange rock and a close inspection is needed to reveal the lines of strength. Steep bold moves of a highly strenuous and technical nature are often needed to overcome the cruxes of many of the climbs.'

We must remember the glint in Moran's eyes when he said, *"It gets in your blood, does the Red Wall."* His Mein Kampf took a fierce and intimidating line up the Left Hand Red Wall giving another crux pitch of 6a standard — a Moran speciality. It required committing moves well above two protection pegs, then lay-away holds on a bulging wall to give a sustained finish in a fine position.

Again on his favourite wall he decided to repeat Mick Fowler's masterpiece, Heart of Gold. On his first attempt at the crux wall, a large foothold became detached and as Williams looked up he saw the hold and Moran both hurtling down towards him. A direct hit knocked Williams unconscious. Fortunately for both of them he had a 'death-grip' on the rope through the belay plate and Moran stopped five feet above him. After Williams came round and stated that he was all right (a massive Tom and Jerry-style lump was poking up through his hair) Moran embarked on his second attempt. Five feet higher than on his previous attempt, splayed out on minute rugosities, a foothold disintegrated — off came Moran again, and as Williams looked up he saw a familiar sight — an airborne Moran — and ducked in. This time Moran stopped five feet below him. After a ten-minute rest, Moran decided on a third and final go. He managed to climb the crux wall and reached a thin crack. He hung around fiddling in two runners, looked down at Williams and announced vehemently:

"These runners are shit."

This did wonders for Williams's confidence as he was by then shivering violently and in a state of shock. Moran then made a difficult and lichenous rightward traverse to a good foothold, reached round into a groove and pulled off a massive layaway hold. Williams thought his final hour had come as Moran for a third time became airborne, scything downwards in a huge arc. Thankfully the dubious wires held and Moran was lowered to the ground leaving Williams to abseil off. They escaped up Vena Cava as a storm swept in and lashed the face. Three pints of tea and a trip to Bangor hospital followed.

Next day the team returned, but this time Williams wore a helmet against further aerial bombardment. Moran cleaned the traverse, then set off on the pitch again, but just as he was moving into Red Wall his footholds disappeared with a loud crack leaving him dangling from his arms above a death fall. Luckily lunch-time factory wall training kept him safe on a route he later described as one of the best in Britain.

Leigh McGinley, who was to do sterling work at Tremadog and eventually produced an excellent guide-book, took time off to look at the impressive unclimbed wall between Ivy Sepulchre and Crucifix. It proved to be a fine but frightening experience which he called Golgotha. On the same day Ron Fawcett was inexorably drawn up to the walls of Dinas Cromlech where he abseiled down for a face-to-face inspection. As Paul Williams so amusingly put it about a previous exploration:

'This line had been inspected by another climber *"The Yorkshire Chipper"* who in spite of improving a few holds decided to leave it.'

The walls of Dinas Cromlech had lured top climbers seductively for decades, the open smooth rock being split, joined and historically connected by Cenotaph Corner. It had been five years since Right Wall, the block-buster from Livesey. Was there a distant thunder clap from a long-dead Alf Bridge with his five-year rule for hard men? If so, Fawcett was the new man whereas Livesey had all but given up hard climbing. Tempted too, by the seductive silver screen, the T.V. hypnotist for millions, Fawcett was intrigued at the thought of having his first ascent filmed for the programme Rock Athlete. As the television cameras rolled, Ron silently struggled to place protection on the hard moves, not able to swear in case he offended the watching beer swillers. Unfortunately the camera-man ran out of film before Fawcett had finished the tremendous route which was aptly to be called Lord of the Flies.

It had been decided that Fawcett would stand on the huge rocking boulder perched right at the top of the climb, the underside of which provided a sinking hand-jam to finish the route. But the world has always had a percentage of vandals and during the night a couple of visigoths armed with crow-bars, car jacks and crude strength successfully prised the boulder over the edge. A tremendous crash accompanied by sulphurous smells were transitory memories of a hitherto perfectly-placed piece of Welsh rock. Dinas Cromlech was a poorer place after the desecration. Perhaps it should be mentioned that after the previous hard winter the boulder had moved about a foot, become unstable and was potentially lethal.

Later another boulder, Y Glocsyn, the famous norber erratic behind Pen y Pass which

---

Opposite: Ron Fawcett on the 1st ascent of Lord of the Flies, Dinas Cromlech.   Photo: Paul Williams.

was enshrined in Welsh myth, was also trundled. £100 reward was offered by Esme Kirby and the Friends of Snowdonia, for information about the incident. However, the culprits, two American teachers from Boston, were never apprehended.

Ogwen was the scene of much activity apart from tree-felling and rhetoric. Nearly all the stars made contributions on cliffs which had largely appealed to the Victorians of nearly a hundred years before. Littlejohn appeared like a will-o'-the-wisp, made some Night Moves on the Devil's Kitchen, then disappeared just as quickly back to the South-West. Ron Fawcett went to the Suicide Wall and produced Mur y Meirwon a sombre name which means Wall of the Dead; perhaps Ron had already thought of the name as he couldn't get the route to be seconded.

There was by then not the same frenzy for new routes that there had been in 1978 but Livesey appeared on the scene again and on Suicide Wall noticed the faintest of direct lines straight up from Preston's route. He inspected it carefully by abseil, cleaning the holds at the same time but the protection proved almost non-existent. In his review of Welsh climbing Livesey said that Zero, E5, was the most serious Welsh route to date. It was Livesey's swan-song in Wales and a fitting pitch to call to mind his major contributions. Andy Pollitt, the teenage limestone-climbing phenomenon, had a hard struggle on the second ascent, but probably it was the old story about repetitions of routes being more difficult without the detailed knowledge and practice gained by abseil inspection.

The next great controversy occurred near the main crag of Clogwyn yr Eryr in the Crafnant valley, which is one of the most beautiful valleys in Wales. A small crag, split in two by a grassy gully, where there was an unclimbed groove with a fierce unprotected start, attracted the attention of Stuart Cathcart. Although the groove was only seventy-five feet in height Cathcart persisted and eventually climbed it, whereupon he promptly graded Crash Landing 6c, then informed the climbing magazines of its technical grading. Cathcart was not acknowledged as one of the front runners but was a fine climber in his own right, although he was neither a trend-setter nor a pusher of technical standards. The claim that his route had a grading of 6c was instantly greeted with derision by the climbing media. His offended reply was that he was in no way being provocative; but the very fact that he graded it 6c caused intense scrutiny, then derision. Cathcart commented:

'A very strong undertone of rivalry and bitchiness exists amongst climbers today. What a shame that the element of puritanical love for tenuous movement and enjoyment on rock is all too rapidly being expelled by the lust for egotism and personal acclaim...'

Very commendable thoughts but 'the lust for egotism and personal acclaim' would seem to fit in with grading the route 6c in the first place. There is no doubt that the route is good, though very short, and now that the dust has settled a grade of E4 6b seems a sensible assessment. Subsequently Cathcart stayed at the sound-hard-climber level and did not elevate himself to get alongside Fawcett, Livesey or Redhead.

The Cumbrian moss-troopers, Cleasby and Matheson, descended from the Lake District to the Llanberis Pass again, to Cyrn Las the crag where they had received much former glory when they snatched the tiny quartz staircase to Heaven on the top pitch of Lubyanka (amazingly later soloed by Gordon Tinnings). It was like a Russian prison,

Andy Pollitt making the 2nd ascent of Zero, Suicide Wall, 1983. Photo: Neil Foster.

entombed in grey ramparts until the Cumbrians unlocked it and its white quartz tip-toeing. In 1979 they looked at an untouched area between the Skull and The Great Buttress, but it was uncompromisingly difficult and didn't yield to a conventional straight-up attack. It needed two days of hard graft to extract Superskull, E5 6a, which they later thought about and renamed Hindenburg.

After two years it was right that someone else should try Midsummer Night's Dream and Bob Berzins felt that he was that man. When he fell onto the ancient peg put in by Ward Drummond it promptly snapped off, but fortunately Berzins was stopped by a bolt — another Drummond appendage which was several feet lower down. The bolt also saved the life of Australian climber Kim Carrigan who took a monster fall just missing the ground; this merited the lampooning headline in High magazine 'Bruce almost bounces'.

Rowland Edwards had spent a considerable time exploring the limestone cliffs of the Ormes and in an article about them he particularly enthused about the routes on Castell y Gwynt. To quote:

> 'The most intimidating of all the routes on the crag is Psychic Threshold, E5 6a. Dave Roberts who made a very impressive second ascent said he found it equal to Right Wall on the Cromlech...the moves over the bulge are the hardest; both Dave and myself have taken falls on this section, but the protection is excellent. Just above is a threaded sling which is used for aid; it was during attempts to free this one move that the falls occurred on the first and second ascents. The line continues steeply for a further fifty feet, but the difficulty is not quite as severe. If the resting point and the sling are genuinely eliminated, without cheating, the climb will be a grade harder.'

The Great Orme sticks out into the sea and along this the Marine Drive road carries its gawping tourists in cars which hiccup their way slowly round each bend as a fresh sight comes into view, of either cliffs or water. Castell y Gwynt is the ace in the pack of cliffs on the Great Orme. There are other crags, but they are not so big: Craig Dinas, Craig Pen Trwyn, Point Five Buttress, Upper Craig Pen Gogarth, St Tudno's Buttress, Craig Pen Gogarth and Hornby Crags — a good enough selection of crags for any area.

One of the finest climbers to come to Wales, John Redhead, was to be better on hard unprotected new routes than anyone else before him. He was 24 years of age, came from Hull, and was a superlative artist on rock as well as on the canvasses in his studios. Soon after moving to Wales he had solo exhibitions in both Bangor and Cardiff. In 1979 Plas Berw was the first E5 on Welsh limestone to be put up by Redhead and it was a harbinger of the type of route with which he decorated steeper rock which had not been solved by previous pioneers. With a respectable 245 feet of difficulty it was extremely strenuous and sustained with a poorly-protected first pitch of 6a which led to a magnificent hanging arete. The second pitch reached the then ultimate 6b difficulty on a long traverse which had been climbed previously by Rowland Edwards using a peg for aid, but which Redhead was able to ignore. The last section did not relent much and was another 6a pitch. The overall impression was that the route was something really special.

Just over a month later, Redhead returned to Castell y Gwynt to look at Central Pillar which had been climbed by Rowland Edwards with some aid. He produced the longest hard pitch that had so far been done on Welsh limestone. The 150-foot Bittersweet Connection needed 6b moves to surmount the enormous roof which barred progress to the upper parts of the first pitch, while the second pitch was only slightly easier and

included an amazing move over another roof which Redhead felt compelled to call 'cosmic'. It has been stated that Redhead is the best climber in the country on any type of rock until it becomes beyond the vertical, but there is little doubt that critics have ignored routes such as Bittersweet Connection which could not be more overhanging.

Psychic Threshold on the same crag had been put up in 1977 by Rowland Edwards using some aid. It was a phenomenal undertaking up the continuously-overhanging prow of the buttress. On the main second pitch a large niche gives a temporary resting place before a roof on the right and a 6b move of great difficulty. Redhead faltered slightly and needed an aid point to solve the problem which reduced the difficulty to 6a. Two years were to elapse before Kim Carrigan was able to dispense with the point of aid to make a companion E5 to Redhead's two other great efforts. Three tremendous routes by Redhead in just over a month were a foretaste of what he was to do on the bigger crags in later years, but although he likes the climbing on limestone and has made many good contributions, he does not regard it as serious — more a training ground for the bigger crags.

In December 1979 Pete Livesey made some sound and relevant comments as to the construction of new routes:

'If any one outstanding feature can be recognised in the routes of the past year it is their all-round poor quality. Good routes have been swamped beneath large numbers of worthless routes. What makes routes good or bad? Certainly not the difficulty nor the strenuousness nor the sustained nature of the route...perhaps the most important being the quality of the movement, the line and the position and the sustained nature of the climbing.

Does the route follow a natural weakness or a strong visible line or maybe the only line of holds up a wall? How close are the next routes and for how long is the route independent? Perhaps the latter question is most crucial for the potential new route. Most new routes in the last ten years have filled in the obvious blank spaces between "strong lines". The blank space itself is a strong line, but once filled with a route the blank can be said to be full...Numerous blanks remain to be filled, but they will require a climbing ability beyond the average.'

Ron Fawcett took some years to reach Livesey's total mental and physical commitment. Livesey was fitter than everyone else in 1974 and just as important totally confident in his own ability. Just to show his contempt for the lower grades of difficulty he soloed Vector in a floppy pair of suede shoes. It was only with Lord of the Flies that it can be said that Fawcett came level with Livesey and then surpassed him.

Perhaps it is fitting that Livesey's last big route should be on the big cliff, the East Buttress of Clogwyn du'r Arddu, where he just beat Pete Whillance to a delectable line that both of them had tried. It was almost a direct version of Troach up the steep wall to the right and he called it the Purr-Spire, perhaps an appropriate name. Livesey transmitted much of his coolness to Jill Lawrence who was his second on The Purr-Spire which undoubtedly was a major factor in Jill becoming the top British woman climber of the eighties. The E4 grade given to the Purr-Spire was too modest an assessment as on a repeat ascent Bob Berzins felt it was easily a grade harder, although Rowland Foster a New Zealand climber led the big pitch with just the clipped peg for protection!

Also on Cloggy, Pat Littlejohn made a fine contribution with an audacious line up the prominent and overhanging arete to the right of East Gully Groove, which gave him The Axe, E4 6a. It had been in the sights of several leading climbers for some time but was

Opposite: Pete Livesey forcing the 1st ascent of The Purr-Spire, Clogwyn du'r Arddu.   Photo: Pete Livesey collection.

clearly an intimidating undertaking. On the successful ascent a full hundred and sixty-foot pitch took all of the available rope.

Eyes were by then firmly fixed on several of the last great problems and John Redhead made some really determined efforts to get up the middle of the Great Wall of Clogwyn du'r Arddu. First he took a tremendous fall onto a tiny nut, then had to accept a top-rope from a party above. He described it all in his article 'Great Wall'.

'I first really appreciated the fabric of the rock from the Great Wall stance: Drummond's brink challenge of *"A Midsummer Night's Dream"* freed by Whillance in 1977 at E6 6b — a fine effort though this was. Drummond's sky-hook blast was the wild fix. Second attempts at the free style ended dramatically: Berzins plummeted above the top peg, stripping it and some of the flake behind which it nestled: Carrigan reached a similar position, flew away on a 70-foot scream: Hall pulled out on a rope; the second ascent in '82 by myself. Drummond's bolt, blessed thing — it failed to be mentioned in the fracas surrounding my own attempts on *"Master's Wall"*, when bolts were an issue. I wonder if a chipped spike for aid might have been more acceptable.

Master's — my own attempts from 1980 have been well wagged about. A vague indeterminate line down Great Wall was inspected and cleaned and the lack of protection soon became painfully evident. With the day drawing in, and the apparently unjustifiable nature of the route looming ever larger in my mind Chris Shorter and I decided to bale out. A last look at the line and a strange impulse took hold of me. I went for it, at 70 feet I woke up. Ghastly! The aggression was dissipated and fear gripped me. I had climbed with virtually no protection and was now eye-balling a tiny shallow crack. I remembered it from the abseil and it had looked pathetic. It was real now. I contemplated jumping on the scree below before the situation got out of control. I fell a million times, my arms unfolding, my breath fading. A No. 1 stopper came to a halt, halfway down this crack, half in, rocking — my weight was on it. I clipped in and sagged down, unable to comprehend the awful consequences should the nut slip through. It didn't, and I was lowered to the ground.

The next day I returned, only to see myself lowering from a sky-hook...I came back on 13 May 1980. The mental preparation was becoming harder and harder. The so-called psyching-up, a pain beyond reason. Out of the naivety which had sparked off this now terrifying enterprise...I knew the score and was unnerved by it...

...I distinctly felt a tiny slide on a friction move lower down and became very insecure, with my feet in Canyon boots. I got to the little crack another twenty feet up and was dangerously pumped because of the extra strain on my fingers. The resin was wearing off the boots. I managed to place an RP 1, clipped in and was about to place a no. 2 when my right foot shot off. The strain came on the RP, ripped it through and I cartwheeled a long way down the wall.

A No. 1 stopper held and, encouraged, I climbed back up. Stuck again I jumped for an abseil rope and pretended to forget the programme — I was more than bored with the whole series. But my pathetic memory became once again in situ on the wall — another failure — no dramatics.'

During these attempts Redhead maintained that he had solved the difficulties of the lower part of the wall but had not been able to make the vital moves going leftwards into the faint groove line which would have constituted the upper part of the route. He could have traversed off right to complete a somewhat lesser route but chose not to, but in fact this is what happened later on the next effort on this blank wall three years later.

Psycho Killer (named from a track by the pop group Talking Heads) was one of the big routes re-discovered by Jim Moran. The line had been known and had been spuriously written up in the Ynys Ettws log book years before, and whimsically named The Final

Judgement. Alan Rouse had already tried it but had come away empty-handed. Moran cleaned the route but realised that the crux was going to be in the first horrifying twenty feet where the rock on the first few feet of the Pinnacle is a loose band with no protection. Moran, who was intimidated by the thought of a nasty fall, offered the lead to Ron Fawcett who led it, thus leaving Moran to bitterly regret his decision to hand over the lead…

An unusual event in 1980 was a first ascent by a woman climber. Bonny Masson had been climbing with Pete Gomersall for some years during which she steadily got better until she put up Emily Street, E2 5b, at Tremadog. What is not known, however, is that the route had previously been climbed by Rab Carrington and Al Rouse who didn't bother to claim it.

Bonny carefully increased her leading standard from 1972, when she was leading Hard Very Severe, to the present day when she is putting up new routes up to E2. She is the most prolific of the women climbers doing new routes and some of these up to Hard Very Severe she has soloed. Sadly there is not yet the recognition for women's new routes, as so far they have been easier than the top men's routes.

The E grading system was still not completely finalised by 1980 and arguments raged this way and that. Eventually Pete Gomersall wrote an article entitled 'Towards a classification of Grades' which made some useful additional comments on the new E gradings. He put forward the idea that the E grade should be only in relation to seriousness — E1 non-serious routes and E5 very serious routes.

Nowadays we have the E grading and technical grading in concert, so that an aspiring leader can tell from the numerical grading whether or not he can say climb a sequence of 6a moves or even one 6a move. If his limit is 5c, then the 6a bracket will mean that the climb is beyond him. Gomersall wrote:

'The E grade should give a general impression of the overall physical difficulties.'

Kim Carrigan, a top Australian climber, made several trips to the U.K. and even found time to put up some of his own hard routes. He too had a useful contribution to make to the intensive E grading discussions:

'At present there are routes such as Strawberries at Tremadog being graded E5 7a. It is not at all serious, nor is it technically 7a, but being one of the hardest routes in the country, another choice might be E7 6b. This same anomaly occurs regularly at all other grades.

Because the E grade has grown out of the adjectival system which is meant to denote overall difficulty, "sustainedness" should be incorporated in the E grade and not the technical grade. With so many of the modern routes falling into this category, there is a pressing need to develop consistency.

The main consequence of this has been a fairly sluggish progression to harder technical moves. Many top British routes tend to be easier technically than their Australian or American counterparts, but are usually less well protected, and hence are more serious undertakings. In Australia alone there are more routes that would be graded 6c than in Britain, but always in the form of "boulder problems" near pre-placed protection.'

A lot of attention throughout the year was centred on Tremadog around Paul Williams, a character who has been at the focal point of Welsh climbing for some years and has played a major part in several of the new route surges that have occurred.

In the middle of winter Williams with Chris Shorter had a look at the Vector Buttress.

Opposite: The Australian climber Kim Carrigan on Cockblock Clogwyn y Grochan.   Photo: Mike Owen.

Brown had criss-crossed it with Nimbus and Vector, Rowland Edwards had put up his excellent Void, and Gomersall had controversially added The Mongoose with a runner high in Void. It seemed almost impossible for there to be anything of a lower grading that could be worthwhile, but Williams made an excellent discovery in The Weaver, an almost direct line up the crag, which belies its name. Perhaps the fact that it weaves its way expertly through the belts of overhangs makes its title self-explanatory. The main crux pitch of The Weaver is one hundred and twenty feet — one of the longest pitches on Craig Bwlch y Moch. Within three weeks the route had been repeated at least a dozen times and within two months there were queues at its foot.

It is not true that Brown had climbed some of it earlier and the only Brown exploration on the line was during the investigations for Vector when Brown had a look at the second pitch and had to have his foot held on to a tiny rugosity by Trevor Jones.

In 1980 there was another explosion upwards in grading towards 7a when Strawberries was climbed by Ron Fawcett. The route follows a hairline crack which splits the headwall at the top of Vector Buttress. It was thought that it was going to be the last great problem of Tremadog and someone said that it would be ten years before it could be climbed — just the sort of comment to inspire Fawcett. He abseiled down to discover that an unknown climber had already been at work in a vain attempt to bring the rock down to his own standard.

After several failures and falls Fawcett placed his three highest runners from his previous attempt by abseil and clipped his ropes through them. It was only like a yo-yo but it was a subtle change in the rules yet again. It eventually took three days, about twenty falls and the three pre-placed runners before he was finally successful.

The very week Fawcett was having such difficulty in plucking his Strawberries, Redhead put up Sexual Salami, E5 6b. He not only surprised the climbing world with the hardness of his new routes but also created a bottom-squirming reluctance to accept his somewhat nauseating nomenclature. Sexual Salami followed a very thin slab, both strenuous and delicate, on the buttress containing Olympic Slab. It still gets three stars for quality, but has slipped down to E4 in standard although precarious protection ensures that it will not become a trade route.

A short time later local climbers came to examine Strawberries and were horrified to find that two bolts had been placed in it. To everyone's delight it was found that someone had stuck them on with glue, a refreshing joke amongst the deadly serious competition.

There was an odd situation when first Redhead then Fawcett tried to repeat Gary Gibson's route Big Bug, which they should have found effortless. Despite a briefing from Gibson, they both failed to climb the line. Somewhat piqued, Fawcett abseiled down the line which had been described in the new route book at the garage cafe below the crag. It was obvious from the scarcity and looseness of the only holds on the described route, that the route had not been climbed. Eventually a possible climbable way was discovered by going some way to the left. Gibson stated emphatically that he had told Fawcett to go left in the first place. There the matter rested.

Almost at the same time as Strawberries, in early March, Redhead put up Bananas which followed the overhanging flakes right of Joe Brown's Croaker. Redhead too thought that it merited a 7a grading on account of knee-locks to maintain stability in a position of incredible difficulty. Eventually Bananas settled down to E5 6b whereas

Strawberries finalised at E6 7a, thus confirming Fawcett's first reluctant thoughts.

In a fine effort Redhead nearly managed to do Strawberries in a day despite the normal number of falls, but eventually seventeen-year-old Jerry Moffatt, a rising star, repeated Strawberries only taking two days as opposed to Fawcett's three. Although he did it in an imperfect style, the fact that he had done it in a lesser time than Fawcett prompted Moffatt to suggest changing the name to Peaches. Some of Moffatt's attitudes were explained by him:

'When Ron Fawcett did Prow, E7 6b, I wanted to repeat that route as soon as possible; it was important to do that route then. As far as I'm concerned that's what competition is all about, you've got to be up with the guy at the time, not a year later because he'll be climbing better then.'

Moffatt had several points to make about soloing:

'If you do some desperate solo you really do appreciate that sense of release, you're thankful to be alive. Sometimes you think, *"Well, is this the end?"*...Soloing gives me a big buzz, it's very addictive, I'm going to try to stop this year.'

There was not much mention of enjoyment or solitude, or the pleasure of being on rock on a warm summer's day.

Moffatt and his contemporary, Andy Pollitt, started to play a major part on the Welsh limestone, both in aid reductions and with new routes. The major joint effort by the two of them was in using siege tactics during the first free ascent of Mayfair, one of Rowland Edwards's routes. The essential point was that without aid it rose to an E4 rating and although they were only seventeen, this route alone elevated them to the upper ranks. Only Redhead had done harder routes at E5.

The pace of putting up new routes was hotting up and with both Fawcett and Redhead living in Wales they were able to take every conceivable opportunity given by good weather to work away at unclimbed rock. In three places they slugged it out for supremacy: the head-wall of Vector Buttress, in Llanberis Pass and out on Gogarth. It could easily be said that Fawcett won on Vector Buttress with Strawberries as opposed to Bananas; and also in Llanberis Pass with Atomic Hot Rod versus Cockblock; but on Gogarth Redhead swept Fawcett away with a stupendous new route. On the steep wall of North Stack the route started up The Cad before trending rightwards to an arete.

The Bells!, The Bells!, E7 6b, was the most daring route put up by Redhead and so far has not had a repeat ascent. It is not so much the sustained nature of the climb but the dubious quality of the rock which might fail causing a leader fall, and worse still the possibility of the protection ripping because of the lack of confidence in the nut placement. Redhead had examined the route and realised that the protection was unsatisfactory and that the technical standard was going to be very high. It was a big risk, but he got committed, kept a cool head and succeeded. He wisely graded it E7 to ensure that anyone who attempted it should climb at that standard to stay alive on the route. In his article on North Stack, Redhead wrote:

'My abstracted involvement in leading a route like The Bells!, The Bells! never ceased to amaze me. In consequence of this abstraction, I could rarely analyse a climb afterwards move by move, even just after the ascent, often to my infuriation. Leading a route is leading a route, being there, in situ.'

Despite not being able to remember the moves afterwards it is quite clear that a route of this seriousness demands the utmost concentration just to stay alive. It is still the top contender for the most serious route in Wales.

Fawcett was not far away and also added major routes to Gogarth when he inevitably joined up with Moran and Williams who were at the ready to grab a few more of the big lines. On The Big Sleep, E6 6b, Fawcett led the first pitch then Moran joined him on the stance. Fawcett was itching to get at the second pitch, but it was Moran's turn to lead and he set off with eyes burning into the back of his head as he felt Ron's impatience at any delay. Jim rushed at the pitch, still not fully recovered from the strenuous first pitch and eventually failed about forty feet up it. As soon as he had lowered off Fawcett promptly snatched the double prize of both 6b pitches.

Ron Fawcett's extraordinary versatility is apparent in a series of ascents on Gogarth when he did his own route The Cad, then The Long Run in a total time of one hour, despite both routes being E5. He then lowered the standard and did Not Fade Away, E4, South Sea Bubble and Talking Heads, both E2s — and on the latter climb he sprinted up in a mere five minutes of explosive action.

On Wall of Fossils, Fawcett was cleaning the top pitch by abseil while Moran was traversing under the overhangs of Mammoth where the crack was seeping with water. Moran had just got to the point where he could pull onto the head-wall above, when a warning shout from Fawcett made him pull back under the overhangs. Ron tipped off a piano-sized block, and from below, 'the sky went dark' according to Paul Williams, who was drenched with a colossal deluge of sea water as the block 'parted the waves as Moses did the Red Sea'.

Concerning Khmer Rouge, Jim Moran feels particularly irritated about publicity surrounding the ascent. He first tried it on a very hot day and couldn't make the necessary moves, so he left it till late in the day when the temperature had dropped a bit. This time the route fell at the first attempt. Phil Thomas, who had witnessed the afternoon failure from Castell Helen, assumed that Moran had used aid (although he could not clearly see what was happening) as Moran had remained in one position for a long time — this was not the case as Moran down-climbed the pitch from his high point. Unfortunately Thomas voiced his opinion to Pete Livesey who published the untruth in a national climbing magazine. To this day Moran still feels very bitter about the whole affair as it is almost impossible to refute the allegations.

It might be said that in 1980 Fawcett was the ultimate technical performer when protection was adequate, but Redhead was undoubtedly untouchable when it came to great boldness allied to technical difficulty — rather like John Streetly nearly thirty years before. This may seem rather hard on Fawcett but one must consider Alien for example. Alien was even harder and more serious than Hunger which was given an E5 rating. (On the latter Fawcett flashed the first pitch in under five minutes seconding Moran and Williams. Williams, who was belaying, could not take the rope in fast enough!) Fawcett tried Alien and failed owing to wet rock, then offered the lead to Jim Moran who went through with Fawcett's runners. It was full circle for Pat Littlejohn who had pushed himself to the limit on Alien; he had been scoffed at in 1976 and now the two mega-stars, Fawcett and Livesey had both failed on one of his routes, although to be fair, Fawcett had not really pushed the lead owing to the adverse conditions.

Opposite: John Redhead impaled on Cardiac Arete, Craig Pant Ifan.   Photo: Paul Williams.

Fawcett had shown superlative soloing ability on several occasions but Cathcart, after his controversial grading of Crash Landing, claimed a solo ascent of The Cad which many climbers openly doubted. This claim provoked widespread amusement and complete disbelief, but a photograph was eventually produced of him on the route. The sceptics spotted an abseil rope in the picture and refused to be swayed in their opinion. Cathcart said that he abseiled down the route to have a look at it and then left the abseil ropes in place as an insurance policy just in case he got into difficulties. The ends of the rope were actually in the sea and while he was climbing the sea slowly but surely took the ropes further and further away from the cliff. Cathcart later commented:

> 'At one stage just above the chopped bolt, I climbed too far right following a false trail of chalk and nearly chopped myself. I did cheat slightly at the bolt, when I stuck my finger through the hole to change feet on a reasonable resting ledge.'

Gomersall and Livesey made the second ascent of Cathcart's Crash Landing and loftily thought it 6a/b, then provocatively said that it was only forty feet...but very good climbing.

Paul Williams had climbed many new lines and at one stage he could see many more desperate ones that were feasible. Teaming up with Ron Fawcett the Welsh scene was blitzed to add Atomic Hot Rod, Ivory Madonna, and True Grip in the Pass, and Crimson Cruiser and Non-Dairy Creamer in the Moelwynion. Fawcett did Precious, E5 6b, on the Right Wall in the middle of winter when there was still good ice-climbing up in Cwm Glas. While party after party were trogging up Parsley Fern Gully in the freezing cold, Fawcett was unlocking yet another hard Cromlech route belayed by Chris Thomas an unsuspecting bystander who just happened to be walking along the foot of the crag.

Williams has given us a rather nice description of the first ascent of Atomic Hot Rod which is high up on the Cromlech to the left of Horseman's Route:

> '...a mind-bending razor-edge crack...it cuts the buttress as clean as a scalpel and is topped by a three-foot roof. Every move on it is at least 6a and it packs a mighty punch requiring a super-thug approach to ensure success.'

It was done with three falls on the first ascent and Fawcett arrived at the top, fingers cut and bleeding, gasping that it was the hardest crack that he had ever done.

Fawcett added more routes to Dinas Cromlech; J.R., E5 6b, (so named because it was 'hard and mean' like the character in the television series 'Dallas') took a tiny gap between Cenotaph Corner and Resurrection. Clearly the walls of Cenotaph Corner were getting more crowded, so Fawcett transferred his attention to the impressive wall, as yet untouched, between Ivy Sepulchre and Jericho Wall. The rock is not so good on this part of the Cromlech but it does have the odd useful pocket for a thankful hand-hold, and occasional flakes which are sometimes loose. Fawcett called the route Hall of Warriors, E5 6b, and found it a harder psychological lead than even Lord of the Flies.

It had been a busy year for Jim Moran in 1980 but he found time to remember his great effort on Tramgo two years earlier and both he and his second Geoff Milburn felt a strong pull to return for the big unclimbed line which was always at the back of their minds. On a windy day at Easter, when there was still a lot of snow on the hills, they went back and Moran abseiled down for a look. It was necessary to swing in to fix slings so that the route could be cleaned as the wall leant in so much. Hang 'em High gave a very frightening

Opposite Top Left: Pat Littlejohn.   Photo: John Mothersele.
Opposite Bottom Left: Ben Wintringham.   Photo: Terry Tullis.
Opposite Top Right: Steve Haston.   Photo: S. Haston.
Opposite Bottom Right: Paul Williams.   Photo: Trevor Jones.

130-foot pitch at E4/5 6a, which Moran described as 'A real pumper'. Later he confessed that he had undergraded at the time he did it, as he was still an angry young man trying to prove something. The route was even more overhanging than Tramgo and he had several falls, while Milburn who was trying to shelter at the foot of the crag had gone numb with cold. When he thought that it was time to call it a day Jim's response was immediate:

"No way! If you think I'm coming down from here, I'm not. No chance. I'm staying here, till I do it, at all costs."

On the way down it dawned on them what a great route it was and they burst into whistles and yells of delight to an empty mountainside, above the beautiful Quellyn Valley.

Dressed To Kill

The recession bit deep into the start of the decade and there was a lull after the stirring deeds of 1980...the great ones paused for breath and the underlying rivalry and competition on the big crags were momentarily stilled in the quiet before the next storm of inspiration. Almost unnoticed, like a whisper of wind at dawn, a new and pure philosophy began to stir and 'Rock Only' as preached by Livesey was gradually preached by more and more teenagers. The move...the technical pleasure...the buzz of soloing...all caused 'House Empty' signs to be hauled up on traditional crags such as Lliwedd and Craig yr Ysfa. There were stirrings of great things just waiting to be done on Pen Trwyn and it felt more like the scene on Derbyshire or Yorkshire limestone cliffs than any of the traditional Welsh crags.

Redhead was the dominant force on the Welsh coast. He was different...being artistic, and older than the teenagers, and somehow they felt uncomfortable about it and tried in a desperate way to side-track him as an oddity. None of them had Redhead's long neck, but they came alongside him in technical stature and even managed the odd route on which Redhead had failed. It took Andy Pollitt and Jerry Moffatt, who were the teenage leaders, to challenge Redhead's unprotected lead with a show of technical brilliance. Although Redhead initiated a sequence of extremely hard climbs, he was swamped by the sheer weight of the number of new routes put up by Andy Pollitt.

At Tremadog the main action was to be centred on Redhead and the much younger Moffatt. The remaining lines were fewer but one stood out like a sore thumb — the impressive black-streaked wall to the left of Vulcan on Craig Pant Ifan. It was a tempting unclimbed prize and Redhead got some way up it before taking a big fall. Undeterred by this Jerry Moffatt, who had done so little on the North Wales limestone compared to Andy Pollitt, forcibly attacked the wall which had rejected Redhead so quickly. After putting in an extra protection peg Moffatt finally succeeded on a highly technical and serious wall which gave him Psych 'n Burn, E6 6c. With this one hard route Moffatt had arrived very swiftly.

Not to be outdone, John Redhead with a distinguished cast which included John de Montjoye, Jim Perrin and Paul Williams, went up to Two Face Buttress on Craig Pant Ifan. There he produced a quite short route, only sixty feet, but it was 6b, sustained and not too well protected. Redhead gave it the typically bizarre name of Hitler's Buttock.

Although the volcanic rock still drew many leaders the major attraction was the North Wales limestone, where about forty new routes were done during 1981. Just after New Year, Andy Pollitt put up High Steppa the first E5 on Craig y Forwyn. It was bold, 6b and quite a long ninety-foot pitch with a small flat-topped spike providing minimal protection. Pollitt persevered with Forwyn throughout the year and picked off another three E4s just for good measure. His contemporary, Jerry Moffatt, could only manage an E2 which was meagre fare compared with Pollitt's big efforts, but Pollitt was not the only hard man on the coast.

Kim Carrigan came from Australia and temporarily deserted his beloved Arapiles to make some trenchant comments on our crags, climbers and climate. He concentrated on Pen Trwyn in the area where Pollitt had already freed Mayfair of its ironmongery the previous year. He squeezed in a route as close as possible to Mayfair, a fierce alternative, which became known as Carrigan's Groove — despite his having failed to repeat Mayfair in its free state. Mel Griffiths, who could impress onlookers by doing a standing back-somersault, did further acrobatics on the wall to the left of Mayfair, partnered by the equally able Leigh McGinley. On the same day and just after each other, they both led another E5 6b, Axle Attack, which quickly acquired classic status for the new generation.

The different natures of two limestone cliffs so close to each other is quite amazing. Craig y Forwyn is surprisingly similar to Stoney Middleton in having such a luxuriant tree belt to soften the approach to each section of crag and continually delight the climber. Its rock is slightly duller however and with more plant growth clinging to any available cracks or fissures which could attract a spore, seed or even an insect; for in from the harsh rock face is a tiny microcosm of life. Pen Trwyn faces the sea and receives the sun hour after hour, day after day. It is also much more compact than Forwyn, with not so many cracks, fissures or pockets. On Pen Trwyn it is even possible to step from the car seat onto the first holds of a route without touching the ground — that is if the ropes, gear and footwear are at the ready.

At another aesthetic level the Central Electricity Generating Board was busily despoiling the mountains with the Dinorwic dam project. Marchlyn Mawr used to be a hauntingly beautiful and lonely lake with the Pillar of Elydir rising superbly almost from its shore. But with a fleet of Rolls-Royces the C.E.G.B. dazzled the local authorities with a few days of roistering and strong drink. Marchlyn's solitude was finished and the water gurgled down into a disgustingly bare Llyn Peris with its painfully obvious shores of bare rock. There was one faint glimmer of benefit however, as the empty quarries that the Board took over became generally more accessible with the new roads, and with the quarry clean-up as well more virgin slate became available.

As long ago as 1971 Joe Brown had explored the Big Hole and started doing new routes with Opening Gambit. Little then happened until 1981 when Steve Haston started to develop the slabs of slate. His best contribution of the year was Comes the Dervish, E5 6a, an obvious tilted slab in the Vivian Quarry on the side of the hillside, close to the car park, near to Llyn Padarn. It was the faintest of cracks with a very hard start, but the heavy use of this immediately popular route caused some splintering and removal of rock on the first tricky few feet, so that it eventually came down in standard and is now thought to be E3 5c. Comes the Dervish was just the start as many highly desirable routes were to be ascended on the slate. Its smooth cleavage and elegant purple surface is not sympathetic even to the latest modern protection techniques and sadly the BOLT had to rear its ugly head again.

It would be wrong to write about this year without mentioning one particularly tragic story about the colourful character Al Harris who was killed when his speeding van hit a wall on the bend near Cobden's Hotel in Capel Curig. A broken rib pierced his heart and he died. There was much that was reprehensible about Harris in that he was brash, promiscuous and into drugs as well, but he was the middle-aged spirit of the sixties which lived on through him till his death.

He certainly gave the best parties in North Wales and the young and not-so-young flocked to them, including his many fans from the U.S.A. Girls, girls, girls — and a fair sprinkling of wives too, that is when he could find time for them. Harris's parties were way out and memorable and if even just a fraction of the unbelievable stories were true they would fill a best-selling book.

Harris on a good day was an excellent climber and even did an early free ascent of The Troach without the sling, but he would hardly have bothered to talk about it. Following Crew up Zukator the clown prince of climbing wore winkle-pickers to amuse the crowd.

And the real foolishness?...Trying to flee from a road accident, he tried to drive off in the police car and was securely handcuffed to the bumper...Fach Wen has a length of over a mile of incredibly tortuous bends. Rumour has it that Harris descended it in fifty-eight seconds.

Harris's funeral was attended by hundreds of mourners who silently acknowledged that the day that Harris died a light went out in North Wales climbing society. It has not been rekindled.

1982 was the year of some great solo exploits by the younger generation. Andy Pollitt enhanced his already considerable aura by soloing both Great Wall, E4 5c, and Quickstep, E4 6a, on his favourite outcrop Craig y Forwyn. That was just a start and astoundingly Phil Davidson, who was Pex-Hill trained, nonchalantly soloed Right Wall on the Cromlech. It was only eight years since Livesey had put up this E5 6a which had heralded the era of modern rock-climbing.

It might be thought that Forwyn was completely under the domination of Pollitt who had his eyes fixed on a tempting wall with an obvious sequence, which would clearly give a fine hard route. On one attempt a hold snapped off and he was deposited painfully on a ledge forty feet below. Ron Fawcett was then brought in to triumph over teenage trauma with Imminent Crisis, E5 6b, an awe-inspiring route.

A few weeks later, Gary Gibson, who might be called the new-route machine, returned suddenly from Cornwall to try one of the biggest unclimbed limestone problems. Both Gary and his brother Phil, having previously criticised Pollitt for over-grading and over-rating, pronounced it a three-star E5 6b. Pollitt was distinctly piqued and declared it to be E4 5c/6a with only two stars. When the dust finally settled it was felt that Gibson deserved his E5 for Space Mountain.

The previous year there had been an Axle Attack but Pen Trwyn was to experience a full frontal assault from Redhead. There were sixty-seven new routes put up on Pen Trwyn in 1982 under the determined onslaught of a host of eager leaders including Wayman, Redhead, Pollitt, Fawcett, Moffatt, Williams, the Lyon brothers, Towse and Gibson, to name just a few of the top performers. One of the most necky routes to be done at Pen Trwyn was Gold Rush, E5 6b, which finally yielded when Bill Wayman pushed the boat out on an impressive lead. Moffatt slipped in a free ascent of Oyster at 6b but it only got a grudging E4 compared to the blitz of routes that Redhead was about to unleash, all of great difficulty and with inflammatory memorable names. Some of Redhead's names are tortured while others are downright anti-social.

The Disillusioned Screw Machine for example was the first E6 on the coast and with pitches of 6b and 6c it was an immediate three-star route. It needed Andy Pollitt to second the line. The route name was inspired by a former girlfriend of Redhead and apart from the climb she has also inspired him to paint a canvas which is similarly named. Such paintings can take him up to six months to paint and this particular one, apart from the visual representation of memories, has many tiny fir trees connected by thousands of thin grass fronds. There does not seem to be much that is abstract, but there is a record of messages and painful visual snapshots. John keeps most of his paintings as he cannot bear to part with them, although he could get a high price for them if he so desired.

Redhead had a hard struggle to produce Burning Sphincter, E5 6a, and too much curry the night before was the reason for the name. Pollitt, who had already pushed things with The Chain Gang, E5 6b, — a route which had few perfect ascents as it was so strenuous — struck back for the local climbers at Craig y Forwyn with Moonwind Direct E5 6b which boldly stormed through two central roofs in an improvement on the original climb to give one of the finest routes in the area. Pollitt also produced a guide-book chronicalling everything from the early days right up to 1982. There was still new-route potential in every direction and the photographs showed all the tantalising gaps between the white lines of existing routes. What was more obvious is that the masses had started to enjoy the satisfying pockets on the bulging walls of Great Orme as well as the superb cracks and horizontal holds of Forwyn.

Increasingly, as the new routes flowered, the problem became one of connecting isolated holds instead of just following thin crack lines which had been so typical up to that time. Bolts started to be used for both aid and protection and arguments which in previous decades had waged furiously about peg protection and excessive aid started to re-surface.

1981 had seen several big roof pitches such as Chris Shorter's intimidating Cobalt Dream, E5 6b, on Drws Nodded. Steve Haston also started to make his mark in North Wales with a series of big leads, often on the steepest rock. In 1981 he had soloed the stunning Weirpig, E5 6b, at Carreg Hyll Drem and made a free ascent of The Grinder on Dinas Mot to give The Red Ring, E5 6b. One of the biggest free roofs to be done was Dumbell Flyer, E4 6a, on Pen Trwyn. Haston then made an amazing lead of Perygl, E5 6b, to free the north side of the Pass of its last aid points. Another tremendous lead was when he freed Obelisk at South Stack. Of his soloing exploits he later did The Pump; and on one occasion it is also said that he soloed Great Slab by moonlight. It was on the slate however that Haston made his greatest contribution and after Comes the Dervish and High Man Snapper he undoubtedly became the guru of Welsh slate climbing.

At one stage Andy Pollitt went down the Conway valley to have a look at the isolated Crafnant cliffs. Connie's Crack has a ferocious start and needed a lot of aid to subdue it in 1961 before Ron Fawcett shook it free of its aid to raise its standard to E4. The main challenge however was an overhanging groove and a sensational arete above the start. This had to wait for a tremendous thrust from Pollitt to create Carousel Waltz, an E5 with a hundred-foot 6a first pitch followed by a ludicrously exposed 6b arete right at the top. Although on the very edge of the big crag area of North Wales, this route put Pollitt into the big league alongside Moffatt who had made his big effort the previous year with Psych 'n Burn.

With the rapid build-up of young talent looming ever nearer, Redhead instantly transferred his attention to the Great Wall of Clogwyn du'r Arddu. He climbed eighty feet

up the wall and was then stopped at the prospect of a possible death fall. The protection was incredibly poor but he managed to reverse back down. He then made the second ascent of Midsummer Night's Dream, which he thought E6 6b, 6b. Another two weeks went by before he went back on Great Wall again. First he made an abseil inspection and dusted the occasional small hold with resin powder, then he worked resin into the soles of his footwear to make them more tacky. With a great effort he then made hard moves above his previous high point but was brought to a halt again. At full stretch he made a discernible mark on the rock with his resin, but then lowered himself off from a runner. Later he made a big decision and placed a bolt at the resin-marked spot from an abseil rope.

Redhead felt strongly that this was a pitch in its own right and called it Tormented Ejaculation which was yet again guaranteed to cause a storm of criticism on several counts. What is clear is that Redhead remarked to Paul Williams that he had only been a few feet from holds leading off right into Mick Fowler's route Spreadeagle. For what purpose was the bolt placed? Redhead still maintains adamantly that the placement of the bolt was solely to protect moves leftwards into the finest unclimbed groove on the Great Wall, and NOT to go right which was merely an escape.

Before long Lord of the Flies had ousted Right Wall as the route to do in the Llanberis Pass and there were at least eight ascents. Fawcett's other 1980 contributions on the walls of Dinas Cromlech were almost as popular. There were falls too and it became almost obligatory for a leader's first attempt on Right Wall to result in a monster fall, usually without physical injury but with severe damage to pride.

One of the more bizarre discoveries of recent years was made by Paul Williams who stumbled across Porth Dafarch, a small crag with a fifty-foot and outrageously-overhanging wall, sprouting from an attractive sandy cove quite near to Gogarth itself. In addition it is only two minutes from the road. Although it overhangs at fifty degrees there are huge horizontal bands of solid juggy flakes which provide superb sport; and not surprisingly the routes have a big feel despite their shortness. Flakes of Wrath, E1 5a and The Smog Monster, E1 5a, are just two of the delights worth sampling. The crag has been used in perfect top-rope safety for youngsters on Youth Opportunity Schemes to try their hand at rock-climbing. Some of those who parachuted backwards owing to lack of finger strength were somewhat sceptical of this particular opportunity.

Six climbers came from the U.S.A. in September at the invitation of the British Mountaineering Council. A powerful British contingent was mobilised including both Jerry Moffat and Andy Pollitt. E5s and E6s were the norm as the visiting ex-colonialists were shown the sights of Gogarth, Dinas Cromlech, Tremadog and the coastal limestone. To the delight of those watching, Dan Lepeska had a colossal fall from Citadel which resulted in the breakage of the ancient loops draped round the etrier rungs which had been hammered in by Jack Street during his mechanical first ascent.

In mid-afternoon towards the end of their stay, and after they had already had an exhausting day, one of the visitors, Randy Vogel, ordered a second mug of tea and settled down at the Space Invaders machine. There he unwittingly came out with a saying which at once captured the innermost feelings of thousands of climbers nearing the end of a season. As he slotted another coin into the machine in quiet resignation he commented:

"You wanna know something... I'm pumped."

At the end of the year yet another climbing wall was opened by Chris Bonington. The Altrincham wall was to provide an indoor opportunity for North-West climbers to do yet more training. Dedication, training and attention to diet were becoming uppermost in the minds of aspirant rock stars. However, it was realised at the time that climbing walls combined with weight-training placed hitherto unknown strains on tendons and muscles of the fore-arms and fingers. It is also unfortunate that some top climbers have trained under the influence of drugs, suppressing the body's natural warning system, so that they are training twice as long and using heavier weight-belts. Sadly this has already resulted in severe and possibly permanent injuries.

1983 saw quite a ripple develop in the Llanberis Pass. Stuart Cathcart first did three quite respectable new routes on a buttress to the right of Plexus, then moved over to the Equator Walls on the right of Cyrn Las. There he put up two new routes but felt the need to put in three bolts in a middle section common to both climbs. Everyone stood back aghast...not one bolt in the previously bolt-free Pass but...THREE! It was too much. Fortunately there were plenty of traditionalists about just waiting to pounce and Nick Dixon, who chopped the offending bolts, obliterated Cathcart's routes and put up his own Mild Steel, E5 6a. The traditional Pass cliffs were safe and climbers breathed again.

With the publication of Andy Pollitt's guide-book, the coastal limestone became more and more popular — particularly Pen Twryn. It was so popular that 1983 saw the greatest number of new routes ever put up in Wales during one year — over 100 — which was much more than even the great boom of seventy-eight routes on Gogarth in 1978. Pen Trwyn became the Tremadog of the eighties, with better weather, a better selection of hard routes, and access that made the approach to the Grochan look like a route march. Even better, the brooding Carneddau massif kept the sagging rain clouds at bay, so that they unloaded their unwelcome moisture onto the Ogwen and Llanberis valleys.

The Happy Valley cafe, near to Pen Trwyn, became a Mecca for climbers and the good weather and unclimbed rock made them happy too. The ice-cream was particularly popular and was made locally by the Parisellas. It seemed right that one particularly gorilla-like overhang should be named Parisella's Overhang. The locals were curious about this sudden influx of young climbers who crowded into the Wimpey bar in the evenings, until the local police could stand it no longer and pulled everyone in for questioning on the suspicion of using drugs. One person however was usually 'above suspicion' in the evenings. Steve Lewis was short of money and couldn't afford to go to the Wimpey bar or the pub, so he passed the evening hours cleaning routes from an abseil rope using a head-torch to illuminate a tiny circle of unclimbed rock.

Routes also multiplied on the Lower Pen Trwyn cliff, as did bolts for protection. Unfortunately bolts are made of two dissimilar metals and frequently salt spray permeates the bolts which causes a battery effect because of the electrochemical series; this can cause rapid deterioration of the bolts to such an extent that they may quickly become dangerous. As there is an exponential decay factor for height and distance from the sea, the Upper Tier bolts should be little-affected as the crag is at a fairly safe distance.

Opposite: Pat Littlejohn on the 1st ascent of The Axe, Clogwyn du'r Arddu.   Photo: Pat Littlejohn.
P. 278: Martin 'Basher' Atkinson on Captain Fingers, Craig Pen Trwyn.   Photo: Dave Lyon.
P. 279: Jerry Moffatt freeing Oyster, Craig Pen Trwyn.   Photo: Dave Summerfield.

Andy Pollitt concentrating hard on Electric Cool Aid Acid Test, Craig Pen Trwyn.   Photo: Dave Summerfield

Tom Jones at full stretch on Magical Ring, Craig Pen Trwyn.   Photo: Dave Summerfield.

While Ron and Gill Fawcett were attempting a particularly difficult overhanging crack at Pen Trwyn, supported by a team of onlookers, a passing holiday-maker remarked to Paul Williams that it was clearly obvious to him that Fawcett was a good climber — to which Williams replied, *"Yes, he is."* The holiday-maker said, *"I bet he could climb Everest,, him"*, nodding to Ron. *"Everest...he could piss up that,"* prompted Williams. The onlooker nodded to himself sagely and said, *"Must be as good as Hillary then,"* to which Williams pointing to the crack retorted. *"Hillary wouldn't stand a chance of getting up that. Don't you know who that is?"* Dumbstruck the holiday-maker asked in awe *"No...no...Who is it?...Who is it?"* In a moment of superb inspiration the reply flashed back, *"That's Charlton Chestwig, the world's finest climber."* A star was born. Of course the route just had to be called Charlton Chestwig (The world's finest climber), E5 6b.

Williams who always seemed to be in the thick of the action at this time proved that even at thirty-eight one can still achieve new targets. Having previously completed the three classic 5a Pass solos — Brant Direct, Diagonal and Cemetery Gates — he then went on to solo Suicide Wall, Silly Arete and finished the Snowdon Marathon in under four hours.

Two noteworthy routes in 1983 deserve mention; Mel Griffiths freed The Prow at Carreg Hyll Drem to give a desperate pitch known as Raging Bull, E5 6b, while Steve Haston fought his way up an offwidth crack in the Upper Dinorwic Quarry. Without any form of protection Fear of Rejection, E6 6a, was well named.

At Pen Trwyn, Andy Pollitt was right in the thick of the excitement but he took time off from the white cliffs to visit the slate slabs of Vivian Quarry. There he climbed an exceptionally bold and delicate pitch to the right of Comes the Dervish — Flashdance, E5 6a. The Dervish has a faint continuous crack which accepts many small wires, which are frequently called upon to take the strain of falling leaders. Although Haston had unlocked the gate with his own route, Pollitt's route was altogether different, being hard, open and a great step forward. It was the first really hard slate climb of its kind.

Pollitt also went for an important ascent when he went round to Ogwen to repeat Livesey's Zero, which was by then accepted to be E6 6a. Although it is only one pitch Pollitt had a hard time, and took two days to do it. On the first day he went the wrong way having foolishly taken the misguided advice of a supposedly knowledgeable spectator. The next day he fell when his foot slipped on some lichen but finally he succeeded. Livesey too had taken two days to complete the route!

Women climbers were gradually improving and working their way steadily up the E grades and Bonny Masson alternating leads with Pete Gomersall put up a new route, China Girl, E2 5c, on Craig Ddu, a very creditable performance. Another determined woman, Geraldine Taylor, led a succession of hard routes including: Foil, E3 6a; Resurrection, E4 6a; Blue Peter, E4 5c; and Wonderwall, E3 6a. Her efforts were remarkable as at one time she was eleven stone five pounds in weight, but she realised that she must shed a lot of weight if she wanted to do harder climbs. Over a period of four months she lost three stone by living on 1,000 calories per day. As a measure of her determination it is worth noting that she confessed to taking a pair of scales away with her at week-ends in order to weigh her food. She also made a few interesting points about her own attitudes:

Opposite Above: Bonny Masson on China Girl, Craig Ddu.   Photo: Pete Gomersall.
Opposite Below: Alan Hinkes on the big pitch of The Grooves, Cyrn Las.   Photo: Alan Hinkes collection.

'A number of the top women climbers prefer to climb with other women. It honestly doesn't bother me who's on the other end, as long as I get the leading. Now and again I'll trade leads, but generally anyone who climbs with me knows that I'm just not interested in seconding. I put a lot of time into training, so when I'm out climbing I want to make the best use of it. I suppose it's a pretty selfish attitude, but that's how it is.

I had a thing about Citadel. I kept going on and on about doing it, and then someone told me that it had a number of long reaches on it, so I decided to have a go at Positron. I just drove over to Gogarth and did it. It's hard, but I was so confident that week. It's a long route too, with 5c pitches before the crux 6a pitches, and I led it all. There's a blind move round an arete on the second pitch which is quite committing — I think that worried me more than the crux. You just have to go for it — it's very steep and quite serious.'

Alison Hargreaves, another fine woman climber philosophised:

'Women are free not only to compete on more equal terms with men, but perhaps offer an elegance and grace to climbing technique that cannot be achieved by their male counterparts.

The mind must be very strong and really it's one of the over-ruling characteristics but you can't build the same muscles, and women's fingers will never be as strong as men's. So you have to pick your routes and compensate with better foot-work.'

A stream of new routes was still steadily pouring out of Pen Trwyn: thirteen E5s, nine E6s and one E7. The old master Fawcett did eight of them, Pollitt six, and Moffatt four. Although Moffatt had the fewest, his route Masterclass had the magic accolade of E7. He had been to America, competing with the young American rock stars, and this brought him to his greatest peak of fitness — all ready for his return to Britain...

The most important event of the year was inevitably on the Great Wall of Clogwyn du'r Arddu. It had been the scene of great efforts by Redhead who actually had not finished a route up the wall but had, over a two-year period, made some spectacular attempts. These had ended in an eighty-foot descent from a sky-hook and a pre-placed bolt. But he eventually succeeded to complete a pitch named Tormented Ejaculation. It was an obvious challenge to add a finish to Redhead's pitch while he was nursing his injuries. His bolt placement had caused general distress. People remembered that Crew had put one in The Boldest more than a decade earlier, but that route was far easier. The route on Great Wall was in a bigger league altogether. Immortality was at stake for the successful leader and possibly also for a failure if the sketchy protection failed to hold a big fall.

In the middle of July at the height of the summer, Jerry Moffatt made his move and provocatively passed the opinion:

'I knew I was climbing better than John Redhead so I thought I might stand a chance.'

A brave comment, but he hadn't made any attempt to repeat The Bells! The Bells!, which would have given some credence to his rather brash statement.

First Moffatt abseiled down the wall and removed the hanger from Redhead's bolt. *"Somebody had to take that damn bolt out, it was a disgrace to British free-climbing."* Very provocative, but after all Moffatt had put three bolts in his own Masterclass on Pen Trwyn and taken five falls. It seemed a case of 'people in glass houses...'

Four times that day Moffatt abseiled down Great Wall, but he only walked up the Eastern Terrace the first time and the last — on the other two occasions he took a short cut and soloed Curving Arete, E3, and also Great Wall, E3. On its own that was no mean feat. Moffatt was then ready for his step into the history books.

Opposite: Gary Gibson making the 1st ascent of Spiral Scratch, Craig yr Ysfa.   Photo: Gary Gibson collection.

He found the first groove which he expected to be easy about 5c, then it became 6b and he had to concentrate to place some precarious protection. He thought about placing a secure sky-hook and lowering himself off as Redhead had done, but after a brief and traumatic period he found that he could stand in balance as the climbing was just off vertical. Some more 6b climbing then led him to the site of Redhead's emasculated bolt.

Stevie Haston, over on the right, shouted to Moffatt to let him know where the vital holds were:

'It was 6a climbing but it felt like 6b.'

Moffatt traversed right into Fowler's route Spread Eagle, a lesser route, which sadly tainted Moffatt's fine effort. At the end of it all Moffatt reviewed the situation:

'Master's Wall isn't the hardest climb I've climbed technically, but it is the most sustained and scary…As soon as I'd got down everybody was asking me what I was going to call it and what I was going to grade it…It might be E7.'

It was an outstanding performance, nearly twenty years since Crew's flawed masterpiece, Great Wall, which originally had been called Master's Wall in deference to all the efforts that Joe Brown had put into it.

Moffatt had been fortunate, or shrewd enough, to have the first pair of Fire (or sticky boots) in this country. The soles were made of butyl rubber and had a tackiness which Redhead had tried to duplicate on his own inferior footwear when he had rubbed resin into them prior to his own efforts. Later Moffatt described his feelings on the hard and precarious moves that were necessary:

'I got to a certain point where I had this imaginary line, where I knew that the runner below me was going to rip out for sure, and the one below that was too low to stop me anyway, so I paused, shook out for bit, assessed the situation in what I thought was a logical manner, psyched myself up and said, *"Right, I'm going to fall, and if I do that runner might hold."* I just looked at things and said to myself, *"Right, I'm not going to die."* You've just got to have this insane confidence in your own ability. It's when you've actually done it, you look back at it in a more realistic manner and think, *"Bloody hell, what would have happened if I had fallen off?"* That's the thing, you just don't know and you don't want to find out. I think the runners would rip out, but you might be lucky, they might hold. It frightens me to think about it.'

In retrospect, if this was an effort to topple Redhead it was premature. One should consider that of the five major E7 routes in Wales in 1985 one of them is of course Master's Wall while the other routes were all Redhead's. Of these, one of them has no runners for the first eighty feet and a fall below it would most likely prove fatal. Moffat's implication that Redhead was bolt-happy is not substantiated. Of the other factors there is no doubt that Fire boots have made a remarkable difference to hard climbing. The tackiness is so pronounced that when they are new, if the soles are rubbed vigorously together, they will stick to each other unsupported when just left to hang. It has been generally agreed that they have made a good technical grade difference in overcoming difficulty, 6b reducing to 6a or 6c becoming 6b. It was fortunate for Moffatt that John Redhead did not have a pair for his determined assaults on the wall.

Paul Williams, who followed Moffatt up Master's Wall, had exhorted him at the start:

"Do this and your name will be in the history books for ever."

Whatever the ethics of the line, Moffatt at the age of twenty carved his niche in history and joined the other great names — Pigott, Longland, Kirkus, Edwards, Harding,

Opposite: Tim Freeman working out on Parisella's Overhang, Craig Pen Trwyn.   Photo: Dave Summerfield.
P. 288: Jerry Moffatt limbering up for his ascent of Master's Wall by making an outrageous solo of Great Wall, Clogwyn du'r Arddu.
                                                                                    Photo: Paul Williams.
P. 289: Jerry Moffatt leading on the 1st ascent of Master's Wall, Clogwyn du'r Arddu.   Photo: Paul Williams.

Brown, Whillans, Streetly, Crew...This apart, the true central line on Great Wall has still not been climbed, the traverse left to get to the tantalising weakness in the upper central part of the wall has still not been made...

After his gripping time on Cloggy, Moffatt descended to the Llanberis Pass to make soloing history with a list which included: Cenotaph Corner, E1 5c; Memory Lane, E3 5c; Left Wall, E3 5c; Foil, E3 6a; and Right Wall, E5 6a — an impressive performance.

The Great Orme is a nature reserve and the home of several rare species of flower. Concern was felt that climbers might threaten the very existence of these plants. With this in mind at Pen Trwyn the Lyon brothers, Chris and Dave, placed slings and in-situ karabiners (with their gates cemented together with super-glue) so that it was possible to abseil off and avoid unnecessary disturbance to the plant life.

The year at Pen Trwyn yielded a heavy crop of new routes, but Moffatt crowned everyone else's efforts on the impossible-looking black-striped wall to the left of Disillusioned Screw Machine. With five falls and three bolts he put up Masterclass, E7 6c, which he felt was his hardest route done anywhere, including the U.S.A. where he had struggled with John Bachar for supremacy. It seems ironic that Bachar, who pioneered the idea of using an overhanging rope ladder for developing the lunge type of training, should be responsible for so many severe injuries to our top climbers.

There were two unusual occurrences in the Llanberis Pass. The first was perhaps to be expected, as Joe Brown showed that even in his fifties his new-route ability was not dimmed with age. For his new route Sidewinder on the West Wing of the Mot he was joined by two other golden oldies, Claude Davies and Paul Nunn. The route was E2 5c and it was good to see the old Master back in action again.

The great event however in 1984 was the discovery of the Rainbow Slab, a beautiful piece of rock in the Llanberis slate quarries above and to the left of the power station entrance. It had been noticed by John Redhead while on the main road from Nant Peris to Llanberis. As an unclimbed piece of rock it was one of the greatest discoveries since Gogarth more than twenty years before. Almost as smooth as a gigantic roof slate it is decorated by a coloured vein of rock which rises in a curve, hence the inspired name. There ought to be a crock of gold at the end of every rainbow and at the end of this one were several cracks of pure gold — superb unrelenting lines which gave the hardest slab climbing in Wales. The rock dries a few minutes after rain, leaving the faintest of mists at the surface. The moisture rapidly goes however, leaving an old-looking dryness that is just waiting for the dab of the tacky butyl rubber of a Fire sole

The development of the Rainbow Slab did not belong entirely to John Redhead as Dave Towse also played a major role. On Cystitis by Proxy, E6 6a, 6b, with two bolt runners Towse led the first and more dangerous pitch, although technically it was easier than the subsequent pitch which Redhead led. Poetry Pink, E5 6b, also with two bolts for protection, was a touch easier, so first Redhead then Towse led it. Raped by Affection, E7 6c, was a different proposition altogether. It had a full 150-foot mind-bending pitch, which tested Redhead's ambitions to the utmost. When he took a thirty-foot fall onto the bolt at eighty feet he ripped his fingers badly. Towse had taken a stance on a ledge six feet from the ground and as Redhead came off he ran down the steep slaty hillside in order to lessen the strain on the thin bolt stem. When they had both got over the trauma

Redhead's fingers were still hurting so Towse leapt into the lead on Naked before the Beast which was still a scary E6 6b.

Unkindly, it was said that the instant popularity of slate was due to the proximity of Pete's Eats cafe and the compulsion to add to the new routes book. Not long after exploration had begun the Central Electricity Generating Board objected to the keen interest shown by the climbing fraternity and promptly banned climbers from the Rainbow Slab. They also surrounded their property with barbed-wire fences to ensure that no harmless sporting activities could take place. Despite the fact that such fences are no deterrent to a determined climber, correspondence did take place:

'...It is the Board's view that the security of the inner area must be maintained.'

Despite the normal inflexibility of powerful bodies in such a situation common sense eventually triumphed and the gargantuan C.E.G.B. reluctantly gave way so that climbing could start again.

Redhead had recovered from his injuries and was back in action so he and Dave Towse spent a few days camping beside Llyn du'r Arddu.

'The lake was cool, and a fine woman brought us food and things. We slept till noon and climbed in the orange of evening.'

Redhead abseiled down one of the walls of the Pinnacle which had an intriguing unclimbed line and investigated the runner placements and the possible sizes. They climbed late in the day when they tried the route, just as the sun was casting shadows on the Pinnacle. As Redhead approached the crux, the shadows lengthened and suddenly he realised that he couldn't find the tiny RP nut placement which he needed for the desperately technical moves that were still to come. He cursed and cursed Dave Towse in an illogical way, in a desperate bid to relieve his heightening tension. Lower down he had a small peg driven in an inch...if he had fallen it would have ripped out. He made the sequence of hard moves then suddenly he was on easier ground and it was done. It had seemed a long, long 130-foot pitch and he finally gave Margins of the Mind a grading of E7 6b/c.

Redhead made the second ascent of Jerry Moffatt's version of Master's Wall and felt that Margins of the Mind was harder but that Master's Wall was a bigger lead. It must have been galling when he repeated Master's Wall to think of his jump for the top rope...the big fall...lowering off the tiny nut. Redhead and Touse also did Womb Bits, E5 6b, which Towse thought to be just as good as Master's Wall, but there was an obstacle which now prevented the next target from being approached. Owing to Moffatt chopping Redhead's bolt it was impossible to replace it, as it would then be on the line of Master's Wall. How then could THE line be protected? The E rating of the unclimbed head-wall will now be far higher, and a different line has evolved, because ethically any bolt placement must be well away from Master's Wall for which it is not necessary. The finest unclimbed line in Wales was thus placed even further from the outstretched reach of the eager fingertips of the elite.

Faced with a Catch 22 situation there seemed to be no way out of Redhead's dilemma. Clearly upset he wrote a letter to one of the national magazines:

'I would like to make certain points clear in defence of my own actions regarding the route on Clogwyn which is generally taken to be the same as that climbed by Jerry Moffatt, and called

Opposite Above: John Redhead on Margins of the Mind.
Opposite Below: Picture taken while John Redhead was still on Margins of the Mind!   Photos: Alan Hinkes.

"Master's Wall".

The line up Great Wall envisaged by myself and others is yet still unclimbed; the historically named *"Master's Wall"*. I placed a bolt at approximately eighty feet after five attempts of trying to work out the moves above and left, hoping to return in '83. However, Jerry chopped the bolt and, in a very fine piece of climbing, eventually traversed off into Spreadeagle, the crackline on the right. Having placed alternative protection in Spreadeagle, he went on to complete his route, just left of the latter route.

Both Chris Shorter and myself saw this traverse into Spreadeagle, and although very hard, dismissed it as another Midsummer Night's Dream in reverse (not taking the real challenge) — the real line, for which the bolt was placed, going straight up the wall.'

The big limestone news in 1984 was the development of Lower Pen Trwyn down at sea level and seven E5s and an E7 were a good ration of new routes for any cliff during a year's activity. Routes were done and there was a lot of swimming, also the sport of making bigger and bigger leaps into the sea. The competition never ends! Eventually Jerry Moffatt outclassed everyone else by jumping from the lip of Pigeons' Cave, a leap of sixty feet into the sea, which has to be timed to coincide with an incoming wave as the water is relatively shallow. However, this was still short of the Welsh record, set by Dave Williams, in 1976 when he plummeted ninety feet from the Castell Helen half-way ledge — into the sea! It should be noted though that this was not on-sight as the landing had previously been inspected during a swim.

Occasionally (!) people were known to cheat on routes. X, who has a great reputation, used to hang on slings, pegs and chockstones. He would move up to a hold, then explain to his second that the hold was good and there was no reason at all for clinging to that piece of protection. Subsequently in the written description he would miss out all the rests.

Bolts were placed for protection, sometimes too liberally, but it had been generally accepted that the Pen Trwyn cliffs were 'fun places', not a place to die, but purely an outdoor gymnasium.

Pollitt was there again and responsible for four of the E5s while Steve Lewis produced Mean Mother, E5 6b. On the latter whilst placing a bolt Lewis created a good finger pocket which he fastidiously avoided on the first ascent, and later filled in with imitation plaster. Pride of place on Lower Pen Trwyn eventually went to Ben Moon with his 'Statement of Youth', E7 6b, which took eight days to make! Protection averaged out at a bolt per day.

It would not be a complete year in the eighties without Paul Williams in some way playing a major part in some development. This time it was Anglesey and the intense development of the cliffs at Rhoscolyn. The cliffs had already had some development, but Williams just happened to pass by on a canoeing trip and immediately recognised the waiting potential. Visiting the cliffs with Jim Moran, he put up Godzilla, E4 5c, and The Sun, E3 5c, then with Moran in the lead the team climbed more classic hard routes: Magellan's Wall, E4 6a, Warpath, E5 6a, Dreams and Screams, E5/6 6a, and finally the stunning prow which became The Jub-Jub Bird, E6 6b, named after the Lewis Carroll nonsense verse, 'Beware the Jub-Jub bird and the Frumious bandersnatch'.

Nick Dixon appeared on the Welsh scene and immediately made his mark on the unlikely walls above the Idwal Slabs where he put up Teenage Menopause, which

follows the cracks to the left of Demetrius. Johnny Dawes, who is probably the best gritstone climber around, repeated it and declared that it should be E7 6b. Apparently Dixon had been hard up at the time and had not been able to buy a vital RP nut to protect the critical move!

During the year there was a joint international women's meet when twenty-one British girls met a contingent of ladies: six from France, Switzerland, Belgium and the U.S.A. They provided the most forceful display of women's climbing ever seen so far. The pressure also extended our own top women climbers, until the highlight when Jill Lawrence led Right Wall. This was followed by further ascents from chunky Rosie Andrews of the U.S.A. and Christine Jambert from France. Many E4s were done including Cream by Jill Lawrence and Resurrection by Rosie Andrews and Catherine Destivelle, whilst Geraldine Taylor led Positron on Gogarth. Jill Lawrence made some telling comments about women climbers:

> 'Women can climb as hard as men, but only women with a light frame where you've got slim hips and broad shoulders...Most women have a smaller frame and therefore don't have as much weight to haul up. But by training you can develop strength and endurance to improve your power-to-weight ration.'

Gill Price, who was also on the international meet had some more pungent comments to make:

> 'Young male climbers, desperate to succeed, are prey to impatience and lack of experience in their relationship with women climbers. The men just want to rush in and take over as soon as they see you might be failing...
>
> ...one oddity is how few women climbers there are given the number of climbers. There seem to be several possible reasons for this. As climbing in Britain is often practised in less than perfect conditions, at least for much of the year, women may be more easily put off. Also with so much of the scene centring around the pub, one of the bastions of male chauvinism, it is harder for women to develop an independent status. Further, there is less militancy among British women in general. Having climbed extensively abroad where this is not the case, the lack of women climbers is a real loss.'

One place that the ladies left severely alone was North Stack at Gogarth. There was one person however, who had decided that he was going to stamp his own brand on North Stack and during 1984 he proceeded to do just that — with three exceptionally hard and serious new routes. One of these routes that John Redhead did with Dave Towse was Demons of Bosch, E6 6b. Redhead had a bolt in for protection and took no gear with him except one karabiner to clip into the bolt. The moves clicked into place and eventually he managed to clip the bolt, but as he moved up past it his karabiner twisted and unclipped itself from the rope. He had just done a 6b move that would have been impossible to reverse in such a desperately unprotected situation. It was a horrifying situation as the margin between life and death must have been minimal. Dave Towse looking up anxiously from far below must have gone through agony but he held his breath and wisely let John get onto the easier 6a ground before he told him what had happened. Later, in his article on North Stack, Redhead's fertile mind recreated the scene:

> 'They keep flying over and they keep missing one. One flew over The Demons of Bosch — it also missed me. Hieronymus with his hellish vision would have cracked his sides at the sight of

Opposite: Without protection John Redhead makes the finishing moves on Demons of Bosch, North Stack.

Photo: Dave Towse.

these creatures. They all flew at me, missed but unclipped my neat little bolt on the 6b crux and threw what was left of me to the top of the cliff. The Demons of Bosch takes a line up the wall between South Sea Bubble and Nice 'n Sleazy. From the abseil it looked fairly improbable but it's deceiving what can hide under lichen and what was hiding was sufficient to piece together some very fine moves.'

Redhead was really climbing well after his lay-off in 1983 when he fell sixty-five feet and broke his wrist at Carreg Hyll Drem. The scaphoid bone is a notoriously difficult bone to heal and had not responded to the 'treatment' meted out by Bangor Hospital. Redhead was in plaster for seven months and had to go to Yorkshire to obtain the critical treatment. Another unfortunate accident had been on the Plas Menai climbing wall right down by the water's edge of the Menai Straits. He and Dave Towse were fooling about on climbing ropes and Towse, who was wearing a weighted belt, cannoned into Redhead causing the fracture of two ribs. Another lay-off period followed.

Not content with Demons of Bosch, Redhead accompanied by Pollitt also found Art Groupie, E5 6a, on the wall to the left of Wall of Horrors. Finally came The Clown, E6/7 6b, another absolutely horrendous Redhead creation — certainly no laughing matter. He had in mind Stravinsky's Petrouchka — The Clown — when he made the route. As a performer on rock, he sees climbing at its highest level as a pure form, a ballet on rock, of which only a handful of people are capable. As an art form it should be a sequence of skilfully executed moves, not a fight or a struggle. If Redhead falls off or fails badly when he is trying to attain this goal he retires back to painting as an antidote to any bad performance he thinks he has been guilty of on rock.

Perhaps Redhead gave that extra bit of inspiration to Andy Pollitt who produced his own Gogarth creation of Skinhead Moonstomp, E6 6b, a three-star performance which solved the much-investigated corner to the right of Alien. The start was up a tremendous flake to the stance of Positron and the route was undoubtedly one of Pollitt's better efforts on a big crag. It certainly made a good transition from the coastal limestone where he had started his meteoric rise to fame. An impressive second ascent was soon made by Joe Healey.

There were basically four acknowledged places for young hot shots to go in 1985, only those places that had been accepted as offering the most popular array of hard problems: Vector Buttress of Tremadog, the Dinas Cromlech walls, the Great Wall on Cloggy when the weather was good, and naturally Pen Trwyn if the weather was bad. The two alternative pubs were the Padarn Lake in Llanberis and the Cottage Loaf in Llandudno for Pen Trwyn habitues.

Johnny Dawes, after his astonishing exploits on Peak District gritstone, made thought-provoking contributions to slate which provided an insight of what might happen in the future. On the second ascent of Naked Before The Beast he straightened it out by climbing more directly, but although the technical grade went up to 6c the route still merited its E6 rating. Later in the year when the monsoon clouds had rolled away, after the worst summer that people could remember, Johnny did a new slab route below the Dervish slabs. One bolt was needed for protection and although the route was a mere seventy feet in height it was clearly an awesome lead of the uttermost difficulty. Johnny daringly rated his Dawes of Perception as being E7/8 6c. Time will tell whether or not it is another step forward in grading...

Opposite: Jim Moran negotiating the big roof of Godzilla, Rhoscolyn, during the 1st ascent.   Photo: Paul Williams.

Dawes also repeated Raped by Affection on the Rainbow Slab and was able to dispense with the sky-hooks that Redhead had needed. When he arrived below the vital bolt at eighty feet it was tantalisingly out of reach. Dawes is quite small, being just over five feet in height, and he had quite a problem. Any other climber in his situation would have attempted to back off or would have called for a rescue rope. He was certainly faced with the distinctive possibility of a fatal fall. His solution was to make a once-only and very desperate lunge to clip the bolt...he made it! Months later climbers were still talking about it and shaking their heads in disbelief.

Another line which although small had a powerful impact was a desperate finish to Strawberries at Tremadog. Martin 'Basher' Atkinson had to work for over a week at what was essentially no more than about twenty feet of head-wall. When he finally finished Dream Topping, E7 6c, the following dry comment appeared in the Pete's Eats new route book in Llanberis:

"I always thought Dream Topping was instant. I didn't know it took eight days to prepare."

Redhead didn't climb very much for a while, then, after a lay-off of about three months, he did a route next to the Dervish called Menstrual Gossip. Supposedly it was so named because at the time his house was full of women gossiping about monthly problems. The young climber Bob Drury made the second ascent and confirmed that it was E6 — for the climbing that is, not the name!

Redhead also did a couple of other things on the Llanberis cliffs. Ryley Bosvil, E5 6c, a short piton-scarred crack to the left of Clogwyn y Grochan, took him two days to climb. Dried Voices, E5 6b, was Redhead's other line on the Grochan. Referred to by Redhead as 'a little technical snippet', it took a slender line between Cockblock and The Pump. Redhead fell twice onto an RP1 which annoyed him considerably as he wanted to climb the route in as pure a style as possible. It didn't help when he completed the crux to discover that he had left his rack of gear on the ground and had to reverse to retrieve it.

In 1985 there emerged a home-grown star from Nant Peris who had obviously inherited some of his father's nimble footwork. Mike 'Moose' Thomas is the son of Dave Thomas, Joe Brown's frequent companion from the sixties, who sadly died from cancer at an early age. Mike made a second ascent, solo, of Pollitt's route For Whom The Bell Tolls, E5 6b, then put up a route on the unclimbed slab to the right. The Spark That Set The Flame was a serious E6 6b with just one sky-hook runner and it added yet another hard route to an ever growing list of desperates on the Welsh slate.

Because of the deadening dampness of the summer, a few pearls were waiting on the watery higher slopes. Long Kesh, E5 6b, the most exposed route in the Pass, was unshelled from Cyrn Las between the top pitches of The Skull and Lubyanka, and it was a fine effort from Boydon and Cardy. Even the unpopular Craig y Llyn yielded a hard route named The Killing Fields, E5 6a, to John Silvester and Martin Crook. Essentially it was an impressive eliminate line on Wailing Wall.

There was a bizarre interchange between two of the top climbers at Tremadog where the Vector head-wall still lured the stars. It is one of those stories that is so typical of the characters of the climbing world. It could so easily be fictitious but is in fact true. One of the climbers who had been involved in the struggle on Strawberries was told by Y that a

Opposite: Jim Moran and John Sonczak making the 2nd ascent of The Mask of Red Death, Rhoscolyn.

Photo: Paul Williams.

famous miler abstained from sex before a big race. He strongly advised Z to do the same to make absolutely sure of an acceptable ascent with a minimum number of falls. Z succeeded having had the minimum number of falls. Y asked him plainly if he had abstained whereupon Z looked round furtively to see if his girlfriend was out of earshot and then answered in the affirmative.

For some time Redhead and Fawcett had been complementary stars of equal brilliance but with the mystical Redhead having a slightly longer neck when the chips were down on bold first ascents. Fawcett had performed brilliantly in many countries and was a real ambassador, perhaps better known in Munich than he was in his own country. A superb climber for a decade, he was not given to outrageous statements — there was no need as his genius on all types of rock speaks for itself.

1985 was not a good year for new routes or innovation and the top level of climbing in North Wales stagnated somewhat. Pollitt and Moffatt were sadly both injured with muscular or tendon problems — or both. Even the weather was bad and after a short beautiful spell in June the heavens opened and the rain never seemed to stop, till the leaves on the trees in Nant Gwynant and the Llanberis Pass turned golden brown when the first autumnal chill enveloped them.

The quarries and the flooded holes in the ground at Dinorwic were in a tumbled mess, and there was just room for the local bus to turn round. Next to the bus stop turn was a deep blue pool surrounded by miniature aiguilles, bracken-covered hillside and white slate slabs. This was the pool which Al Harris used as a last resting place for insurance claim vans, vehicles which had reached the end of their natural life-span — and often ended their lives as mobile funeral pyres having been set alight just before they crashed into a watery grave. A skin diver investigating the depths came upon a mini-van, poised quite delicately on top of a pinnacle, where it was rocking slightly in the watery depths. He had gone to look for an expensive camera left by Harris in one of his moving infernoes.

The pool was filled up as part of a landscaping project for the whole hillside and it soon became obvious that there were attractive and unclimbed slabs. Paul Williams was again at the forefront in the development of these with Massambula, E3 5c. Bill Wayman his partner raised the standard with Scarlet Runner, E4 6a. Then came the superb joke name of the year — Virgin on the Ridiculous, E5 6a. The Dinorwic Bus Stop Quarries have provided a fine new ground for the keen local activists.

The star Australian woman climber Louise Sheperd came for a quick visit and it seemed natural that she should climb with Paul Williams. In spite of her stated preference for crack-climbing she led Lord of the Flies, the first E6 to be led by a woman, and only a year after Jill Lawrence had led Right Wall, E5. With E7 being the top grade Louise could stand quite proudly amongst the top echelon of male climbers.

Water seemed to dominate in 1985 and there were endless wet week-ends. It began to feel as if the high crags would never again be in condition, although in early summer the weather improved briefly to allow one good effort on the left-hand edge of Great Wall by Nick Dixon which gave Dinas in the Oven, E6.

The bad weather certainly prevented John Redhead from making more big efforts on the Great Wall of Clogwyn du'r Arddu — his one great obsession. He states quite seriously that he wouldn't mind dying there. There are still remaining lines for him to

Opposite: Paul Trower the Scarlet Runner, E4 6a, in Bus Stop Quarry.   Photo: Andy Newton.

complete — the direct and true finish to Great Wall, a direct finish to Womb Bits, and a girdle traverse of the whole wall from right to left.

Great things were being done in the Peak District in 1985, but in North Wales there was a pause...a time to reflect on what had gone before, and more important what was still to come. All climbers will one day feel Welsh tradition gnawing at them and sooner or later will come to the Cromlech walls, Pen Trwyn, Gogarth's jagged coastline and the slate quarries where there is still so much left to be done. And for some there will be the Great Wall of Clogwyn du'r Arddu, the brooding cliff where it all began, with the mists swirling round and the harsh croaking of the ravens high overhead.

Opposite: Steve Lewis contemplating how to clip the gear on the 1st ascent of Rompsville, Craig Pen Trwyn.
Photo: Dave Summerfield.

Epilogue — The Tilt-Yard

Robin Smith, the scintillating star of the sixties, wrote in an article in the Scottish Mountaineering Club Journal:

'You've got to go with the times.'

And how much more relevant is that sentiment today. If the tidal flood of better technique with sticky boots, better protection, chalk etc. goes with the wind it is useless to try to resist. White Knight Pat Littlejohn tried to hold back the waters with *his* rejection of chalk until his principles too were enveloped in ever-increasing white cloud puffs. With this greater intensity, light-heartedness and riotous behaviour (although reprehensible) are sadly in decline.

Although each generation manages to break the unwritten rules in order to subdue some piece of rock, at some stage standards are still preserved and there is an underlying aim towards purity. In his article 'Great Wall' John Redhead wrote:

'Of tradition, the words here are plentiful, joined together for your indoctrinal logic, steeped in the Establishment quagmire. I care very little, play to my own parameters. However abstract these lines appear, they form a discipline.

An historical account? The Black Cliff is your neat package. Indulge yourself; Boysen Quasimodo-esque, a cartoon-photograph on Troach, swinging on a long sling. Climbing? Banner on an attempt on Troach, spending hours chipping a spike. I don't believe it! Braithwaite hammering nuts into cracks; Yates pre-placing chocks; and Crew, so desperately obsessed to burn Brown off, abseiling, chipping, pre-placing. Is this comedy? Are they real? Still with the audacity to talk about the ethics of today...

"Great Wall" itself is a classic route, with a history of much nonsense and debate I don't care to take too seriously: Brown with his allocation of two pegs and two balls; Kid Crew in dubious style and trendy sunglasses; "John Allen climbs Great Wall free with chalk" at E3 6a; eventually soloed a classic tale.'

Professionalism has now gripped the sport in its monetary talons and for a select few under the spotlight there is commercial sponsorship. Deeds recorded, photographed cheating or unethical behaviour, are all reported in climbing magazines. For others, the dole, so that they can climb all the time. The Government climbing grant is the thin humour that envelops this style of climbing life. What was it that Edwards said? *"We laughed and laughed until we could not laugh."* The laughter seems a lot less now.

Perhaps there is a lesson to be learnt from the old master, Kirkus. He walked up to a crag, to a new line, struggled on the crux, overcame it, descended the hillside and quite possibly cycled back to Liverpool. Then of course here was Peter Harding who soloed Spectre, one of the hardest routes in Wales at that time, to check his description and grading after John Lawton's terrible fall. It wouldn't now be possible to have such attitudes; the change in strength and mental approach to the hardest climbs forbids that. On the present top routes at the very limit of human capability it often isn't possible to rest except by continuous moves upwards in a dynamic sequence...no question of lungeing for holds...power and timing are vital...an instinct for the degree of adhesion. A sloping hold may be used at full strength but as the body moves up it can become useless and at some point in the dynamic sequence another transient hold may have to be used. A jump upward may be necessary to perhaps two side-pulls at the same time…one may not be good enough, so a wild swing will be necessary onto the other side pull.

These techniques are not new, they were developed twenty years ago in Colorado by John Gill — the supreme boulder-problem expert. He could do seven one-arm pull-ups with his right arm and six with his left — even a one-finger pull-up on a narrow radius bar. He developed the theory that acrobatics, aerobatic and controlled lunges were legitimate although they needed to be co-ordinated with control. Developments of Gill's techniques have channelled aspirant stars into long deadening hours…days…weeks of training to achieve the ultimate. Will we ever see another Al Harris?

People are now taking quite big falls onto the smallest of nut placements — certainly to a degree not even contemplated ever before. The length of rope run out is an important factor as during a fall the natural elasticity will absorb a substantial proportion of the potential energy generated by the falling leader. A lot of rope out when falling onto a small wire will have much less impact than a fall when perhaps only ten feet of rope is out. This is undoubtedly a good thing as the advent of smooth slate climbs with minimal protection will almost certainly lead to serious falls. John Redhead tried to make an on-sight lead of Dawes of Perception and a fall agonisingly close to the only protection bolt resulted in the breakage or ripping out of five pieces of protection — including the shank of a Friend which he thought was perfectly placed. He was stopped close to the ground by an indifferent runner and sustained only a broken finger from a potentially fatal fall. There already seems to be a trend away from the over-protecting bolts, but a highcasualty rate seems a strong possibility.

The era of the nineteen-eighties dawned and holds became smaller…so small that it was almost impossible to climb a route from the ground without prior knowledge — particularly if there was a loose flake, unstable vegetation or any other barrier to the magic sixth degree of technical difficulty. It became impossible to garden and lead a new route from the bottom of the crag and climbers started to abseil down to clean routes prior to an ascent. Multiple falls too became the norm in desperate bids by leaders to claim the first ascent of the faintest of cracks. Furious arguments raged as to whether a smaller number of falls could be counted to justify the renaming of a coveted line. An unknown madness crept into the surges forward as teenagers in star-spangled tights jostled for triumphs in the tilt-yard.

The gap between the generations was nowhere more poignant than in 1985 after a white-haired Trevor Jones had just led Ichabod, a modest E2 on the East Buttress of Scafell. He was approached by a star spangler who congratulated him and confided that he knew who he was — Menlove Edwards (Edwards had in fact died in 1958).

When the sun comes out there will always be an exodus to North Wales. The beckoning unclimbed groove at the top of the Great Wall will still call from afar and the slate will yield more desperate new routes. In time it will be realised that Gogarth, the fallen idol, still has a lot of unclimbed rock. Happily that will be for the future star, who may even now be making his first tremulous lead on the white limestone cliffs of Pen Trwyn.

Opposite: Andy Pollitt leading the main pitch of Skinhead Moonstomp on the 1st ascent. Steve Andrews is on the stance below.   Photo: David Jones.

INDEX OF CLIMBERS

Abraham, Ashley   17
Abraham, George   17, 18, 20
Alcock, Dave   168, 170, 174
Allen, John   197, 221, 307
Allen, Nat   100, 103, 107, 108, 124
Andrews, Rosie   296
Armstrong, Dave   221, 237
Atkinson, Martin   205, 300
Austin, Allan   141, 154

Baldock, Jancis   168
Bancroft, Steve   197
Band, George   118, 120
Banner, Hugh   128, 132, 135, 141, 142, 145,
   149, 154
Barber, Henry   185, 205
Barford, John   77
Beard, Roy   81
Belshaw, Doug   128
Berzins, Bob   248, 252
Bicknell, Peter   36
Birtles, Geoff   173, 185
Birtwistle, Arthur   76, 92, 103
Biven, Peter   197
Bonington, Chris   124
Bourdillon, Tom   116
Boysen, Martin   131, 137, 141, 149, 150, 153,
   154, 163, 167, 168, 170, 197, 238, 241, 307
Bridge, Alf   39, 46, 56, 59, 76, 93, 244
Brown, Joe   81, 85, 100-135, 145, 149, 150,
   153, 163-198, 206, 219, 233, 254, 268, 286,
   290, 307
Brown, Robert   188
Burke, Phil   205

Campbell, Jock   78, 81
Cannings, Frank   197
Carr, Herbert   29, 30, 35
Carrigan, Kim   248, 251, 254, 268
Carrington, Rab   254
Carsten, Arnold   90
Cathcart, Stuart   247, 262, 276
Chapman, Don   103
Chorley, Roger   118
Churchill, Johnny   104
Cleare, John   167
Cleasby, Ed   247
Clements, John   164
Collomb, Robin   154
Cowan, Don   114
Cox, David   76, 78, 81, 205

Cram, Geoff   170
Crew, Peter   130, 135, 137-198, 237, 285, 307
Crook, Martin   300
Crew, Peter   130, 135, 137-198, 237, 285, 286,
   307
Crook, Martin   300

Davidson, Phil   205, 271
Davies, Claude   149, 150, 290
Dawes, Johnny   296, 299, 300
Destivelle, Catherine   196
Disley, John   97, 98
Dixon, Nick   276, 294, 302
Dodd, F.R.J.   75
Dolphin, Arthur   154
Drasdo, Harold   75
Drummond, Ed   181, 185, 188, 191, 192, 198
Drury, Bob   300
Dwyer, George   90
Dyke, Gordon   98, 99
Dyson, W.S.   53

Eckenstein, Oscar   11, 13
Edge, Sandy   27
Edwards, Menlove   27, 40, 49, 61-82, 86, 93,
   94, 100, 307, 308
Edwards, Rowland   167, 168, 209, 212, 219,
   238, 243, 248, 256, 259
Evans, Al   222, 231, 233, 234
Evans, Ray   195, 197, 222

Fawcett, Ron   128, 205, 216, 219, 226, 233,
   234, 244, 247, 251, 254, 256, 259, 260,
   272, 285, 302
Fisher, Macraith   89
Fowler, Mick   237, 243, 275, 286

Garlick, Adrian   216
Gibson, Gary   256, 271
Gill, John   308
Gomersall, Pete   206, 234, 238, 254, 262
Greene, Raymond   29
Greenwood, Peter   124
Gregory, Dave   137, 141, 142
Griffin, Joe   205
Griffiths, Mel   268, 283
Guinness, Maurice   29

Haines, Jack   78, 81
Harding, Peter   53, 83-99, 104, 107, 108, 113,
   198, 205, 307
Hargreaves, Alan   39, 40, 45, 49, 50, 53, 54, 56,
   62, 65, 67, 104

Opposite: Chris Lyon on Old Sam, the Little Orme.

Photo: Dave Lyon.

Cleaning the Second Coming prior to the 1st ascent.   Photo: Andy Newton.

INDEX OF MAJOR ROUTES

Top left: Johnny Dawes.
Top right: Martin Boysen.
Bottom left: Jill Lawrence.
Bottom right: Geraldine Taylor.

Photo: Trevor Jones.
Photo: John Cleare.
Photo: Lawrence collection.
Photo: Trevor Jones.